Advance Praise for *Intermission*

"FINALLY someone has written a YA for all of us m
nerds! *Intermission* will pull you in like a big Broadway
swoony romance and a heroine you can root for. Serena
the theater world alive with this tale of first love, famil
a character who's searching for her place in this world.

Jenny B. Jones, award-winning author o
and the Katie Parker Production series

"This book sings! A masterfully written story that broke my heart
one moment and had me cheering for the main character the next.
If you're looking for a stunning and emotional read, look no further
than Serena Chase's *Intermission*."

Heather Burch, bestselling author of *One Lavender Ribbon*
and the Halflings series

"With *Intermission* Chase has penned a brilliant and moving story
that honestly explores first love, finding your voice, and family
drama. Every moment feels authentic as the story's compelling
narrator walks through that precarious time in life between being a
teen and becoming a young adult. Chase has skillfully developed a
romance rife with obstacles, weaving a story that is both
heartbreaking and healing. All the while, the pulse of *Intermission*
thrums with hope, even during the most tumultuous moments. I
cried, hugged the book, and happy-sighed my way through reading.
This is Chase's best work to date. I highly recommend it."

Jess Evander, author of the TimeShifters series and
multi-published romance author (as Jessica Keller)

"A multifaceted coming-of-age love story that explores the depth of self-doubt, difficult family dynamics, and a faith built in the midst of heartache. Beautifully-crafted prose with a timely message."

Nicole Deese, author of the Love in Lenox series
and *The Promise of Rayne*

"*Intermission* is a singularly captivating YA novel. It delivers a wistful holding of breath while exploring the emotions experienced in the gap between what happened *before* and the hoped-for promise of what might happen *after*. This book, as with all the very best coming-of-age stories, will resonate with readers of all ages as it encourages us to come out from behind the curtain, step into the spotlight, and have the courage to live without masks. Certain to be a career-changing novel for accomplished author Serena Chase, I expect reader reviews will be a chorus of praise and, with her other fans, I eagerly await the encore."

Sandra Byrd, author of *A Lady in Disguise*
and the London Confidential series

"*Intermission* is both heartbreakingly real and poignantly hopeful. Dipping her pen into issues of faith, friendship, and family, Chase had me holding my breath and experiencing the highs and lows as if I was personally involved in Faith and Noah's lives. Brava!"

Jill Lynn, author of *Falling for Texas*

"*Intermission* is a love story for the heart and the spirit. You'll fall head over heels for Faith and Noah!"

Lorie Langdon, author of *Gilt Hollow*

Also by Serena Chase

To the Public Library—
Waverly Public. I enjoyed my time
with you♪

intermission

HOLD ON.

Serena Chase

SERENA CHASE

INTERMISSION
Published by Candent Gate LLC

A pair of small-town teens dream of careers in professional musical theatre but come against strong opposition to their plans and their romance.

Editorial input from: Jenny Quinlan, Historical Editorial – Sandra Byrd – Charity Tinnin – Amanda G. Stevens – Jess Evander

Copyedit by Erynn Newman, A Little Red Ink

Proofread by Charity Tinnin, ibleedbooks freelance

Cover design by Jennifer Zemanek, Copyright ©Jennifer Zemanek/Seedlings Design Studio
Formatted for electronic and print publication by Polgarus Studios

For every aspiring young
performer,
inventor,
writer,
artist,
& creative visionary
brave enough to give voice to a dream
but strangled by the phrase,
"but you need something to fall back on" . . .

Hold on.

. . . & when you're certain that what you're holding on to is something true,

leap.

OVERTURE

August 9th
Present Day
Somewhere between Michigan and Iowa

T*ick-tick-tick-tick.* Thrum-bum-bum. *Tick-tick-tick-tick. Tick-tick-tick-tick.* Thrum-bum-bum.

White dashes cut the interstate lanes like staccato sixteenth notes, arguing time signatures with a Rodgers & Hammerstein waltz, the current selection on my Broadway playlist.

Tick-tick-tick-tick. Thrum-bum-bum. *Tick-tick-tick-tick. Tick-tick-tick-tick.* Thrum-bum-bum.

Ugh. So annoying. At least my car's iffy power outlet is cooperating with the ancient-but-necessary adapter today. I can ignore background static as long as the tunes flow from my phone to the car's speakers without interruption.

Tightening my grip on the steering wheel, I press the pedal down. The dashes blur, but only until I glance at the speedometer. Oops. I ease my foot off the gas. The clock confirms what I already know. I'm two hours ahead of schedule, and a working college student's budget leaves precious little wiggle room for unnecessary extras, like speeding tickets.

Setting the cruise control at an almost-law-abiding number, I turn up the volume, hoping the encompassing magic of Broadway will transport my anxious mind to the stage and speed the hours of this long-awaited trip.

It works. For three or four songs. And then a random pothole euthanizes the show tunes I spent hours arranging into playlist perfection.

The sudden silence pulls two unbidden exhalations from my lips. "No-ah." My Broadway illusion shatters on those shallow syllables, yanking deep cords of an aching hope.

He was my Noah once.

Back then, any doubts that arose were quickly snuffed.

Today, they own me.

I pull the adapter from the power outlet and blow on it, though I doubt there's scientific evidence of why that might help. I stick it back in. Static. I try again, twisting left, right . . . nothing.

My pulse increases as desperation builds in my throat. Music. I need music!

Remove. Blow. Replace. I repeat the process with the end attached to my phone. Nothing but static. With a groan, I unplug both and toss them onto the passenger seat.

My five-year-old Siberian husky mix lifts her gray and white head from the back seat and pants a smile.

"Well, Janey," I say, glancing at the blue-eyed beauty in the rearview mirror, "looks like we're at the mercy of the radio."

Clearly, Janey is unconcerned, but her calm does not stop panic from wrapping a chokehold around my windpipe. I was counting on that playlist to distract me from the "what-ifs" of this long-awaited road trip, from thinking about what may or may not be waiting on the other side of the promise I'm in the process of keeping.

"He said he would come."

I repeat the reminder like a mantra as I hit the seek button.

"He said he would come."

Janey barks a happy sled-dog sort of sound that seems not only out of place on this hot August day but entirely too optimistic, all things considered. I guess she's forgotten the part that lets Noah off the hook if he—

No, I can't think like that. Not yet.

But neither can I handle the twangy country station the radio finds. I hit the seek button again. And again. Do they *make* another kind of music in this part of the world?

After tapping the button five more times, each tap a little more desperate, a little stabbier than the one before, the smooth caramel croon of an old Michael Bublé song saves me from the clutches of a desolate musical landscape.

Saves me . . . and wrecks me, because it floods my mind with the memory of another crooner—Noah—and his spot-on Bublé impression.

Tears threaten above the smile I cannot contain. I blink away the blur, but it doesn't clear the view in my mind's eye.

His eyes, a shade of blue so honest they should have a crayon named after them.

His hands, entwined with mine. His fingers, callused from guitar strings and hard work.

The sound of his laugh, genuine and warm.

Each memory is torture . . .

And bliss.

Memories of him. Of us.

Of hikes. A creek. A waterfall.

A stage. A duet.

A frozen pond. That first kiss.

Our song.

My ribs squeeze around each golden moment of a friendship that expanded, overflowed, stretched, and then leaped . . . into a love cut short.

No, not cut. Paused.

Please, let it be a pause.

In its first act, our romance delivered everything a theatre-lover could hope for: star-crossed lovers, a killer songbook, touches of comedy, a cruel villain, and—of course—an emotional cliffhanger leading into the intermission.

A very long intermission.

But tonight, *finally*, the curtain will rise. And if Noah—

Hot moisture stings my eyes. "Breathe," I remind myself.

The radio plays a different song now, a current Top Forty tune in four/four time. The tempo is swift. The sixteenth-note dashes could pass for eighth notes if I watch my speed.

Tick-tick. Tick-tick. Tick-tick. Tick-tick.

Tick-tick. Tick-tick. Tick-tick. Tick-tick.

Maybe those dashes aren't so bad. Each series of ticks is one less measure I'll spend waiting backstage.

Eight, nine. Eight-seventeen.

Two years ago, on the night we said goodbye, today's date—August ninth—and that time—8:17 p.m.—became the earworm refrain that has held me together since.

Eight, nine. Eight-seventeen.

In just a few more hours, the curtain will rise to reveal the players for Act II.

But it's been two years.

Two. Long. Years.

When Noah left, my world imploded. I was gutted—in so many ways—but I survived. I'd like to think I'm stronger now, but if the appointed time arrives and he doesn't . . .

I'm not ready for that script.

I'm not ready to admit Noah could have discarded his promise during the intermission.

I have to hold on. Just a little while longer.

ACT I

November 5th
Nearly 3 Years Ago
Kanton, Iowa

The blue-black sky squeezes the edge of a nearly full moon as I exit Kanton High School, trading musical rehearsal for the rare luxury of having the house all to myself this weekend. Rehearsal began right after school, but it was tech night—with a freshman at the sound board, no less—and lasted much later than normal for a post-football-season Friday night. A few friends from the cast invited me to go with them to catch the late movie in Sommerton, but for the first time in a long time, I can hardly wait to get home.

I click the remote that lets me into Parre Hills, the gated golf course community I call home. The iron gates open . . . and an invisible vise loosens its hold on my chest.

I draw in a fuller breath than I've taken in a long time, envisioning the peaceful night stretching before me. The last few hills and curves often tense up my shoulders, but not tonight. I usually dread going home to my mother's "*How was your day?*" greeting. More often than not, that seemingly innocuous question becomes a lecture, complete with verbal bullet points outlining how I could better use my time at Kanton High and how I should channel my energy toward leadership opportunities instead of singing, acting, dancing—the sorts of things intelligent people do not pursue as careers.

"*You could be Class President next year,*" she might say. Or, "*Remember, every grade counts toward your cumulative G.P.A. Don't get distracted with your hobbies.*"

Hobbies. That's how she interprets the passion that drives me toward the stage. As a hobby. Thanks for the vote of confidence, Mom.

I am the unexplainably artistic Prescott, the strange child who shies away from nets and bats and balls but hungers for the stage. Academically speaking, I do almost as well in school as my brother did and slightly better than my sister. But it's never good enough. I never quite live up to my potential—at least not in my mother's eyes. Call me a slacker, I guess, for being *Vice* President of the sophomore class with a 3.8 G.P.A. Since I don't play sports, like my brother and sister did when they were in high school, and my parents did before them, there's no excuse for anything less than a 4.0.

This weekend, however, Mom went with Dad to one of his medical conferences. I have the house all to myself. No one will be breathing down my neck about homework or complaining about the "unnecessary volume" of the music seeping out from under my bedroom door.

Freedom.

Since I don't want the camera-monitored security company to send my parents another warning listing my license plate, I'm careful to follow the artfully posted speed limit. After curving through several paved hills, I reach the private drive that leads to my family's sprawling Craftsman-style bungalow.

Light breaks through the evergreens lining our long driveway.

What? I slam on the brakes. The house should be dark, but as I inch the car forward, more light breaks through. Too much light.

Mom would never leave more than the porch and foyer lights on, a fact that offers two possibilities. Either Mom and Dad didn't go to the conference after all . . . or they called in one of my two older sibs to watch the house—and me—while they're away.

"Let it be Ryan." I grip the wheel. "Please, let it be Ryan."

Eleven years my senior and in the second year of a surgical residency at the University of Iowa Hospitals and Clinics, Ryan already answers to Dad's title of "Dr. Prescott." Regardless of the age gap between us, we've always been close. But Ryan is busy being a doctor. He just got engaged to his longtime girlfriend, Danielle. What are the odds he would be able to answer Mom's beck and call?

Slim to none.

When my headlights illumine the U-shaped driveway in front of the house, there are at least six cars crammed around the curve, leaving no doubt as to the identity of my Zen-breaker.

"Gretchen," I growl my sister's name like a curse word. "Great."

So much for solitude.

All I want is an empty house where I can relax. Maybe even practice my songs and lines somewhere other than behind my closed bedroom door. Instead, I have the pleasure of dealing with my party-crazed sister and her obnoxious friends. Again. Yay, me.

My headlights catch on a six-pack of silver and blue-labeled bottles awaiting retrieval on the roof of one of the cars, which means there must be enough alcohol flowing inside already that its owner hasn't missed his beer yet.

At least I know what I'm walking into.

Gretchen will be twenty in January, but her pre-law major is a tad ironic considering the level of respect she gives certain laws. Such as the legal drinking age.

And I'm the one who needs supervision?

As I pull around to my assigned parking spot, a single-bay carport by the garden shed, I'm glad it's a safe distance from the other vehicles. Mine is a hand-me-down car, but it's mine. Besides, I don't want to have to try and convince my parents it's not my fault if a dent shows up overnight. Again.

I clench my teeth and shove the gearshift into park. Even if Mom and Dad are aware of their middle child's abuse of their trust, they'll never let on.

When I open the car door, my ears are assaulted by a thumping bass beat. If the neighbors complain about the noise, my parents will assume it was me, the music lover. I won't bother correcting them. Neither will Gretchen.

Gretchen is the golden child. Literally. Whereas Ryan and I take after Dad's side of the family, Gretchen inherited Mom's blue eyes and the entirely unfair combination of blonde bombshell femininity and athletic prowess. Her gilding is figurative as well, at least according to my blind, deaf, and really dumb—*as in ignorant, not mute*—parents, because Golden Gretchen can do no wrong.

Muttering a few choice words, I slam the car door, but my temper fizzles when a cold wet nose presses into my palm.

"Hi, Janey." I kneel and kiss her fluffy gray and white head. "Looks like Gretchen's at it again, huh?"

Janey makes a throaty sound. Affection. Agreement. Solidarity. She doesn't much care for Gretchen or her loud crowd. I don't want to make her go inside, but . . . maybe we don't have to. At least not yet.

"Whaddya say we hike up to the waterfall?" It's November, but not really winter yet. And even a cold hike through the woods beats subjecting myself to Gretchen's drunk and handsy friends in the house.

Janey's warm tongue wets my face from chin to hairline. "Okay, okay." I laugh. "We'll go."

I pull out my phone and send my sister a quick text.

> **Faith:**
> **Got home at 8:45.**
> **Taking Janey for a hike.**
> **Be back later.**

I don't expect a response, but because *someone* around here needs to be responsible, I send a follow-up.

> **Faith:**
> **Be safe, k?**

Before stowing my phone in my pocket, I pick a playlist and put my ear buds in. The November wind has taken the night off, and although its absence keeps winter's coming chill at bay, it is far from warm. I pull the hood of my sweatshirt from beneath my insulated vest and grab my gloves from the passenger seat. "Okay, Janey. Let's go."

Four miles west of the small town of Kanton and fourteen miles east of Sommerton, the closest city big enough to have a decent hospital, the Parre Hills subdivision includes over a hundred wooded acres with manicured trails for walking, running, and biking. The location appeals to professionals like my parents who make their living in Sommerton but prefer the relative peace of "rural" life, the social status of living in a golf course community, and the quality education afforded their children in the smaller Kanton school district.

What I like about Parre Hills is how the west and north sides of those carefully kept woods are bordered by a not-so-tidy nature preserve. This is where Janey and I usually trek. Our most frequent destination is, of course, the waterfall—my secret stage. It's not much of a waterfall—this is Iowa, not Oregon—but it's mine.

As we wind our way up through the woods, I silently review the night's practice of *Annie*. Earlier this fall, against the warnings of my Drama Club friends, I tried out for a named part—a daring deed, virtually unheard of for a lowly sophomore. The underclassmen of Kanton High are almost always relegated to the chorus. But . . . my risk paid off. The drama coach broke tradition and cast me as the bimbo airhead, Lily St. Regis.

Yes, it's a smaller part, but playing a character role is crazy fun, and even though I did make temporary enemies of a few junior and senior girls by snagging the role "away from them," most seem like they're over it now.

I duck under a low-hanging branch, smiling as I mentally replay how I vamped it up at practice tonight, scoring a wink from the senior boy cast as Daddy Warbucks.

At the top of the hill, I veer to the left, following a familiar deer trail rather than the carefully maintained Parre Hills paths. Without needing my command to know where we're headed, Janey crawls under the dilapidated wire fence separating our gated community from the county nature preserve. I follow, climbing over it. A few moments later, the steep bank of the creek welcomes us to follow it to my favorite perch.

Glad for the moon to light my path, I find a few outcroppings of rock to use as footholds, and I descend the creek bank. Tracing the water's path, I don't need to think about where I'm going, but it's nice to have that ambient light to point out fresh obstacles that have fallen in the creek bed since the last time we were here.

Several yards ahead of me, Janey stops, on point—or as much "on point" as she can with that tail curling over her back.

I creep forward. What is it? A deer? Wild turkey? Bobcat? Coyote? We've seen or heard all of those around here, but we've never come too close.

I pull out my ear buds. "What is it, girl?"

Her low growl jolts me to a halt, but it's a different sound that shocks me into clumsiness.

No, not a sound. A *song*.

I catch my balance in time to avoid dipping my shoe in the shallow water. I know this tune. It's a song not from the radio but from a Broadway musical. *In the Heights*.

I lean forward, tilting my head as if that will help the words I know align with the words I'm hearing. It doesn't. The tune is right, but whoever this guy is, he doesn't know the lyrics at all.

Still, I can't help but listen. Even sung with the wrong words, the delivery is incredible. Almost . . . painful. But in a good way.

"Wow." As I breathe out the word, one of Janey's ears perks slightly back toward me, but the rest of her remains in complete stillness.

I almost don't care that this guy is murdering Lin-Manuel Miranda's lyrics. He's emoting those wrong words with such . . . *truth*, it's almost as if he's changing them up as he goes, improvising the lyric around his heart.

Curiosity takes wing. I feel a little like a Peeping Tom, but without the skeeve factor.

This is private. I should leave.

Instead, I move forward stealthily, so as not to spook the singer.

Janey slinks forward as well, staying just ahead of me. After we round the final curve of the creek, revealing the waterfall, she growls again.

It's a longer sound this time. Louder.

The guy stumbles to his feet. My gloved hand fists at my lips.

I'm sure he's about to go right over the edge, but he doesn't.

Janey braces herself between me and the stranger and inhales saliva through her snarl, accenting it with a deep bark before continuing the rumbling threat.

"Nice doggie," the guy says, glancing over the ledge as if he's considering it as a possible escape route. He backs toward the creek bank instead. "*Niiice* doggie."

Janey lets out three tonal barks and resumes her slobbery snarl. If I didn't know better, I'd think she was kind of scary. Maybe borderline rabid.

That's my girl.

With her by my side, I'm not afraid.

It's kind of satisfying, actually. But . . .

"Janey, hold."

"Oh!" The guy startles. "Uh . . . hi. I didn't see you behind the— Is that a-a *wolf?*"

"Siberian husky, mostly. With a little Akita mixed in. Janey, heel."

"A dog. Good. Wow. I thought I was alone out here, and then . . ." He chuckles, but it's a nervous sound. "I won't lie. Your dog almost scared me over the ledge."

"Why did you come all the way out here at night anyway? To *my* waterfall?"

"This is your—? I'm—I am so sorry. I didn't realize this was private property. I'll leave. That is, if your dog isn't opposed to the idea." He clears his throat. "I apologize, sincerely. I didn't mean to trespass. I thought this was part of the nature preserve."

"It is." I cringe, glad my embarrassment won't be obvious in the color-cancelling moonlight. "It's not really *my* waterfall, I just . . . well, I've been coming here for years, and I've never seen another person here after dark." I bite my lip. "Probably because the sign posted at the entrance says the preserve closes at dusk."

Not that I used the actual entrance.

"It wasn't dark when I got here. Unfortunately, the night crept up on me pretty quickly once I ventured off the marked trail."

His almost-an-accent elocution proves he's known a bigger world than most of the people in my little town. His diction is too perfect to be a local boy, but his speaking voice is vaguely familiar. As was his singing, now that I think about it.

A face pops into my mind, and with it, a memory of the rest of him, doing a little soft-shoeing on the Kanton High stage.

"You're Noah Spencer."

"I'm sorry?" The words of apology carry a bewildered tone, making them seem more like a greeting. Tilting his head, he takes a step forward. When my dog growls, he stops. "Er . . . do we know each other?"

"No. At least, I don't think we've met." He graduated with my sister, and I did go to all three performances of *Guys and Dolls* that year, so . . . maybe? "Sorry. I saw you perform in *Guys and Dolls*. And some other stuff at Kanton High. I recognized your voice."

"Wow. *Guys and Dolls*, huh?" The smile of a memory filters through his voice. "That was a long time ago."

"Uh . . . not really. It was, like two years ago."

"Yeah. I suppose you're right. Huh. Seems like a lot longer."

"Yeah. I guess."

I take a deep breath. I don't want to go home, but he was here first, so . . .

"Look, I'm sorry we bothered you. We'll go. Janey, come."

"Wait. You don't have to leave if you don't want to. There's a dry spot here by the ledge. We could share the rock, if you'd like. If your dog isn't going to kill me, that is."

I laugh. "Janey's not going to kill you."

"That's a relief. But since you've hiked all this way, you might as well enjoy the view." Noah lifts a hand to gesture toward the sky. "It's a beautiful night. And there might not be too many left before winter."

He's right. And I really do *not* want to go home to Gretchen's beer fest.

Noah has the reputation of being a good guy—which is more than I can say for the collection of douche-canoes that usually show up to Gretchen's parties. I think it's safe. If Noah Spencer turns out to be bad news, I'm betting it wouldn't take much for Janey to rip out his throat.

But I'm hoping that isn't necessary, because the loss of that singing voice would grieve the world.

I toe off my shoes and remove my socks to cross the stream. Several achingly cold, wet steps later I arrive on the only dry spot of the overhang.

"Smart." Noah nods at my shoes. "I got my boots all wet." He offers his hand. "Hi. I'm Noah. But I guess you already knew that."

He wants to shake hands? Odd, but . . . okay. It's kind of charming.

I tuck my shoes under my arm and meet his hand with my own. "Nice to meet you. I'm Faith. And this is Janey."

Noah offers an open palm to my dog and is rewarded with a deep-throated growl.

"Be nice, Janey." I stroke a hand over her head but speak to Noah. "Don't worry. She'll warm up to you."

Janey growls again.

I laugh. "Or not."

"Protective, is she?"

"That's the Akita in her. She's a good dog." I sit down to put on my socks and shoes. "We're not used to running into anyone up here. Not a lot of people come to the preserve this time of year, you know? Especially after dark. You've messed with her routine."

"So it would seem." Noah sits as well. "But like I said, it wasn't dark yet when I hiked in. I guess I lost track of time and then I . . . well, I got lost." He shakes his head. "It's kind of silly, actually. I was nearly ready to write this waterfall off as an urban myth—"

"Or a *rural* myth, as the case may be."

"Right." He laughs. "Anyway, I finally stumbled—and that's a literal statement," he says with a slight groan in his voice, "upon the creek. I decided to follow it. I figured I'd discover either a trail out or the elusive waterfall I've heard so much about."

"You're not injured or anything, are you?"

"No, no. Nothing like that. Well, unless you count my pride. I've been sitting here for the past hour wondering if I'll be able to find my way out . . . or if I need to channel my inner survivalist and construct some sort of short-term shelter."

"Your rescue service has arrived." I give an abbreviated bow, tilting my head. "I know the way to the entrance. Just say the word when you're ready to go."

"Really? Thanks. I feel like an idiot for getting lost, but I'm not stupid enough to turn down an offer of help. And even though it was something of an accident, I did find the waterfall I guess, so . . ." He shrugs, smiling. "Mission accomplished?"

"I don't think very many people know it's here. The county's website has a map that lists it, but since there's not an official trail that leads to the waterfall, it's not easy to find unless you've been here before."

"A map. Now that would have been handy. I wish the guy who told me about this place would have mentioned there was a map."

"I'd guess he doesn't know about it. Most people probably don't even realize the county has a website."

"True. And nature tromping isn't really Mr. Barron's style. Do you know him? The KHS choir director?"

"Sure."

"I guess one of his vocal students comes out here a lot to practice, and she said the acoustics were really good."

Uh, yeah. That would be me.

"I have to say, she's on to something. It's like God's own amphitheatre out here. If I'd known about this place sooner, I would've been out here all the time. I'm glad you mentioned the map, though. I doubt I'd be brave enough to try to find it again without one."

A ping of possessiveness slides through my brain, tensing my muscles. This is not my waterfall, but I've thought of it as mine for as long as I can remember.

When Noah sighs, however, an odd weariness seeps through the sound, and compassion replaces my selfish emotion. I'm just about to ask if he's all right when he breaks the silence with a question of his own.

"What brought you to the waterfall tonight?"

"Me? Oh, too many people in my house. I thought I'd use the stage—er, the waterfall, that is—to practice."

Noah tilts his head.

"That vocal student Mr. B told you about?" I tap my gloved hand against my heart. "Yours truly."

"Ah. Of course! And you're practicing for . . ."

"I'm in *Annie*. The performance is next weekend."

"You go to KHS?"

I nod.

"Huh. What part do you play?"

"I'm the dumb hotel."

"The dumb . . . ?" He barks out a laugh. "Lily St. Regis."

"Yep."

A grin stretches my cheeks. When I used that line on my parents, Mom consoled me, believing I had been cast as a building. A *building*! I tell Noah the story.

His laugh is softer this time, a sound of genuine amusement. "Your parents aren't big fans of the theatre, I take it?"

"No. They're all about sports, as are my older siblings. I'm something of an anomaly. The artsy one. The family oddball."

"Lily St. Regis must be a pretty fun part to play."

"It is."

"Have you seen the version with Kristin Chenoweth?"

"I *own* the movie. I've watched it so many times, it might be permanently burned into our TV screen."

He chuckles. "*Annie* isn't my favorite musical, but it's a good one. And Chenoweth is fantastic in that role."

"Which musical is your favorite? No. Let me guess." I put my hand on his arm and then pull it back. "*In the Heights*. Wait." If that were his favorite, wouldn't he sing the correct lyrics? "Or . . . is it?"

"I like it okay, but I wouldn't say it's my—Oh." His head drops, and his shoulders jump. "You heard me singing 'Inútil.'"

"I heard you singing something that sounded like the *melody* of 'Inútil,' but the lyrics? Not so much. Er, sorry. That sounded rude."

"Not at all. You are . . . one hundred percent correct. I—" He breaks off. Clears his throat. "I do know the correct words. Sometimes I . . . Well, I adjust lyrics to fit the mood of the moment."

Okay . . . I guess I interrupted a pretty dark, mournful moment, then. Wow. Awkward much, Faith?

His knees are raised, his feet crossed at the ankles, and his gaze is glued to the rock. Surely he's not insecure. Is he? With that voice?

Hmm. Maybe I'm not the only one feeling like the poster child for "awkward" right now.

"You sounded great," I offer. "Your vocal was spot-on."

"Thanks."

"So . . ." I've embarrassed him. I should change the subject. What were we talking about? Oh! Right. "We've established that you like *In the Heights*, but you haven't told me your favorite."

"There are so many elements that make up a good musical." Noah absently rests his hand on Janey's back. She pants happily. It sure hasn't taken her long to warm up to him. "*Wicked* is funny. And it has some really poignant moments, too. A good message. The special effects are cool."

"Not to mention the music. That last bit of 'Defying Gravity'? Iconic."

"Yeah," Noah agrees. "I love that show. And *Hamilton*. I mean . . . wow. Everything about it is just so revo—"

It takes me a second, but . . .

"Oh, no." I laugh. "You were *not* going to call it 'revolutionary,' were you?"

"Guilty." He ducks his head. "But it wasn't on purpose. I wasn't trying to resurrect an old pun. It's just . . . well, it's true."

"Yeah," I concur. "It is. Have you seen it? Live?"

"Ha! I wish."

Longing escapes on my breath. "Same."

"It's definitely a bucket list item. But since I haven't seen the live production, it wouldn't be fair to try and rank it yet."

"True. I love the story and music from *The Pirate Queen*, but I've never seen it. And hardly anyone's ever heard of it. At least around here."

"I know that one!" He's nodding. "Short run. Lots of criticism. Some of it valid, I suppose. To be honest, though, I might not have made the connections, the comparisons to the composers' other works, if they hadn't been pointed out by critics in reviews. But what a great story, right? And I love how the musical style shifts between Irish and English. Very cool use of the harpsichord."

"Right?" Finally! I'm actually speaking to someone who *gets it.*

He's nodding, not in a head-bobbing way but like he's considering the show, thoughtfully. "I wish I could've seen that one, as more than just random clips online." Noah reaches into his coat pocket and then offers something to me. "Gum?"

"Sure." I unwrap the stick and inhale the scent of cinnamon. "Big Red?"

"Yep." In the moonlight, Noah's bright smile looks ready for a toothpaste commercial. "The only gum worth chewing."

He continues, "I like all kinds of theatre. Plays, one man—or woman—shows, experimental theatre, all of it. But musicals? That's where my heart lives. I was raised on them. My mom's a fan of classics like *Fiddler on the Roof* and *My Fair Lady*. My dad, on the other hand, loves the nostalgia stuff like *Rock of Ages* and *Hairspray*. But *my* favorite?" Gloved hands against his knees, he executes a muted drumroll. "*Les Mis*. Hands down. It has everything."

I nod. It's one of my favorites. "It's a beautiful story. I have that DVD, too."

"The movie is okay," he agrees. "But there's something about the energy and emotion of a live stage production that can't be duplicated."

"I haven't seen it live, but I know what you mean. I have the original London cast recording, and even that is, I don't know . . . *bigger*, somehow, than it felt in the movie theatre."

"The touring company is coming to Des Moines in a few months," he offers. "You should go. You'd love it."

I've already asked—no, begged—Mom to take me, to no avail. Big surprise. "Are you going?"

"Not this time. *Les Mis* tickets—not to mention the gas money to get there—don't fit into my budget right now. I'm trying to save enough money to move to London."

"London? As in England?"

"The very same." Noah's next sigh is heavier. "I guess I should say that I'm *hoping* to move to London."

"What's in London?"

"The London Academy of Musical Theatre. I had an audition in Chicago a couple months ago, but I'm still waiting to hear if I got in."

"Really? The London Academy?"

"You've heard of it?"

"A little." I nod. "Freshman year we did a careers unit in . . . I don't remember what class it was for, honestly. Doesn't matter. Anyway, we had to research schools that offered training for a job we thought we were interested in. Since my job choice was," I bend my fingers into air quotes, "'Broadway Star,' I researched musical theatre programs. The London Academy was one of the schools that came up."

"Ah. I didn't move to Kanton until eleventh grade. I guess I missed out on that assignment."

"Not really. As assignments go, it was pretty lame." I smile. "That's cool you got an audition."

"Yeah. It would be cooler if I knew if I bombed it or not. I haven't heard a word out of them. Not a rejection, not an acceptance . . . nothing."

Janey perks one ear and swivels her head toward him. She must have caught the same things in his tone I did. Frustration. Exhaustion. Sadness.

Like his wrong-worded song.

"I'm not the most patient person, I guess. I just want to know if I made the cut. Or if I should throw in the towel and become a . . . a pipefitter or something."

"What's a pipefitter do?"

He groans. "I have no idea."

"If it helps, I thought you were awesome in *Guys and Dolls*."

"Thanks."

Noah scratches Janey's chin, and she stretches her neck forward to give him better access.

"I auditioned for the London Academy once before," he says. "My senior year of high school. I got in, but I couldn't afford it then."

"Your parents wouldn't help you out?"

"They would if they could. My parents are missionaries with five kids. I'm the oldest. Not a lot of extra money lying around. And there aren't a lot of scholarships for B students wanting to train in musical theatre overseas, so . . . it's all on me. And that's okay. Really. I'm willing to pay my dues. I just wish I knew . . ." He trails off.

The silence is heavy. I lift it. "So . . . your parents are missionaries." So weird. "In Kanton?"

"No." Noah laughs. "They serve in the Czech Republic. We were in the States for my last two years of high school because my parents were on furlough."

"I thought furloughs were for people in prison."

"Yeah, they are." He laughs again. "*As a prisoner for the Lord, then, I urge you to live a life worthy of the calling*— Sorry. Randomly quoting the Bible is one of the hazards of being a missionary's kid. A furlough is what they call it when a missionary comes home to raise financial support." He sighs. "Anyway, I graduated from Kanton around the same time my parents' furlough was up, and I decided to stay here. I thought it would be a lot easier to earn money for school in Iowa, where I already had a job, than halfway up a mountain in the Czech Republic. But since I haven't heard from the school, I'm beginning to wonder if it was the right choice. I guess my faith is failing me or—" He breaks off with a laugh. "No offense, of course."

"Believe me, I've heard them all. But since Faith is actually my middle name, I don't let it bug me too much."

"You go by your middle name? Is your first name really embarrassing or something?"

"Not at all. Madeleine. I like it, actually. I was named after my grandmother."

"Madeleine Faith. It has a nice syncopated rhythm. Kind of melodic. It's too dark for me to know if it fits your face, but I'd have to say it fits your voice."

"Thanks." I bite my lip, warmed by the compliment, however oddly framed.

"Why don't you use it?"

"Long story. Family politics."

"Sounds interesting." Noah shifts position to face me, cross-legged.

"Believe me, it's not. I was the unplanned third child, the family's fifth wheel, as my sister likes to say. Mom claims she was all hyped up on pain meds and thought it would be sweet for me to share a birthday and a name with my dad's mother, but that she regretted it as soon as the drugs wore off. According to my older brother, all was well until I was a few weeks old. Apparently, Mom and Grandma Maddie got into a huge fight about something—I have no idea what it was—but after that, Mom refused to call me by Grandma's name. She decided it was too much of a hassle to change my birth certificate, so I'm still legally Madeleine, but I can't recall her ever calling me anything other than Faith. The end."

"Ouch."

"Yeah. My mom is the world's foremost authority on how to hold a grudge. So if you need *faith*, then you may have to wait a little longer. Technically speaking, I'm not it."

"Ah, well. It was a pretty cheesy straw to grasp." He doesn't sound too upset, though. "So, you need to practice, right? Go ahead."

"Really?"

"Sure. Do you want to sing 'Easy Street'? I can fill in the other parts, if you'd like. You're the dumb hotel, so I guess that makes me Rooster."

In my dreams. I cough over the thought. "Rooster and Miss Hannigan. And, honestly, most of the song. My part is pretty small. Just harmonies and a few nasally-delivered lines." I frown. What felt like an awesome achievement for a sophomore at KHS a little bit ago seems a bit pathetic now, considering my present company.

"I guess it's not the best song to duet," he says. "We could give it a try . . ."

"Nah." I sigh. "It's okay. I guess we could sing something else if you wanted. A real duet."

Did I just suggest we—?

Oh, I did. I *did.* I cannot believe I—

Kill. Me. Now.

"Forget it. Sorry." I squeeze my eyes shut, glad again for the darkness.

"No, we should. I mean . . . the acoustics here are phenomenal. It would be a shame not to use them. Let's sing something. Do you have a favorite duet?"

I've been addicted to show tunes since age three when a family vacation to Orlando introduced me to some princesses, a life-sized mouse or two, and a show featuring selections from the Broadway version of *Disney's Beauty and the Beast*, but my mind is a sudden blank. "Umm . . . you pick."

As if he caught the theme of my princess-y train of thought, he says, "Do you know 'Ten Minutes Ago' from *Rodgers & Hammerstein's Cinderella?*"

I nod. "Mm-hmm."

Noah shoots to his feet, singing the opening line before he's even fully upright.

My jaw drops. I mean . . . dang. He's all so . . . Prince Charming. I close my mouth in time to take his offered hand, and he pulls me to my feet just before my part—Cinderella's—begins.

It's a fairly short little song—thank goodness! And somehow, *somehow*, I manage to pull it off, even while my brain is mushy-mcmushkins that this amazingly-voiced Prince Charming is singing to—I mean, *with*—me in the moonlight, on top of a waterfall.

"That was fun," Noah says as we sit down, both of us dangling our legs over the waterfall's ledge. "Your voice is . . . rich."

"It's the acoustics here. They're—"

"No, I mean it. Sincerely. You're good. I wonder why you didn't get cast in a bigger role for *Annie*? Speaking of that, are there still tickets available for the show next weekend?"

"Last I heard."

"I'll have to get one."

"Really? Mr. London Academy of Musical Theatre wants to come to a measly little high school musical?"

"Sure." His grin widens. "I know the girl who's playing the dumb hotel."

"I'm honored." And my face is on fire. He wants to see me on stage!

Noah pulls his phone out and wakes the screen. "Oh, man." He groans. "I have to be on a job site in six hours."

"A what?"

"I work for MacIntosh Contracting." He covers a yawn. "Sorry. I also wait tables at The Smoked Salt Grille in Sommerton. I worked the lunch crowd shift today after school. I'm taking a few classes at Sommerton Community College. You know, general ed requirements. Just in case I don't get in . . ."

He winces.

"Wow." I fill the gap. "You're busy."

"It's not as bad as it sounds. I like to be busy. But I should probably call it a night." He stands, offering his hand for the second time. "It was very nice to meet you, Madeleine Faith." He tilts his head. "Sorry. I don't remember your last name."

"I don't think I told you." I take his offered hand to rise. "It's Prescott. Madeleine Faith Prescott, of Faith & Janey's Rescue Service, at your service. Come on. We'll walk you out."

The hike to the entrance of the nature preserve is a lot longer than—and in the opposite direction of—the hike home. But because I'm talking about the theatre with someone who not only *gets* my obsession, but also shares it, the trail seems half its normal length. I'm almost surprised when we reach the gate.

"Nice truck."

"Yeah." Noah moves around to the tailgate. "Too bad it's a loaner." He peers to the left and then the right. "Where's your car?"

"At home." At Noah's blank look, I explain. "I walked. I live in Parre Hills."

"That's pretty far from here, isn't it?"

"If I were walking by road, yes. But it's not far at all from the waterfall." I smile. "This was . . . fun. Thanks for sharing your rock with us."

"Thanks for sharing your waterfall."

"Any time." I mean it, too. "I guess I'll see you late—"

"Wait. I could drive you home. If you want."

My stomach does a little jump. "Really?" Noah Spencer spent the evening with me . . . and now he wants to drive me home? Uh, yes, please! *Act cool, Faith!* "I mean, I don't want you to go out of your way."

"It's the least I can do after you rescued me and all. Will Janey mind riding in the back, though? It's my boss's truck." He pats Janey's head. "No offense, girl."

"She won't mind. In fact, she'd be offended if she *didn't* get to ride in the back."

He opens the passenger door, and I climb in. Sudden shyness has me looking at my lap when Noah gets in the driver's seat, but once he climbs behind the wheel and the dome light goes off, our conversation resumes . . . and my brief moment of shyness disappears.

When we reach Parre Hills, Noah pulls up to the manual code entry box. I recite my gate code, and he punches it in.

"Turn left at the Y," I say once we're through the gate. And then, "Take the next left." A few curved hills later, "Turn right, there. That's our driveway."

"Are you sure there's a house down here?"

"Fairly certain," I quip. "There's a little curve to the driveway. That and the trees block it from view. But it's back there, I promise."

I'm surprised the house is dark. Gretchen and her party must have moved elsewhere. It happens sometimes. Another upturn for me.

I cringe at the selfish thought and shoot a silent prayer into the night, hoping there are a few designated drivers mixed in with Gretchen's party crowd. Considering the number of cars that were here but are now gone, however, it's doubtful.

Noah pulls into the now-empty U-shape in front of the house, and the motion light kicks on, illuminating the area. "Is here okay?"

"Yeah. Thanks." I open the door and slide to the ground.

"I'll get the tailgate for Janey."

After he lets the dog out, Noah comes around to where I stand. He puts his hands in his coat pockets, rocks back on his heels, and smiles. "Ah, so *that's* what you look like."

"What? Oh. Right." I squint up at the motion-activated light and back down. The harsh artificial glow makes Noah's skin seem pale next to his sandy-blond hair. There's a hint of stubble on his chin and a few specks of dirt on his face.

Remembering the feel of splatter from one of the times Janey shook herself dry, I touch my own cheek, finding texture uncommon to my skin. "I have mud on my face, don't I?"

"A little." Noah rubs his hands down his cheeks. "Probably no more than I do." A dimple tugs his right cheek inward as he smiles. "I guess I'll see you next Sunday."

My mind is a sudden blank. "N-next Sunday?"

"I'm coming to see the dumb hotel at the Sunday matinee, remember?"

"You're really going to come?"

"Well, I can't *promise*," he hedges. "Sometimes my work schedule changes at the last minute, but I usually have Sundays off."

"Cool." My grin is a little too wide. I try to contain it. "Can you find your way home from here?"

"I'm not *that* directionally challenged." He chuckles. "I do okay out in civilization."

"Okay. Well . . ." I glance toward the house. "Thanks for the ride."

"My pleasure. Besides, if you and Janey hadn't come along, I'd probably be cutting branches to build a shelter right now."

I laugh.

"Goodnight, Madeleine Faith. Thanks for a great evening."

"You, too."

After turning the deadbolt on the door, I peek out the sidelight window. To my surprise, Noah Spencer stands exactly where I left him, staring at the door with a thoughtful, almost bemused expression.

Suddenly, he wrinkles his nose, gives a slight shake of his head, and moves toward the truck.

As he rounds the driveway, I press my cheek against the window, watching until his red taillights disappear, thinking of Sunday, and wondering if he'll like my version of a dumb hotel.

If he likes . . . me.

When I rise from my final bow as Lily St. Regis during Sunday's curtain call and the house lights come up, my eyes are drawn to a two-fingered whistle coming from the back of the auditorium. Noah smiles and gives a salute. I grin. Still feeling a little in character, I lift my hand to bounce the curls of my short blonde wig and give him an impulsive—and rather outrageous—wink. His head tilts back, but he is too far away for me to hear the chuckle that shakes his shoulders.

I expect Noah to come up to the stage and talk to me, but when the crowd clears, he's gone. I'm more disappointed than I should be. But what did I expect? I'm just a sixteen-year-old girl in a high school musical. He's Noah Spencer, future star of London's West End.

Ah, well. Back to my regularly scheduled life-after-musical, I suppose.

On Monday morning, at the end of my second period class, I'm called to the principal's office.

The. Principal's. Office.

My stomach swirls. What have I done? Am I in trouble? Have they called my parents?

I've never been called to the office before. Never. I wrack my brain for something, *anything*, that might explain the summons. I'm a model student. Respectful. Even my friends have occasionally called me a prude. I can't remember the last time I had my phone out during class without permission. This has to be a mistake.

As I pass the gym, the reek of hormone-laced sweat almost overpowers the unpleasant aromas wafting from the adjacent cafeteria. Coupled with my nerves, the government-issue food products, ever-present scent of moldy dishcloths, and testosterone-on-crack boy-stink is almost enough to make me gag.

I pause at the glass office door, swallow hard, then push it open and walk to the counter to wait—*respectfully*—while Mrs. Tulley, the secretary, finishes her call.

"Hi, Faith. What can I do for you?"

I hold up the yellow slip of paper. "I got a notice to report."

"Oh, right. Right! How could I forget?" The secretary beams, as if getting called to the office is some sort of honor. "You look worried. Don't be, sweetie. You're not in trouble." Mrs. Tulley scoots backward on her wheeled chair. "You have a delivery."

Swiveling to the table behind her desk, Mrs. Tulley grabs a long white box with a purple bow.

"For me?"

"Mm-hmm." She nods, her eyes sparkling. "See? Nothing to worry about at all."

I let out a deep breath.

"Great job in the musical, by the way. I almost didn't recognize you in that blonde wig. And what a fun accent! What was that? New York?"

"*Joi-zee.*" I take the box from Mrs. Tulley's grip. "Thanks. Do you know who it's from?"

"Your boyfriend?"

"Nope. Don't have one."

"Oooh . . . a secret admirer, perhaps?" She winks. "There's a card. Go on, Faith. Open it."

I put the box on the counter and pull the card out from under the bow. The envelope is sealed with *Madeleine Faith Prescott* scrawled in cursive on the front. I don't recognize the handwriting as my grandma's, and no one else in my family would put "Madeleine" on the card.

I pull the card from the envelope, but it's simply the contact information for Kerri's Flowers & Gifts.

"Noah who?" When the secretary speaks, I jump. "Sorry." Mrs. Tulley has the good grace to blush. "I don't mean to be nosy. There's writing on this side."

I flip the card over to read the message.

Great show, Madeleine Faith! Sorry I couldn't stick around after. Hope to see you at the LCT auditions on Saturday.

The message is written in a tiny, precise script. Below the message, a bolder signature leaves only his first name, but those four letters almost fill the remaining space.

Noah.

I read the message again.

Auditions? What auditions?

"So . . . ?" Mrs. Tulley looks like she's going to burst with curiosity.

My stomach, which had just started to recover from being called to the office, flutters. "Um, they're from Noah Spencer."

"Noah *Spencer*." Mrs. Tulley squints as if trying to put a face to the name. "Noah Spencer, Noah Spencer." Her eyes widen. "Oh! *Noah Spencer*. The missionary boy. Such a sweet kid. Always so polite. Wasn't he in your sister's class?"

"Mm-hmm."

I slide the bow from the box, pry the lid up, and draw in a fragrant breath. Inside, five long-stemmed, lavender-colored roses nestle in a soft bed of baby's breath. I run a finger over one of the velvety petals. No one has ever sent me flowers before. Not even on Valentine's Day.

Valentine's Day? What am I doing, thinking about Valentine's Day in November? This isn't a romantic gift. It can't be.

Can it?

No, it isn't. Stage performers are often given flowers at the end of the performance. Even Mom knew enough to present me with a small bouquet after the curtain call when she came to see the show on opening night. Noah's gift is a simple act of courtesy from one actor to another. That's all.

A bright orange piece of paper, folded in half, rests across the roses' stems. It's a flyer advertising upcoming auditions for the Leopold Community Theatre's winter production of *The Sound of Music.*

I read the card again. A smile tugs my cheeks. *I hope to see you at the LCT auditions.*

He's auditioning. He wants me to audition.

He wants *me* to audition. He . . . believes in me.

It's not something I have a lot of experience with. And coming from *him*? A guy once accepted to a London theatre school? I'm . . . floored.

The bell for third period rings. I replace the flyer and slip the box's lid back over the roses. "I'm going to be late to class."

Mrs. Tulley grabs a small piece of lavender paper—not as pretty a shade as the roses—and scribbles a note. "Here you go, honey. Excused tardy. I added a couple extra minutes so you have time to go to your locker if you need to."

"Thank you." I slide the bow back around the box but stick the card in my pocket. "Can I leave these here until the end of the day?"

"You bet." Mrs. Tulley nods, and I nearly float to my locker. I exchange books quickly, so I can text Jenna.

Faith:
Noah sent me roses!

Jenna:
Noah Filchman?
Eww.

Faith:
No, you dope. Noah Spencer. Cute waterfall guy.

Jenna:
Oh riiight! THAT Noah. Gimme the deets!

Jenna:
Gotta stash my phone before Mr. G sees. C-U @lunch?

Faith:
YES!

As soon as I get home, I add Noah's flowers to the vase holding my opening night bouquet.

"There." I smile, pleased with how the additional flowers perk up the slightly-wilting arrangement Mom most likely nabbed from a grocery store display on her way home from work Friday night. "Perfect."

I pull the card from my pocket and re-read Noah's note before pinning it to my bulletin board. The dry-erase calendar above my desk shows nothing but an open square for next Saturday, so I grab a marker and fill the square with *LCT Auditions*. I surround the words with a heart.

Shooting a glance toward the mixed bouquet on my desk, I wrinkle my nose. "How old are you, anyway?" I wipe the childish doodle away with the tip of my finger. "It's a theatre tradition. It's not a romantic gesture. It doesn't mean anything."

But as I pull my homework from my bag, I can't help the dreamy little smile that tilts my lips upward, because maybe . . . maybe it could.

I'm not generally a morning person, but Saturday finds me wide awake a good ninety minutes before my alarm is set to go off. Dusky sleepiness surrenders to the buzz of excitement hurtling around in my brain. It takes me a moment to remember why I'm so fully awake. When I do recall the reason, I grin.

The auditions are today.

Since I'm too wired to go back to sleep, I throw off the covers and go downstairs for a bowl of cereal.

"You're up early." Mom, dressed in a turquoise and gray tracksuit, is putting on her gloves. "I'm going for a run, but I can wait if you want to go with."

"Um, not really." I open the cupboards. "But thanks."

"Okay. Would you mind starting a pot of coffee?"

"Sure." I reach for a brightly colored box.

"One of these days, I'm going to make you start buying that stuff for yourself. You have no idea how ridiculous I feel buying cereal with a cartoon character on the box. If I ran into my trainer at the store, I'd be mortified."

"But Mom, they're magical *and* delicious." I reach in the box, grab a handful, and then tip my head back to drop the cereal in my mouth.

Mom shakes her head, but I smile and offer the box to her, careful to keep my lips closed, lest I ruin a rare relaxed moment with her.

"Thanks, but no." Mom gives me a half-smile. "Don't forget about the coffee."

"Got it."

"And don't talk with your mouth full."

"'Kay." Oops. I swallow. "Are you taking Janey with you?"

"Yep." Mom nods and heads for the door.

I fill the coffee maker before seeing to the rest of my breakfast. By the time Mom returns from her morning run, I'm showered, dressed, and sitting at the table, ear buds in and music on.

Mom peers around my cup of herbal tea to look at my playlist. "What are you listening to?"

I pull one ear bud out. "*The Sound of Music.*"

"I didn't think you liked that one."

"It's okay. Not my favorite." I'm surprised she remembers. "I'm listening to it for the Leopold Community Theatre audition. Remember? It's this morning."

"Right. You mentioned that." Mom takes a sip of her coffee. "Mmm. This is good, Faith."

"It looks like tar."

"As it should." She takes another sip. "Sounds like your dad's up." Mom leans back in her chair. "The paper's on the kitchen counter!" She turns back to me. "What time do you need to leave?"

"Around nine. The auditions don't start until ten o'clock, but I want to be early."

"Well, good luck."

My eyes round. I wince.

"What?" She sets her cup down. "What did I say?"

"You said 'good luck.'" I shudder, maybe a little more than necessary.

"And? I may not be into all this artsy business of yours, but can't a mother wish her daughter good luck?"

"Well, sure. Just . . . not like that. Remember when I studied the Scottish play in Mrs. Whetstein's A.P. lit class last year?"

"Which Scottish play?"

"*The* Scottish play."

"She means *Macbeth*." Dad's slippers make a *slish-slish* sound as he crosses the slate floor from the kitchen to the breakfast room.

"Thank you." I tilt my head, acknowledging Dad's unexpected Shakespearean Theatre knowledge.

"Oh, good." He takes a seat and reaches for the carafe. "Coffee."

"Anyway," I continue, "Mrs. Whetstein taught us about theatre superstitions. One famous superstition is that you're not supposed to say the name of the Scottish play when you're in a theatre. Another is—"

"We're not in a theatre."

"Okay, okay. *Macbeth*. There. I said it. Happy?" I roll my eyes but only the slightest bit before I remember how much Mom hates it when I roll my eyes. "And another is that you should never, ever wish an actor good luck. Saying 'good luck' is considered *bad* luck. That's why people say 'break a leg.' It's the law of opposites or something."

"Well, *that* makes perfect sense." Mom shakes her head, frowning. "So if I said, 'Faith, I hope you fall, bump your head, get a concussion, and have to get nine stitches across the bridge of your nose,' it would mean you would get the lead role?"

"Sweet!" I laugh. "But, no. It's just a silly superstition. I don't believe it or anything. But some people are superstitious in the theatre, so I don't want to say something at auditions that's going to make someone else freak out."

"What's this about you trying out for a role in *Macbeth*?" Dad already has the paper open and is perusing the financial section.

"Not *Macbeth*. *The Sound of Music*. The Leopold Community Theatre is putting it on this winter, and I'm trying out for the part of Liesl."

"What's that got to do with *Macbeth*?"

"Nothing, dear. Read your paper." Mom grants me a silent smile. "So, did you eat a good breakfast?"

"Yep."

"Protein?"

"Um, I guess. I'd have to check the box."

"Faith, protein is brain food. You need protein in the morning. How about I whip up a couple of egg white omelets?"

"But it's *Saturday*."

"So?" Mom arches an eyebrow.

"I don't use as much of my brain on Saturday. Besides, egg white omelets are gross."

"Hear, hear!" Dad raises his mug.

"You should practice what you preach, *Doctor* Prescott." Mom points a finger at her husband. "What would your patients say if they knew what you—"

"Janet, I really don't think it will kill me if I have a yolk in my omelet on Saturday morning." He sets his paper down. "Besides . . ."

Like clockwork, the regular Saturday morning argument begins. Regardless of his title of cardiologist, I'm pretty sure Dad would go for donuts and frothy cappuccinos on the weekends if he could get away with it, but Mom doesn't believe in varying nutritional content based on the day of the week.

41

I see my opportunity to escape and take it. My parents will likely debate weekend nutrition for the next fifteen minutes at least, and by the time they're finished, Dad will be choking down three spears of asparagus wrapped in a tasteless, unsalted white omelet, just like Mom. Neither will notice that their youngest child has left the table.

Once upstairs, I finish drying my hair and brush my teeth. After a quick but careful application of blush, mascara, and ice-pink lip gloss, I dock my phone and soak in *The Sound of Music* soundtrack until it's time to go.

It's about a seven-minute drive from Parre Hills to Kanton and another fifteen or so minutes to the slightly larger small town of Leopold. The Opera House, located off the town square, is easy to find. Nearby parking, however, is not. On my fourth time around the square, I finally spot someone's reverse lights in front of a small pharmacy.

I can see my breath as I cross the square and mount the granite steps of the Opera House. Once inside the large building, I'm greeted by a middle-aged man who directs me to a table to collect a questionnaire card and a practice schedule.

Pulling a pen from my purse, I inscribe my contact information on the card, wondering if my address alone will disqualify me from serious consideration. Leopold's community theatre has a reputation for casting hometown leads for every production, often leads who also contribute generously to the theatre fund. It's unlikely a sixteen-year-old girl from the rival school will be cast in a role larger than "chorus," if she's cast at all.

But it doesn't hurt to try.

I hand the completed card to the smiling, gray-haired lady sitting behind the table. The woman scans the information and then looks up at me with a raised eyebrow—and a cooler smile than before.

"You're from Kanton, I see."

I hold in my sigh. "Yes."

"And you're trying out for the part of Liesl."

"Yes."

The woman sniffs and sets the card in a stack. "They'll call your name when it's your turn. You'll be asked to read with Dr. Hitchings, and then you'll be asked to sing."

"Dr. Hitchings?"

"Our new director. He's not from Leopold." The woman's frown suggests that to originate from anywhere but Leopold is the eighth deadly sin. "We certainly miss Mrs. Arbuckle. Francine Arbuckle, our old director. Twenty-two years she directed our little theatre. She was born and raised in Leopold, you know. Spent her whole life here." The woman shakes her head. "But her health forced her to move in with her daughter this past winter. In Arizona."

"Oh."

The woman arches an eyebrow and looks as if she expects more.

"Um, that's too bad."

"Yes. Yes it is. It took four years to get the theatre renovated, and now she won't even be here to see the first post-renovation production." She clicks her tongue. "Here's a brochure about the theatre's history and the renovations. Since you're from Kanton, you probably aren't all that familiar with our town."

"Thanks."

"Dr. Miller had these printed up for us. Donated the cost. He's the veterinarian here in Leopold and has starred in *several* past productions, you know."

"That was very, um, generous of him." I take the brochure and try to think up an exit strategy.

"He's a lovely man. He'll audition for Captain Von Trapp, of course. His daughter Brittany is trying out for the part of Liesl. She has a *beautiful* voice. Plans to be a music teacher someday, or so I've heard."

"Oh." My stomach drops. If LCT royalty is auditioning for the same part, why should I even bother?

I take a breath. Even if I don't get the part, I gain experience auditioning. "Okay. Well, thanks." I swallow. "I guess I'll go find a seat now."

Before the woman can start in with another paragraph, I make for the auditorium doors.

The three rows closest to the stage are already filled. A few children run around squealing and chasing each other through unoccupied rows. Others stand at attention while their mothers give last minute directives.

Everyone looks like they know each other, of course.

My gaze roves the architecture of the old building. It truly is a remarkable structure for such a small town. Up front, rich red curtains have been retracted to the sides, and a black backdrop hangs at the rear of the stage. On the auditorium floor, dark red and gold patterned carpet leads to ornate balustrades that support red-curtained box seats. It's like something you'd see in a classic movie.

If Kanton had a theatre like this, I would want to move in.

I take a seat in the back of the auditorium and observe, unsurprised to recognize several faces from last year's district and state speech team events. In Leopold, the Fine Arts are as big of a deal in the high school and community as school sports are in Kanton. And they prove it, year after enviable year, earning top awards at state band, choir, and speech contests. I can't help but sometimes wish Parre Hills was in this school district.

An electric tingle travels up my back, lifting gooseflesh as it grazes my arms on its way out. I glance over my left shoulder where the door has slivered open.

A pause. A familiar voice says, "Thanks."

It's him.

Another jolt crackles against the hairs on my neck, my arms. I hold my breath as Noah Spencer steps inside the auditorium, letting the door swing shut behind him.

Scowling at the practice schedule in his hands, he takes three steps down the aisle and halts. His head lifts. He examines the gathered crowd up front and then slowly, *slowly*, he turns to the right and finds . . . me.

"Madeleine Faith Prescott." His instant smile grabs for my breath, which comes out in a *whoosh*. "You came."

I nod. Swallow. "Yeah."

"Is that seat taken?"

I move my purse.

Noah leans back in the seat and gazes around the auditorium. "Wow. They've really done something here. It's like stepping back in time. Or walking onto the set of a film from the days of classic Hollywood."

"I thought the same thing."

"I'm glad you decided to come. I wasn't sure you would. You were great in *Annie*, by the way. You nailed it."

"Thanks. And thanks for the flowers, too. That was really . . . nice." Nice? *Lame, Faith. So lame.*

"You're welcome." His dimple catches like it's a switch, lighting sparks in his blue eyes. Noah's smile expresses pure delight, as if sending me flowers gave him even more pleasure than I'd experienced receiving them. "I'm glad you liked them."

"They're beautiful. Such an uncommon color, too."

"For an uncommon girl. But why didn't you go out for the plays back when I was in school? I would have loved the chance to perform with you."

"I wasn't even in—"

"Your attention, please." A deep voice booms from directly in front of the stage. "Everyone take a seat, and we'll get started."

The crowd falls silent and obeys.

"As I'm sure most of you know, I am a newcomer to the Leopold community. My name is Jeremiah Hitchings. I'm pleased to have been chosen as the director of *The Sound of Music* here at the historic Leopold Opera House."

There is an awkward smattering of applause.

"Ours will be the first production to grace this stage in several years," Dr. Hitchings says, "and, as such, I intend for it to be perfect."

"No pressure," Noah whispers.

I toss him a quick grin before returning my attention to the director.

"If today's turnout is any indication, I expect I'll need to schedule callback auditions sometime next week. When I call your name, please come to the stage. My wife Nancy," he says, gesturing to a petite woman who stands and waves to the crowd before taking her seat again, "will give you a script and direct you to the correct page. You will read first and sing after. There may be a slight pause between actors as I take notes pertaining to your performance. Shall we warm up a bit?"

I am more than a little self-conscious to be singing through scales next to a guy who's bound for a London theatre school, but I try to ignore the butterflies in my stomach and sit up a little straighter. I need to warm up my instrument. This is an audition.

Dr. Hitchings sits at the piano and leads the assembly in singing "Do-Re-Mi." Finally, he calls the first person to read.

An attractive, heavy-set woman, whose short, silver-going-white hair is set off by a lavender sweater, announces she's auditioning for the role of the Mother Abbess and proceeds to read through the lines with perfect inflection.

The bar is set. Until the woman opens her mouth to sing. *Or not.*

"Next." Noah's low whisper tickles my ear. I glance over, and he grimaces, adding, "*Please.*"

I stifle a giggle and turn my attention back toward the woman in the lavender sweater.

Lavender, like the roses Noah sent.

The director belts out, "Brittany Miller!" A perky blonde takes the stage.

Her reading goes well, I guess, though the delivery of those lines would have benefitted from a little more expression. *Liesl's* lines, I note. But when she sings? *Beautiful.*

I slump back in my chair.

"She's good," Noah whispers. "Great voice."

"Mm-hmm. I think she's the vet's daughter."

"Huh?"

"The vet. Dr. Miller. The guy who donated the flyers." I point at a line printed on the back of the leaflet that says, *Donated by Miller Veterinary Hospital.* "Her name is Brittany *Miller.*"

"Ohhh." Noah catches my meaning. "Hmm. She sounds a little like Jackie Evancho."

It's a good comparison. "She sounds like an *angel.*" I almost groan.

"I guess that's good news for you then." He gives me a sideways smile. "Liesl von Trapp is no angel."

I straighten. A rather non-angelic smile pulls my lips upward. He's right. Liesl is the kind of girl who sneaks out her bedroom window to meet a boy. She's a flirt. A rule-breaker.

Noah shifts in his seat. His hand rests on my forearm. "I meant that as a compliment on your acting skills, not as an insult to your character."

"No worries. That's how I took it." It didn't even occur to me otherwise.

"Good. After I said it, I thought . . ." He shrugs and gives my arm a quick squeeze. "I've seen you on the stage. You've got this, Madeleine Faith."

Our eyes lock. A rich, sweet sensation—a rush of blissful, childlike glee that is at the same time oddly ancient and wise—constricts my chest. I hold completely still, almost afraid to breathe and lose it.

A name is called. The auditorium hushes. A piano plays. Someone sings. But the song and the singer are someplace else, where time is fluid and in motion, a place set apart from the warm and welcome bubble that's captured me and Noah.

The dry, wintry air forces me to blink. Noah blinks, too, and the spell is broken. He pulls his hand from my arm. Shyly at first, as if we're both embarrassed to be caught within such an unguarded, mysterious thing-of-a-moment, we smile.

"Madeleine Prescott!" A male voice calls from the stage.

"That's you," Noah whispers when I don't respond. He winks. "Break a leg."

That is a distinct possibility. I can't even *feel* my legs.

"Madeleine Prescott!" The voice calls again. "Is there a Madeleine Prescott here?"

I shoot to my feet. "Here!"

Noah smiles. "You can do it. Just believe that you're still sixteen going on seventeen."

Easy enough, since it's true. "I *am* sixteen going on seventeen." I give a firm nod, and with a little smirk, I add, "and I'm no angel."

"Attagirl." His wink is melt-worthy, yet fortifying. "You've got this."

Buoyed by Noah's confidence in my abilities, I make my way to the stage, refocusing my mind as I trek up the aisle.

By the time I read Liesl's first line, I own it. It only remains to be seen if the director agrees.

And if the town of Leopold will accept a Liesl who comes from Kanton.

"**I** got a call back!" I do a little happy dance and then run down the stairs. I'm not all the way down yet when I shout toward the first person I see. "Mom! I got a callback!"

"Who called you back?"

"Dr. Hitchings! The director of the Leopold Community Theatre!" My phone's glittery pink case winks in the light as I wave it around. "He asked if I could come in Tuesday evening for a callback. A second audition."

"Aww," Mom says, laying a hand on my shoulder. "Did the first one not go very well?"

"No. It went fine. Great, even! I mean, *I got a callback!*"

"So a callback is a *good* thing?"

"Yes! It's awesome."

Mom laughs. "Well, congratulations, honey. I hope you need a big old cast and at least nine stitches from all the broken legs."

"Right." I laugh, a giggle, really. I'm breathless. "Thanks."

Mom's brow furrows. "But don't you have Show Choir practice on Tuesday?"

"Show Choir is right after school." My lips almost hurt from smiling so widely. "My callback isn't until six forty-five."

"You won't be out late, will you? Didn't you say you have a test on Wednesday?"

"I was planning to study with Jenna and Cole anyway, and I'll be there by eight at the latest, home by ten, ten-thirty. No big."

"Everything counts toward college." She crosses her arms. "One bad test can wreck your whole semester's G.P.A."

"I know, I know." My shoulders slump on a sigh. "But it's U.S. History. With the extra credit I turned in last week, I'm already over a one hundred average. Don't worry."

"Any score below a B+ and your drama artsy stuff gets nixed. No show choir, no dance team, no community theatre. Got it?"

"Got it." My enthusiasm wanes. Whenever Mom whips out the word *artsy*, I know I'm on thin ice.

Too bad I don't always heed the warning.

"Gretchen never had to quit volleyball when *she* got a B."

As soon as the words exit my lips, I regret them. Athletics are almost a religion in the Prescott home. My mom was a volleyball and track star at her high school in Nebraska. Dad played intramural sports in college, all the way through med school. My brother Ryan declined three different full-tuition baseball scholarships from smaller schools when he chose to forego playing college sports and focus on his pre-med studies at the U of I instead. And Gretchen, Golden Gretchen, set dual records for serves and kills at Kanton High that have yet to be broken, as far as I know.

Mom's lips form a thin line. "Your sister graduated in the top two percent of her class."

"I know, but—"

"And her college tuition would have been paid by a volleyball scholarship if she hadn't torn her ACL the third time."

Colleges have music and drama scholarships, too, but I know

better than to take the argument further. You can't prove the value of the arts to someone who has no love for them.

Mom can't carry a tune in her gym bag. She thinks dancing should be reserved for four-year-olds in tutus and the occasional wedding reception—and it is certainly *not* to be considered a *sport*. School sports impart valuable life skills, but the arts are expendable luxuries for flighty airheads with no sense of healthy competition.

No sense of competition? In the theatre department? She has no *idea*.

Still, I know her threat has teeth. Last year, right before Christmas break, I got a B- on a Biology test the week of my ballet recital. I was the Sugarplum Fairy in *The Nutcracker*, and regardless of the fact that mine was the second highest score in the class—and I still ended up with an A for the semester—that was my last ballet recital.

"Don't worry, Mom. I'll have plenty of time to study. I prom—"

Pink glitter vibrates in my hand, and I look at the screen. *Unknown caller.*

"Go on." Mom sighs, shooing me away. "But remember what I said, okay?"

"I will." As I turn to go back upstairs, I push the button to answer. "Hello?"

"Hi, Faith. This is Noah Spencer."

"Hi!" Too enthusiastic. I sound like an idiot. *Don't be an idiot, Faith.*

"I asked Dr. Hitchings for your number. I hope that's okay. I can't believe I didn't think to get it from you the other day."

The thrill Mom doused flares high. I force down a giggle. To let it out would be worse than uncool. "No. I don't mind. Did you get a callback, too?"

"I did. He wants me to read for Rolf. So I was wondering . . . I'm going to be working a tiling job in Kanton on Tuesday afternoon. Would you like to carpool with me to Leopold?"

I go into my room and shut the door. "Do you need a ride?"

"Uh, no." Noah laughs. "I was *offering* one. I thought maybe we could grab a sandwich or something before the audition. My treat."

"Your treat?"

"Um, yeah." Noah clears his throat. "I'm, uh, trying to ask you out. Pretty smooth, huh?"

I answer his laugh with my own, but words fail me. Noah Spencer is asking me out.

Noah Spencer, who sings like a dream, who loves the theatre, who is kinda hot and totally nice, is asking me out. Me.

Noah Spencer, who graduated two years ago with my golden sister . . . is asking *me* out?

Is that weird? Or just . . . amazing?

"Faith? Are you still there?"

"Oh! Yes."

"So . . . would you go out to dinner with me before our callback audition?"

"I'd like to, but . . ." I bite my lip. My parents rarely get home from work before a quarter to six, which means there won't be time for him to meet them—a Prescott dating requirement—and still leave time for us to have dinner before the audition.

"You have a boyfriend, right?" He sighs. "I should've known. Sorry. I didn't think to ask."

"No, I don't have a boyfriend." I press a hand against the heat of my cheek. "But I have Show Choir rehearsal after school. I won't be finished until around 4:30."

"Perfect. I get off at four, so that will give me a chance to clean up a little. Should I pick you up at school?"

"That should work." Guilt pricks me, but what are my options, really? "Around 4:40? That'll give me time to gather my stuff in case Mr. Barron goes over time."

"You mean there are times he *doesn't* go over?"

"Right." I laugh. "A quarter to five then. I'll watch for you from the front doors. Will you be driving the truck?"

"Unfortunately, no. I got my car back. It's a somewhat ancient Buick four-door. Three-door if you only count the ones that open. It's a rusty shade of blue, but I imagine you'll hear it before you see it."

"Ah. A classic, huh?"

"More of a beast, actually, but I'm sure she'd appreciate the compliment."

"Does *she* have a name?"

"Of course. I'll tell you, but you have to promise not to laugh."

"I can't promise that."

"At least you're honest. I call her Eliza. As in Doolittle."

"Ah. *My Fair Lady.*"

"The same. She's crass and loud and regularly threatens to do me in, but," he half-sings the next few words in a British accent, "I've grown accustomed to her . . . pace."

"I don't think that's how the song goes."

"Forgive me. I'm a habitual hack. And that, I must admit, was one of my very worst lyrical hacks. You can smack me if it gets annoying. Most everyone does."

I'm glad to be on the telephone instead of in person. My smile feels like it's stretching toward something goofy.

"So, on that sour note," Noah continues, "I'll say goodbye for now and plan to pick you up at the high school at a quarter to five on Tuesday."

"Great. In the meantime," I affect a brash cockney accent, "please give Miss Doo-li-ul me regards."

I can still hear him laughing when I hang up.

I glance at the clock for the fortieth time since school let out. "Mr. B, I'm sorry, but I've really got to go."

"But it's only—" The choir director glances over his shoulder at the clock in the back of the auditorium. "Oh. I guess we went over time. Again. Sorry, guys. Okay, I'll see you all back here Thursday after school."

I fly off the stage and out of the auditorium to my locker.

Just outside the high school's front entry doors, Noah stands with his hands in the pockets of an unzipped, sturdy brown jacket. Looking like he's stepped off the cover of an L.L. Bean catalog, he wears a blue and white flannel shirt over a navy t-shirt and faded jeans with dark brown lace-up boots. His gaze is directed toward the parking lot. He hasn't seen me yet.

I glance down at my own outfit of skinny jeans with a dark pink hooded cardigan over a black fitted tee. On my feet, black high-top Converse.

"It'll do." I push through the doors.

Noah turns. "Hey."

"Hey. Sorry I'm late. Mr. B kept us overtime."

"Big surprise." Noah rocks back on his heels. "So . . . do you need to go get your coat?"

"I didn't bring one."

"Here. You can borrow mine." He starts to slip off his coat.

"No, it's okay. Really. I'm warm blooded. Besides, we'll be inside most of the time."

Noah squints at me, as if trying to gauge what to do. At last, he puts his coat back on. "My car's been running for a while, so it should be warmed up by now." He does a little half-bow and gestures to where his car is parallel parked.

"There's a certain trick," he says, lifting the door handle at the same time he presses a foot against the bottom seam of the door, "to opening this door." When the hinge gives a painful groan, he adds, "And an apparent need for a little WD-40."

"Thanks." I slide into the seat.

Noah shuts the door and walks around to his side. As he pulls away from the school, I say, "Oh, would you mind dropping me off at my friend Jenna's house after the audition? I left my car there this morning and rode to school with her. I promised to help her study for a history test later."

"No problem. Where does she live?"

"Out on Twin Oaks Drive."

"That's near where I was working today. Mac's got me tiling a foyer in a new house out there."

"Mac?"

"John MacIntosh. My boss. He owns MacIntosh Contracting. And he's my landlord."

"That's handy."

"More than you know. When my parents went back overseas, Mac let me move into the apartment above his garage in exchange for mowing his grass and stuff. It's a pretty good deal. Plus, he throws these little construction jobs my way." Noah turns the heat up a notch. "Truthfully, I think he's hoping to turn me into a carpenter so I have something to fall back on if I don't make it in show business."

"That sounds familiar." I let out a sigh. "My brother's a doctor, my sister's pre-law, and I'm planning to major in Musical Theatre." I give a wry laugh. "My parents are hoping I'll 'come to my senses'"—I make quote marks in the air—"before I graduate."

"Where are you going to go to college?"

"I'm not sure yet. I suppose I'll go to whichever school is willing to take me. I'd love to go somewhere in New York, of course."

Noah nods. "N.Y.U. has a fantastic program. And you're right there, in the heart of N.Y.C." He sings the letters like the song from *Annie*. "Er, sorry."

"No apology necessary. You're speaking my native tongue. But you'd rather go to London?"

Noah turns onto the highway. "At the risk of sounding like a snob, theatre is . . . well, *older* in England. There's such a rich history there. And I want to be a part of that theatre-life before I tackle Broadway."

It makes sense. "So you plan to come back some day?"

"Not back *here*, other than to visit, of course. But the States? Yeah. I'll stay in London for a while, most likely. Build my resume around the connections I'll make at the London Academy. Granted I get in, that is."

Conversation flows so easily that when I finally turn my face forward I'm surprised we've already reached the edge of Leopold.

Noah smiles. "Good company makes time fly."

He turns left, toward the business district. "I thought maybe we could eat at that little café on the square. They make great sandwiches. And this time of year, they have a peppermint mocha that's really good."

"Mmm. That does sound good, but since we're going to an audition, I'll probably just get a salad and some lemon water."

"Killjoy." He wrinkles his nose. "But your idea is better." Noah pulls into a diagonal spot across from the café. "Now," he turns to me, "you sit tight and let me be chivalrous."

"What?"

"I'll come around and open the door for you."

He doesn't wait for my reply. A moment later, he wrenches the door open with the eardrum-searing twang of metal on metal.

"Well, it's not the most elegant form of chivalry," he says with a wink, "but a guy has to work with what he's got, right?"

I slide out of the car, jumping a little at the force with which Noah slams the door shut.

"Sorry. Eliza requires a strong hand. It's part of her charm. Do you want my coat?"

"Thanks, but I'm fine. We're just walking across the street."

The café is comfortably warm, and the aromas of baking bread and foamy coffees make it cozier.

"I've never been here before." Each wall is painted a different playful hue. The dining area features a mismatched collection of distressed tables and chairs. "It's charming."

"Yeah, I guess it is. I never noticed. The food is really good, though." Noah looks around the room as if seeing it for the first time. "What? Did I say something funny?"

"You sounded, well, *normal* there for a second."

Noah's eyebrows go up—way up—and I realize what I've said.

"Not that you're not normal." Heat flames in my cheeks. "I mean, well, you sounded like a regular teenage boy there for a second. Like the guys at school. They all act like they're completely famished all the time. When food enters the room, they see nothing else. I usually get out of the way. Someday one of them is going to bite off one of my fingers, if I'm not careful."

"I'm nineteen, so technically I *am* still a teenager." He shrugs.

"True. But you don't really act like one. That's a good thing," I'm quick to add. "It's nice to talk to someone who has more on his mind than the big game or who might buy them some beer."

"Ahh." Noah gives me a cockeyed smile. "I do suffer from a ravenous appetite occasionally, but I promise to try and restrain myself from biting or otherwise endangering your fingers."

"My fingers appreciate your interest in their safety."

We examine the chalkboard menu, then order and find a table while we wait for our food. Our drinks are delivered. Out of habit, I reach for the salt shaker and sprinkle some onto my napkin. When I look up, Noah's head is tilted at on odd angle. His expression, puzzled.

"Salt keeps the glass from sticking to the napkin," I explain. "Seriously. Try it."

With a shrug and a sideways smile, he lifts his glass and shakes a bit of salt onto his napkin.

We chat about everything from school, to his job, to family, his move from Eastern Europe to Iowa . . .

"You're very easy to talk to, Madeleine Faith." Noah tilts his head. "Something wrong?"

"No. It's just . . . nobody calls me Madeleine Faith except my Grandma. It's a little strange to hear it from anyone else."

"Sorry. It just has a ring to it. It rolls off the tongue. I can stop if you—"

"No. I'm not used to it, but I like it." I take the lemon wedge from the side of my glass and squeeze it into my water. "Want to know a secret?"

"Do tell."

"I was thinking of using Madeleine Faith as my stage name. You know, like Faith is my last name instead of Prescott."

"I like it."

"I signed up for the musical with my full name. If I get the part, everyone's going to call me Madeleine, so I guess I'd better get used to hearing it."

"I think you'll get the part."

"Leopold has a lot of talent." I lower my voice. "If it comes down to me or a local girl, I'm out."

"I wouldn't be too sure. Dr. Hitchings is new here. He doesn't know who's from Leopold, who's from Kanton, or who's from Timbuktu."

Our food arrives, and once the waitress departs, we dig in.

I look up from my salad to find a smile playing on Noah's lips. "What?"

He gestures to my bowl with his fork. "Not a fan of the tomato?"

"Not remotely." I look down at my salad, which I've habitually separated into edible and nonedible sections. "Do you want them?"

"I don't want to be a pig, but if you're going to leave them . . ."

I take Noah's fork and, one-by-one, spear my discarded tomatoes and place them into his bowl. They disappear almost as fast as I deliver them, no utensil necessary.

He reaches for his glass, which is now sweating condensation. It does not cling to his napkin.

"See?" I point my fork at his glass. "The salt trick really works."

"Huh." He smiles. "I'll have to file that under the 'Life Hacks' tab in my brain."

I flourish my hand and give a mock bow. He grins.

We eat quietly until I notice Noah is eyeing my discarded croutons.

"Should I be watching my fingers?"

"What?" He swallows. "Oh. Sorry. Tell me I wasn't drooling."

"Only from your eyes." I laugh. "Noah." I enunciate each syllable slowly, like a preschool teacher might. "Would you like my croutons?"

"Yaaaasss."

"Help yourself." I glance at the oversized clock behind him. "It's already 6:15!"

Noah looks at his phone. "Wow. I guess we'd better hurry. Are you about finished?"

"Yeah. I'm good." I dab my lips with the napkin and glance at the ticket the waitress delivered a few minutes ago, upside down on a little black tray. Should I offer to pay?

"Don't even think about it." Noah swipes the bill with one hand and reaches for his wallet with the other. "My treat, remember?"

"But you're saving for school, and—"

"And I've done a good job of it. Don't worry. After all, how often do I get the chance to take a pretty girl out?"

My cheeks heat. "Well, I don't know the answer to that, but . . . thanks."

Between the café and the Opera House, we warm up our voices using exercises we both learned in Show Choir. "*Charlie Chester chews cheddar cheese.*" We sing up an octave and back down. "*Susie Simmons saves small sweet seeds.*"

When we finish a third time through our tongue twisting scales, Noah says, "Mr. Barron *still* makes me do those every week."

"How? You graduated."

"He goes to my church. I have a voice lesson with him every Wednesday night, after Bible study. I thought it would be good to keep working my instrument until I go to . . . wherever I end up."

"Good idea." It's hard to picture Mr. Barron anywhere outside of the school, but I guess he actually does have a life. A life that includes Wednesday night Bible studies and . . . Noah.

Does my church do things on Wednesday nights? If they do, I don't know about it. The Prescott family darkens the door on Christmas and Easter and maybe one or two other times throughout the year.

"Do you want to go through it again?" Noah's question snaps me out of my church wonderings. I follow his lead, and we change keys and repeat the exercise two times before we mount the granite steps of the Leopold Opera House.

Once inside, I wait by the ticket booth as Noah sheds his coat and hangs it on a rack. The muffled sound of a piano filters beneath the auditorium door.

"Are we late?"

Noah checks his phone, which I could have done instead of asking him. Between dinner with a fellow musical theatre nerd—who happens to be hella cute—and the callback, I guess I'm a little distracted.

"We're still a couple of minutes early," he says, then tosses me another melty wink as he opens the auditorium door. "Break a leg."

"Right back atcha."

A triangle of light creeps into the auditorium ahead of us, widening to let us in.

"Where is everyone?" I whisper, but my voice must carry—thank you, wonderful acoustics—because the woman sharing the piano bench with Dr. Hitchings turns her head and stands.

Dr. Hitchings rises as well. "Ah, Mr. Spencer. Miss Prescott." His reddish-white beard crimps the edges of his smile. "Excellent." His eyes move back and forth between Noah and me as we follow the aisle to the front.

He casts a gaze at the woman I now recognize as the accompanist from the initial tryouts.

She nods. "Yes. Excellent."

Dr. Hitchings's grin widens.

"Dr. Hitchings." Noah reaches a hand forward.

The director gives it a firm shake. "Call me Jeremiah." He offers his hand to me, and I match his grip. "This is my wife, Nancy. She's taking charge of choreography for the show. Nancy, this young man is Noah Spencer, and this charming young lady is Madeleine Prescott."

Nancy Hitchings shakes our hands. "Very nice to meet you both."

Dr. Hitchings hands each of us a music book and directs us to the correct page. "Shall we warm up a bit?"

I glance at Noah before saying, "We did some vocal warm ups on the way here."

"Good, good. But to soothe me, we'll do few little scales, eh?"

Dr. Hitchings sits down at the piano and guides Noah and me through a series of "La-la-la" and "Do-re-mi" scales.

"Good. Now let's try the song."

After one time through the duet "Sixteen Going on Seventeen," he sends us to the stage and describes what he has in mind for the basic blocking of the scene and then retreats, taking the center seat in the front row. "Let's take the scene from the top and lead right into the song."

Blocking is always awkward. With no costumes, scenery, or props, my character is not as easy to grasp. I close my eyes and inhale, giving myself a moment to find her.

I am Liesl von Trapp. I am innocent, but not quite as innocent as everyone thinks. I am a naïve little flirt longing for my first romance. I am sixteen . . . going on seventeen.

I open my eyes. *I can do this.*

We read the scene once through, take a few directorial suggestions from Dr. Hitchings, and run it again.

"I believe it." Nancy Hitchings's comment fills the silence after the last note is struck.

"My thoughts exactly." Her husband stands. "What do you say, Noah? Madeleine? Are you ready to join the cast?"

We exchange a glance. "Don't you have other callbacks?" I ask.

"Done. Political formality." Dr. Hitchings waves a dismissive hand. "I'd already made my decision. And now I know I was right. But just so you know," he pauses, giving us a big smile, "if you two were a few years older, you'd be my Maria and my Captain Von Trapp, no contest."

Surprise is a mild word for the emotion that steals my breath, but Nancy calmly nods, saying, "I agree. Such talent!"

"Honestly, if it wasn't for your work schedule, Noah, I would risk the tarring and feathering and cast you anyway." Dr. Hitchings winks. "But since your evening availability is limited, and I'm less-than-comfortable with the idea of casting Madeleine opposite a fifty-year-old veterinarian, I hope I can count on the two of you to apply your considerable talents to the roles of Rolf and Liesl. What do you say?"

He had considered me for the lead? The *lead*? I mean, Noah is amazing. He could absolutely carry the Captain Von Trapp role. But me?

I nod, feeling like my blood is made of glitter and light, and try to sound cool. "I'm in."

"Me, too." Noah nods, too, grinning. "You bet."

Not only was I considered for the lead, not only have I been cast in the exact role I auditioned for, but I will also be acting opposite— and kissing! Well, stage-kissing, anyway—*Noah Freaking Spencer*, the hottest, nicest theatre nerd I know?

Yes, yes, and Y.E.S!

"Terrific! I'll see you both next Tuesday? At 6:30?"

"We'll be here." Noah answers for both of us. I just nod, absently wondering if I look half as bobble-headed as I feel.

The director dismisses us, and we head out. When Noah suggests a celebratory peppermint mocha, on him, I gladly agree.

"Too bad you didn't bring your coat," Noah says after I refuse his again. "It would be a nice night to sit out on the waterfall."

"Yeah." Pleasure lifts my cheeks as, mochas in hand, we hurry toward Noah's car. "But I promised my best friend and her boyfriend I'd help them study, so even if I had my coat, I wouldn't be able to go tonight."

"Right. I forgot." Noah goes through the necessary routine to open Eliza's passenger door. "What are you doing this weekend?"

"Let's see . . ." I wrack my brain, a task made more difficult with Noah's blue eyes so near, so focused on me. "Um, on Saturday my family is going to Iowa City for the Hawkeye game. My brother got us tickets. But that's about it, I think."

Noah moves around to his side of the car and gets in. He turns the ignition. "What about Sunday afternoon? I'm leading worship at church this week, but I should be finished around 11:30."

"Which church?"

"Fellowship Community."

"Is that the big one just off the highway?"

"Yep. Halfway between Sommerton and Kanton. So . . . are you free Sunday afternoon?"

"I think so."

"It sounds like it's going to be pretty nice weather. We could take a picnic to the waterfall."

"Sure." A picnic. With Noah. "That sounds like fun. Do you think you can find it?"

"I'm sure of it."

He bites his lip and lets it go so quickly I almost don't notice. Almost.

"I, uh, went online and found that map you told me about. I've gone out there a couple of times since and made it out alive." He grins. "What time should I pick you up?"

My racing blood stills. My parents expect my dates to come in and meet them, but I'm not sure what they'll think of him . . . with me. "Why don't I meet you there?"

"What? Don't you want another chance to ride in my luxurious automobile?"

I laugh. "Eliza's a peach, but Janey loves to walk in the woods. If I go to the waterfall without her, I'll feel guilty."

True enough, but if I'm being entirely honest, the thrill of Noah Spencer wanting to spend time with me is probably stronger than any guilt I might feel over leaving my dog at home.

Or telling my parents about him. Probably.

Maybe.

"I don't want to be responsible for a dog's sadness. How about this. Since you won't let Eliza and me come pick you up, you have to let me provide the picnic."

"Deal."

"Then it's a date." Noah smiles. "Well, sort of a date."

Sort of. I swallow. Technically, I'm not supposed to date any boy my parents have not met. But *sort of a date* means *not entirely a date*, doesn't it?

It's finally Sunday. Mom and Dad are having brunch with friends at the Parre Hills clubhouse and staying to watch some game on the big screen TVs in the bar area after. Football? Basketball? I have no idea. Also, I don't really care. Normally, I would be basking in the wonder of an empty house, but not today. Today, I can't sit still.

I'm pacing between the grandfather clock in the foyer and the cuckoo on the fireplace mantel in the family room, but the clocks' hands are not moving fast enough. I grab my coat and gloves, call for Janey, and start up the hill, a full hour before I'm supposed to meet Noah.

He's already there.

"Hey! You're early."

"So are you." He grins. "Pastor Lewis wasn't feeling too great today. It was a short sermon." Noah cringes. "I guess I shouldn't sound so happy about that."

"I won't tell if you don't."

"Deal." Noah fills a mug from a thermos and hands it to me. "I hope you like hot tea. It's either that or what Janey's drinking." He gestures to where my dog is lapping water from the creek.

"I'll stick with the tea, thanks."

"Wise choice." Noah pours himself a mug and lifts it. Closing his eyes, he takes a deep breath. "This smells like the color of your hair."

I laugh. "Color doesn't have a smell."

"Sure it does." Noah reaches over, lifts a handful of my hair, and lets it fall. "Okay, maybe not. But if it *did*, the color of your hair would smell like cinnamon."

"Cinnamon." The breeze pushes the tea's spicy fragrance toward my face, and I inhale deeply. "Random Noah factoid," I say, pretending to write in a notebook. "Dude likes cinnamon. Evidenced by a preference for Big Red gum, cinnamon hot tea, and the belief that the color brown has a smell."

"Brown? No, not brown. Brown is boring. The color of your hair is much more cinnamon-y than brown."

"Also," I write in my pretend notebook again, "he creates new adjectives derived from the word, 'cinnamon.'"

"That Noah guy sounds like a nutjob," he says, grinning. "Okay, so . . . I brought subs. Turkey on wheat with white cheese, mayo, lettuce . . . and some other stuff for you. I didn't think to ask you what you liked, so I figured turkey was safe. No tomatoes, though." He smiles, as do I, because he remembered. "You can pick off any toppings you don't like."

"Perfect."

"Not to be weird, but . . . do you mind if I, uh, bless the food before we dig in?"

"Go ahead."

Noah bows his head. I follow suit.

"Thanks for a beautiful day and a beautiful girl to share it with, Lord. Please bless our time, this food, and those who prepared it for us. In Jesus's name, Amen."

"Amen," I echo. It's not the first time I've talked to God from this ledge. But it *is* the first time I've done it with a friend.

Or whatever Noah is.

The creek's thin flow dives from the ledge and into the little pond below, and the sun's reflection dances across the surface ripples like the kicks of a chorus line. Squirrels chatter and scamper in search of nuts to fill their winter stores. A slight breeze stirs the scattered leaves.

I take a bite of my sandwich. Noah's simple prayer was perfect for this setting.

"We sometimes say a prayer before dinner at home, but not like that."

"Oh? How does your family pray?"

"Bless this food for our good, help us do as we should, may we know you today in our work and our play. Amen." As I finish reciting my family's usual meal prayer, my cheeks heat. I break eye contact and let my gaze trail down the narrow creek which flows out of the pool below us. "It's kind of embarrassing. I'm pretty sure it came out of a book of nursery rhymes or something. Your prayer seems . . . more real."

"That doesn't mean it was." He sighs. "It can be pretty weird to pray aloud. Whenever I pray with other people, I have to fight the temptation to try and sound churchier than I am."

"What do you mean?"

"It's a pride thing, I guess." Noah gives me a lopsided grin. "I'm a performer, right? So I should be eloquent. And I was raised by missionaries, so I should know all the proper, church-approved lingo, you know?"

"Um, not really. I was raised by an accountant and a cardiologist."

"Right. So . . . in your case, people who know your parents probably assume you're good at math, right?"

"I *am* good at math. But yeah. I guess it's a fair assumption."

"My parents are missionaries. God is their business, their life."

"So people expect you to have a direct line to Heaven."

"Something like that." He nods. "And when I know people are listening, my prayers sometimes lose their authenticity. They become like . . . a kind of performance, I guess. More about what other people are thinking about me and my mad prayer skills than about me connecting with—talking to—God. It's like they're not really prayers, but . . . soliloquies."

"To pray or not to pray," I quip in my best Shakespearean accent, "*that* is the question."

"Now who's the hack?" Noah picks up a little stick and traces a design in a small patch of sandy mud in the cleft between our rock and the next. "But enough about me and my pride." He sets the stick down. "What's new in your world?"

"Not much. Oh! Well, I'm playing Liesl in *The Sound of Music.* That's new."

He chuckles. "Have you been accepted at any of the colleges you've applied to yet?"

"I haven't *applied* to any colleges."

Noah tilts his head. "Why not?"

Oh. My breath catches as I remember the conversation that was interrupted at our first audition. *Noah probably thinks I'm a senior. That I'll be going to college next year.*

"I wasn't kidding when I said I was sixteen going on seventeen. I *am* sixteen."

He blinks. Squints. His eyes round. "You're . . . *what?*"

"I'm a sophomore. Next fall—and the fall after that, when I actually *do* apply to colleges—I'll still be at Kanton High."

This fact falls between us like cymbals dropped on the floor of the orchestra pit.

"You're a—" He stares at me. "You're *sixteen? Years old?*"

"Mm-hmm." The warmth that so recently moved within me dissipates like the fog of my breath on the wintry air. "I turned sixteen on October sixth."

Noah is silent. "*That's* why I don't remember you from high school," he says at last. "Because you weren't even *in* high school with me. You were in, what, *eighth grade* when I was a senior?"

He graduated with Gretchen, so . . . "Yes."

"Wow. That's just . . . *super*."

The sarcasm stings. I look away.

"I'm sorry. It's just that I thought—never mind. It's not like you can help it." Noah rakes his fingers through his hair and lets out a long breath. "Sixteen. Wow. I'll be twenty in September."

"You must have been the baby of your class."

"Yeah." He agrees, but his voice carries a sense of deadness. "I was."

"That makes you only three years and . . . a month older than me." I resist the impulse to bite my lip. "If you would've been born a few days later, you would've been a senior when I was a freshman."

"Yeah. I guess so." He nods, but his eyes are on the ground.

"I tried to tell you at the audition, but . . ." I shrug. "I got called up to the stage. I guess I forgot about it until now. It didn't seem important." I let out a heavy breath. The age difference did seem a little weird to me at first, but since I've gotten to know him? No. "It *doesn't* seem that important. Not to me, anyway."

"When I saw you in *Annie*, I just assumed you were a senior," he says, still looking at the ground. "Mrs. Thomas and Mr. Barron *never* cast underclassmen in named roles. It's like, an unwritten rule or something."

He sighs. When he glances at me, a gentle frown puts a crease between his eyes.

"To be honest," he says, "that first night we met up here, well, I was surprised when you told me you were still in high school. Even in those few minutes, I'd assumed you were college age. My age." He pulls at the collar of his coat. "But you're six*teen*. A sophomore. In high school."

"Don't feel bad. People usually think I'm older than I am. Some even think I'm older than Gretchen."

"Gretchen?"

"My sister."

I wince at Noah's telling, sharp inhalation. "You're *Gretchen Prescott's* little sister?"

"We're very different."

"Well, *yeah*." Noah snorts then cringes. "Sorry. I didn't mean—"

"It's okay. I know my sister's reputation. And I know she's earned it."

"Sorry. Wow." Noah shakes his head. "You have two and a half years of high school left."

I nod and fiddle with the drawstring of my hood.

"Sixteen. You're only sixteen."

"Yep. Pretty sure we've covered that."

Again, Noah shakes his head, as if the two sides of his brain are arguing with each other. He gazes out over the creek. Finally, he lets out a long stream of air and turns back to face me. "Does it creep you out that I'm so much older than you?"

"Only a matter of days kept us from being in high school together. So, no. It doesn't."

"Maybe it should."

I open my mouth, but Noah holds up his hand to shush me.

"But . . . that being said, there's a part of me that doesn't care about your age. I knew *you* before I knew your age, and I think . . ." He takes a breath. "It's weird, Faith, but this week I was thinking . . .

maybe you're the reason I've been stuck here in Kanton."

"Uh . . ." *Not sure how to take that.* "Sorry?"

"No, it's not a bad thing. At least I didn't think it was before I knew your age." He frowns. "I like you. A lot. I've never met anyone like you. There's no one around here who gets it, you know? The theatre, performing . . ."

I nod. I *do* know.

"From the moment we met, we connected in a way that doesn't have to do with age so much as . . . as fate. Except I don't *believe* in fate." He makes a gruff sound in his throat. "I don't know how to explain it. You're pretty, you're smart, you're easy to talk to. But it's more than that. I can't put my finger on it, but there's something . . . something almost magnetic going on here. Between us. It's like I'm being drawn to you by something beyond my ability to comprehend."

"I feel the same way." He's put into words every disorganized, random thought I've had about him—us—over the past couple of weeks. "Every time I've seen you, it's been like, '*I know him,*' you know?" I take a deep breath. "It's like you're a favorite old friend that I just met. I feel like I've known you forever. No. It's more like this sense that I *will* know you forever." I nod, more to myself than to him, because it feels good to say it. "You're right that it's weird. But I think it's weird in a *good* way."

"A favorite old friend I just met. I like that."

In a swift, surprising motion, Noah stands and holds out his hand. I slip mine into his grip and let him pull me to my feet.

"So, Old-Friend-That-I-Just-Met," he says, and although his smile seems true, it still holds the tiniest hint of caution, "beyond the required hours we'll spend upon the Leopold stage, are you willing to be seen 'round about with an old man like me?"

"I think I can manage."

"Good." Noah lets go of my hand and begins packing the sandwich wrappers, thermos, and mugs into his backpack. "Would you like to go for a walk?"

"Do you think you can keep up with me, *old man?*"

He laughs. "I think I can manage."

A sudden wind rustles the branches of the overhead trees, and their leafless arms creak in muted, arthritic pops of applause that swell as the breeze gains strength. A light, swirly feeling of almost-deific approval stirs within me.

"What time should I have you back home?"

A corner of my stomach twinges, and a bit of its warm comfort escapes.

Noah hasn't said anything about dating since he found out I was sixteen. Neither have I. We've mentioned friendship. So . . . we're just friends, right?

"Let's make our way back here by about three-thirty," I say. "That way we can both get out of here in the daylight."

"Still worried about me getting lost, eh?" Noah arches an eyebrow, and his smile tilts the same direction. "Don't worry. I can make it out on my own in the daylight. But I'd be happy to drive you home."

"Nah." I look away. "It's actually shorter if I walk."

"Really?"

"Really. From here I can be home before you even get back to your car." *And you won't have to meet my parents.* Not that it should matter, if we're just friends, anyway.

"No wonder you come here so often. It's like having a waterfall in your back yard."

"Yeah, it is. That's why I've always kind of claimed it as my own. Discovering its acoustical awesomeness was by accident, though." I chuckle. "This was my first, and remains my most frequently used, stage." I gesture to the waterfall ledge. "And these," I spread my arms and turn a circle, encompassing the banks, the weeds, the rocks, the trees, "make for a rather captive audience."

"It's pretty perfect for that." He gazes around my "stage," and a gently bemused smile reveals his dimple.

He probably had a pretend stage or two of his own as a kid.

I whistle for Janey, and we set off, hiking upstream.

A little bit later, when I realize my hand has found its way into Noah's, I have to wonder what sort of "friendship" we're embarking on.

The first official day of winter break finds me up in my room, listening to an online playlist of Christmas music Noah shared with me and texting back and forth when he's between customers.

> **Noah:**
> **A kid just squirted**
> **ketchup in his**
> **chocolate milk and**
> **drank it.**

> **Faith:**
> **Gross.**

> **Noah:**
> **He drained the cup.**
> **With a straw. Time**
> **for a refill.**

We text all the time, and I suppose we've been spending a lot of time together, but most of it is either during rehearsals at the Opera

House or on our way to and from on the nights we share a ride. Since I'm in more scenes, I have more rehearsals, so I don't always see him, but considering how much we text, he never seems too far away.

> *Noah:*
> **What's your favorite Christmas song?**

> > *Faith:*
> > **All of them.**

> > *Faith:*
> > **I take that back. I loathe "Jingle Bells."**

> *Noah:*
> **Loathe? Strong word! Why?**

> > *Faith:*
> > **3rd Grade Music Class. Recorders.**

> *Noah:*
> **Say no more.**

He hasn't met my parents yet. But since I don't consider a rehearsal a date, I hardly see a reason to invoke the dreaded "meet the parents" rule. We're talking, yes. But talking doesn't always result in a dating relationship. Sometimes, it's just . . . talking. Most of the time, we discuss music and theatre-related things. We don't talk about love or romantic stuff or . . . whatever couples talk about.

When Mom calls me down to dinner, I'm humming "O Come, All Ye Faithful" while texting Jenna about my evening plans.

Faith:
What should I wear?

Jenna:
How about that silver thing your sister wore last New Year's Eve?

Faith:
Singing at a nursing home, Jen. Not clubbing.

Jenna:
Do you have a cat sweater with jingle bells sewn on? There's a crowd pleaser.

Faith:
LOL. But seriously.

Jenna:
Hmm.

I wait. And wait. Still humming, I take my seat.

"No singing at the table," Dad reminds me as he reaches for a wheat roll.

I stop humming. "Shouldn't we pray before we eat?"

My parents look at me and then at each other. Mom shrugs. "It *is* almost Christmas. Go ahead, Faith. But put your phone away first. You know the rule."

I slide it under my leg. Of course it vibrates immediately. Most likely Jenna's reply, but I won't know until dinner is over.

After listening to Christmas music all day, our family's traditional, rhyming blessing seems even more ridiculous.

"Thank you for Christmas vacation, Lord," I begin. "And for Christmas music that makes me feel so warm and loved and joyful. Thank you for our home and for our dinner. Please comfort those who aren't as blessed as we are tonight and help us to remember the real reason for Christmas is the birth of Jesus." Forgetting the "no singing at the table" rule, I end my first extemporaneous, non-rhyming dinner table prayer, singing, "*O come let us adore hi-im, Chri-ist the Lord,*" and adding a quick, "In Christ's name, amen." before lifting my head.

When I open my eyes, Mom and Dad are staring at me.

Dad clears his throat and picks up his fork. "Well, ah, thank you, Faith."

Mom does not make a move toward her own dinner. Instead, she crosses her arms and leans back in her chair. "What was that?"

"Sorry about the singing at the table part. It wasn't on purpose. I've been listening to Christmas music all day, and . . . I guess I just felt like praying differently tonight. Sorry. I should have asked first."

"No, it's fine." Mom blinks a few times, shakes her head, and turns her attention to her dinner. "We all suffer from the Christmas Crazies sometimes."

Dad, who already has a fork and knife poised to cut his second or third bite of steak, looks up. "Where is Gretchen?"

"She went out to eat with some old friends from high school."

"Again? She's been home on winter break for almost a week," Dad says, sawing a bite of steak with hard, quick motions, "but she has yet to grace us with her presence at the dinner table. This is getting ridiculous."

Someone besides me is unhappy with *Gretchen*? Shocking.

"Oh, give her a break, Joseph," Mom says. "Gretchen hasn't seen her friends in ages."

Dad scowls, but doesn't argue. Not that I expected him to.

Back to the status quo. May Her Golden Highness's reign remain unhindered.

I cut into the center of my steak and almost gag as reddish liquid escapes from a bright pink center. "Seriously, Mom? Rare? Do you know what kind of bacteria and parasites can transfer into the human body when meat is undercooked?"

"Oh, not this again. It's *medium rare*, Faith. I used the meat thermometer. It's fine." Mom cuts a piece of her own steak, sticks it in her mouth, chews, and swallows. "See?"

I look at my plate again, where cow blood is spreading across the surface. "Would you be really offended if I nuked this for a minute or two?"

"You want to microwave filet mignon?"

I nod.

Mom lets out a long breath. "Is it going to make a difference as to whether or not you eat it?"

Again, I nod. "It's oozing blood, Mom."

"It's not oozing. And that's not blood. Those are the meat juices. It's *supposed* to be that way." Mom sighs and cuts another bite off her steak. "Fine. Microwave the flavor right out of it, if it makes you happy."

"Thanks." I take my plate to the kitchen and set the microwave for three minutes. When it's finished, I rejoin my parents.

"Did I hear you tell your mother you're going out tonight?" Dad takes a sip of his water. "With Jenna?"

"Yes and no." As usual, Dad has absorbed small parts of multiple conversations and then combined their content incorrectly. "Yes, going out. Not with Jenna."

"With a *boy*?" A teasing tone enters Dad's voice.

"Girls *and* boys. Also, men *and* women. I'm going caroling at the nursing home with a bunch of people."

"Look, Janet, she's blushing."

"Dad!"

"Is that Davidson boy going caroling, too? The one you went to Homecoming with?"

"No." I laugh. "Tanner doesn't sing. Let me correct that. Tanner shouldn't sing. Believe me, I've heard him." I give an exaggerated shudder. "It should be prohibited by law."

"Tanner's a football player, isn't he?"

"Yeah."

Mom perks up. "I think he had a sister on the volleyball team with Gretchen. Tonya, right?" She leans back in her chair and smiles. "Yes. Tonya Davidson. Tiny little thing, but what an *excellent* setter! Remember how she would set that ball just so and . . . wham!" Mom spikes an invisible volleyball in the air. "Gretchen would get the kill."

Sure, no singing at the table, but sports pantomime? No prob.

Mom's gaze moves back to me. "I wish you would have stayed with volleyball, Faith. You were pretty good in middle school."

"I was horrible, and you know it." I cut into my now-rubbery but totally brown piece of meat. "It wasn't my thing, Mom. Besides, I don't want to live in Gretchen's shadow any more than I already do."

"You don't live in Gretchen's shadow."

"Right."

81

"You could have been good at sports, if you would have stuck with them. Put forth a little effort."

"Dance is a sport."

"You know what I mean."

I do. And she's wrong. But I'll have a headache later if I don't relax my jaw.

"You have no reason to be so jealous of your sister. You're every bit as intelligent as Gretchen, and you're just as attractive, too. In your own way."

I jab my fork into my steak. Hard. "What is *that* supposed to mean?"

"Nothing! For goodness sake, Faith! Why does everything always have to be drama, drama, drama with you?"

"Why does everything always have to be Gretchen, Gretchen, Gretchen with you?"

"That's enough, Faith." Dad's sigh is of the longsuffering variety, but his quick glance toward Mom precedes a much more pointed one toward me.

I swallow. Does he see how white Mom's knuckles are around her knife and fork?

Dad is oblivious most of the time, but I'm glad he's here right now. I know he's probably going to chew me out—something I'd gladly take in place of one of Mom's ice-outs or volume-enhanced *let-me-set-you-straight* lectures—and I also know he'll never stand up for me against her and risk having that mega freeze ray directed at him. But he's usually a pretty good buffer and skilled at calming her down when necessary, too.

It's been necessary a lot since Gretchen went off to college, leaving only the "artsy" kid at home.

"Your mother simply meant that you're a brunette, and Gretchen's a blonde. You have brown eyes, she has blue. Right, Janet?"

After an exaggerated huff, Mom opens her mouth, but Dad clears his throat, beating her to the punch. "So, Faith. Tell us more about this caroling thing."

I shift in my seat. "What's to tell? About twenty people are going to the nursing home to sing Christmas carols and hand out gifts to the old people."

"The elderly, Faith," Mom corrects, her voice tight. "Or residents. Nobody wants to be called old."

"Okay, *residents*," I amend. "After we hand out the gifts and sing to the *residents*, we'll head back to the church to play games and have cocoa and cookies and stuff."

"I don't remember seeing anything about that in the church newsletter."

"That's because it's not First Church doing it. I'm going with a group from Fellowship Community."

Mom wrinkles her nose. "How did you get hooked up with that bunch?"

"Pass the mashed potatoes, would you, Faith?" Dad's request spares me from answering Mom's question. "Fellowship Community," he muses as he takes the bowl and scoops out a big helping. "Amanda MacIntosh said something about Fellowship Community when I saw her in the cafeteria the other day."

I brighten at the familiar name, suddenly making a connection I hadn't before. "Does Dr. MacIntosh's husband own MacIntosh Contracting?"

"Yes, he's a builder. Now, what was it? Something about Christmas Eve, maybe?"

"Was it about the candlelight service on Christmas Eve?" I supply.

"That's it." Dad's brow relaxes. "Amanda mentioned her daughter was home from college and that she's going to sing at the candlelight service. She invited us."

"As if we wouldn't go to our own church on Christmas Eve?" Mom's facial expression is almost as acidic as her tone. "I suppose she thinks we're heathens or something."

"We're going to church Friday night?" After last year's debacle, I didn't expect that.

"Of course we are." Mom takes a sip from her glass then sets it back down hard enough that it sloshes just short of over the lip. "We always go to the Christmas Eve service."

"We didn't last year."

"Yes, we did."

"No, we didn't. Gretchen couldn't find her black boots, remember? And she thought I'd taken them, and then you started looking through my closet, and we got into that huge—"

"Oh. Right." Mom's lips press together. "Okay, so we missed one Christmas Eve service in twenty-nine years. That doesn't make us heathens."

"Nobody said we're heathens, Janet. It was an innocent invitation for us to hear Amanda's daughter sing. Faith, please pass the gravy."

"Maybe we should go." I pass the dish to Dad. "I mean, is it written in stone that we can only go to First Church's Christmas Eve service? I've heard Fellowship Community has a full band and—"

"We don't go to church to be *entertained*, Faith. We go because it's Christmas." Mom's tone is firm, with a layer of frost as an accent. There's no use arguing. "We've always gone to First Church of Kanton. Besides, we just donated to the building fund."

Dad looks up. "We did?"

"Yes, dear. A fairly sizable chunk. We needed an end-of-the-year tax deduction."

"Oh," he says, spooning more potatoes onto his plate, "right."

Disappointed, I reach for a wheat roll and the tub of butter. I had thought that, with all the peace and goodwill to men and what-have-you floating through the Christmas season, it would be the perfect chance to introduce Noah to my parents. Plus, he told me he's singing at the service, and I really want to be there.

"You said Dr. MacIntosh goes to Fellowship Community, right, Dad?"

He nods.

"My friend Noah goes there, too."

"Nora Johnson? I thought the Johnsons were Methodist."

"Not Nora. *No-ah.* Noah Spencer. *He,*" I emphasize the word, "is in the community theatre with me in Leopold."

"Ahhh." Dad arches one eyebrow, a teasing glint in his eye. "I take it this *Noah* is part of your caroling group tonight?"

I nod, hating the heat that brushes my ears when the corners of his mouth lift. Why did I put my hair in a ponytail today?

"Ah-ha! And now we get to the *real* story. I believe our little Faith has a crush on this boy."

"We're just friends." We are. "We're . . . talking. Tonight, we're just singing. Hanging out. That's all."

So why do I feel like I'm lying?

"Just friends. Talking friends. Mm-hmm." Dad leans back in his chair. "That's why your face is turning red."

"Da-*ad!*"

"Oh, stop teasing her, Joseph. She's sixteen. She's bound to have a few crushes now and then."

The dinner conversation continues along other veins, but I tune out. When I put my fork down on my empty plate, I realize I consumed the entire meal without tasting it.

If this is how Mom and Dad behave when Noah is *mentioned*, how will they act when—I mean, *if*—we get beyond talking, and he actually comes here to pick me up for a real date?

And how will they act when they find out his age is a lot closer to Gretchen's than mine?

noah meets me just inside the nursing home doors, a guitar case in his hand. "Hey there."

"Hey yourself. I didn't know you played guitar."

"Yes, ma'am. You?"

"No." I shake my head. "A little piano, but no guitar."

Noah sets the case down, takes my coat, and hangs it on a nearby rack.

In one corner of the nursing home's large front living room, a group of residents clusters around a television, watching *Wheel of Fortune*. In another corner, a pair of men gaze at a battered checkerboard while several white-haired women sit at a card table, working yarn through plastic mesh squares.

Noah picks up his guitar case. "Are you ready?"

He leads me through the maze of walkers, wheelchairs, and workers in the front room and down the hall where he pauses, frowning.

"What's wrong?"

"Nothing. Well, maybe nothing. I should probably warn you that there might be a few people who, um, stare at us."

"Oh, that. No worries. I volunteered here when I was in middle school. It doesn't bug me." I start forward again, but Noah stops me with a touch on my arm.

"No, I don't mean the residents. I mean people from my church."

"What? Why?"

"Well . . ." Noah licks his lips. "When I told the music director I was bringing a friend, some of the guys in the band overheard and asked, 'Bass, baritone, or tenor?'"

"None of the above." I laugh.

"Right. When I said, 'alto,' well . . ." He shrugs. "I warned the guys to be on their best behavior, but you know how guys are."

"Gotcha. Thanks for the warning."

As Noah predicted, the men in the group, especially the older guys, participate in a good bit of elbow-ribbing when we arrive. Even Pastor Jack, the music minister, laughingly accuses Noah of being too cheap to take a girl out on a real date. The guys' teasing continues off and on throughout the evening, but it's friendly, and in the end, I feel more flattered than uncomfortable. The older women smile, but while most of the girls near my age seem friendly, there's a weird vibe coming from a few. It puts a tang of awkward in the air that has nothing—or maybe everything—to do with the guys' teasing.

We make the rounds, singing through every hall of the nursing home before ending up back in the front living room. After small gifts are handed out to the residents, the carolers find places to sit on the floor while Pastor Jack reads the Christmas story and gives a short message.

"Why don't you grab the hand of the person next to you, and we'll pray."

One of my hands is already clasped in Noah's, but for the life of me, I can't recall how or when it got there. From the look on his face, Noah is as surprised as I am to find our fingers entwined. With a half-smile and a little shrug, he takes the hand of the resident on his other side. I reach for the frail, wax-paper-skinned hand of the sweet woman in the wheelchair beside me. A hush moves through the room.

At the conclusion of his prayer, Pastor Jack looks our way. "Noah, would you lead us in 'Silent Night'?"

With a nod, Noah begins, soon joined by the rest of the carolers, as well as many of the residents.

In the adjoining hall, beyond the circle, a lone woman stretches her legs and pulls her feet against the floor, but the brakes must be set on her wheelchair, because it's not moving her forward. She stops, leans back in the chair, and sighs. A tear glistens on her cheek.

I look around to see if anyone else has noticed her plight, but all the workers and residents—even the choir members—are watching Noah.

Not that I blame them, but . . . she looks so alone.

I rise, careful not to disturb anyone more than necessary, and cross the main room into the hall.

"Do you need some help?"

Her eyes well. "I wanted to hear the singing, but I fell asleep in my chair. I thought they'd wake me."

"I can push you in, if you'd like."

"I don't want to be a bother."

"It's no bother. I'm glad to do it." I release the wheel brakes. "I'm Faith. What's your name?"

"Mrs. Harvey Welch. Gloria. I'm a widow."

I push the wheelchair forward. "Can I call you Gloria?"

"Sure, honey. That'd be fine."

I settle her into a spot as close as I can get to direct line-of-sight to Noah, the main attraction, at least in my opinion, and set the brakes.

I sit cross-legged on the floor beside her, and as I reach for her hand, I find Pastor Jack watching me. He gives me a slow nod as the song ends.

"Noah," Pastor Jack says, his gaze swiveling that direction, "how about a couple more songs?"

"Sure." Noah stands. "Does anyone have any requests?"

The residents pipe up with suggestions as if they've been waiting for the opportunity to hear their favorite Christmas carol. Noah leads us in "Away in a Manger," "Deck the Halls," "It Came Upon a Midnight Clear," and "Angels We Have Heard on High"—all songs we sang earlier—before I follow his gaze to a nurse who's looking at him with a sour expression and tapping her watch.

Wow. Scrooge much?

"Okay, one more request," he says, sending a million watts of warmth around the room with that smile, "and then we'll finish up."

"Amazing Grace!" Gloria's near-shout makes me jump.

"Excellent choice." Noah lowers his chin toward his chest and takes a deep breath. When he lifts his face again, his eyes are closed. He sings a few words, and everyone joins in.

At the end of the first verse, I'm forced to bow out because I don't know the rest of the song. But as I listen to the words and watch the emotion of the lyric play across the wizened faces of the nursing home's residents, I determine to learn the rest. It's beautiful. I see why Gloria wanted to hear this song along with the Christmas carols.

This isn't just a song. Not to them. When they talk about grace leading them home, they know the journey's not that far away.

Christmas has always seemed like an ending point to me, probably due to its positioning on the calendar. But tonight, in the words of that song and the faces of those so close to realizing eternity, I recognize my error. Christmas is not the end at all, but the beginning of something beautiful and sacred. This is hope, revealed. Renewed.

Gloria's eyes are closed, but there's a fresh shiny path on one cheek. I'm moved by the confident awe giving depth to her time-shaken voice as she sings the second-to-last verse. Tears well, but somehow I manage to hold it together. Barely.

"*Yes, when this flesh and heart shall fail, and mortal life shall cease, I shall possess, within the veil, a life of joy and peace.*"

By the end of the sixth and final verse, my throat is tight with the beauty of the song's lyric as a whole, as well as how I've heard and seen it sung here tonight. Tears sting my eyes. It's almost a relief when Pastor Jack takes a seat at the piano and plays the opening bars of "Joy to the World," signifying the program's close.

I wheel Gloria back to her room myself, visiting with her a little bit and thanking her for requesting that song before returning to the main room where Noah waits for me.

"You're awfully quiet," Noah says as we make our way to the parking lot.

"Just thinking. Thanks for asking me to come. It was really nice."

"Thanks for bringing that lady in. *That* was nice." At my look, he says, "I wondered where you were going when you got up, but I couldn't ask. Then I saw you wheel her in. Pastor Jack told me the rest. That was very cool of you."

I shrug. "She seemed so lonely."

When we arrive at Fellowship Community Church, Noah takes my coat to hang it up. As soon as he's out of sight, two of the younger carolers approach me.

"Hi, I'm Kaitlyn Roscoe. This is Bailee Stevens."

"Nice to meet you. I'm Faith."

"You're Gretchen Prescott's little sister?"

I nod. "You played volleyball with her, right?"

Kaitlyn nudges her friend. "I told you."

"Yes," Bailee answers. "We both did. We were a grade ahead of your sister."

"Faith," Kaitlyn says, frowning in a way that sets off warning bells in my mind, "you do know that Noah is a good Christian guy, right?"

"The best," Bailee adds.

"Yes. I know."

They exchange a look. "We, uh, don't want to see him get hurt."

It takes a moment for the implication to make sense.

Oh. They assume I'm like my sister.

Bailee nudges Kaitlyn, whispering, "Here he comes."

"You have a beautiful voice, Faith." Kaitlyn's voice is louder now, friendlier, and it's certainly not for my benefit. Her smile is twenty kinds of fake. "Thanks for singing with us tonight."

So that's how you're going to play it. "Thanks for having me." I smile stiffly. "It was fun."

"Pastor Jack is setting up *Pictionary,*" she addresses Noah, who has arrived at my side. "Do you guys want to play with us?"

"I already told Kev and Darren we'd play *Guesstures,* but . . ." He looks at me. "What do you want to do?"

"*Guesstures,*" I concur, maybe a little too quickly to be polite.

Kaitlyn and Bailee go their merry way, not a moment too soon for my taste.

"Faith?" Noah's expression is one giant question mark of concern. "Did I miss something? What happened here?"

"Nothing. It doesn't matter." I force a smile. "So, where do we find this *Guesstures* game?"

Noah puts his thumb under my chin and gently turns my face

up. "What did they say to you?"

I sigh. "I guess they're worried about your reputation."

Noah wrinkles his nose. "Why?"

"Because they know my sister."

His lips round. "I'm sorry. They shouldn't judge you by—"

A low chuckle sounds, and Noah takes a step back as one of the older choir members approaches. "Hey, Al."

The large-bellied, gray-bearded man laughs and then grabs one of my hands and one of Noah's hands and sticks them together. "That's better. Don't get embarrassed, kids. We've all been there. And everybody knows," he clears his throat and sings an improvised melody, "*Christmastime is the perfect time for fall-ing in love.*"

Every head turns our direction.

"Now, you keep an eye on this rascal, Miss Faith. And focus a wary glance upward now and then. You never know where that pesky mistletoe might show up this time of year!" Al winks at me, and then, with a slap to Noah's back that almost takes him off his feet, Al moves toward a cluster of people closer to his own generation.

"Uh, sorry about that." Noah squeezes my hand but doesn't let go. "You okay?"

"Yeah. I'm good." Al's just messing around. But Kaitlyn and Bailee were not, and I feel a little smaller, and the evening is a little soiled now, knowing that Gretchen's shadow lurks over me even within the walls of a church.

Christmas Eve arrives. The stockings are hung. I'm all dressed up, ready to attend First Church of Kanton with my family, as is tradition.

> **Noah:**
> **Wish you were here.**

> **Faith:**
> **Me too.**

> **Noah:**
> **But I'm sure your**
> **service will be good.**

> **Faith:**
> **Still...I'd rather be at**
> **yours.**

Noah:
**Variety is the spice
of life, or so they
say.**

Faith:
**The Prescotts prefer life
blandly seasoned.**

Noah:
**Says she with the
cinnamon hair…
and eyes. Have I
mentioned that your
hair and eyes are the
same lovely shade
of cinnamon?**

Faith:
**Once or twice. Or 50
times. Whichever.**

Noah:
Well, it's true.

With my brown leather boots under my arm, I take a chair in the breakfast room where Mom and Dad are waiting with their wool dress coats slung over the backs of their chairs. They're sipping coffee—it's decaf, so what's the point?—until it's time to leave for the service. As I slip my foot into the boot and pull up the side zipper, a swish of slippers crosses the breakfast room's slate floor.

My sister's golden hair is tousled, as if she's just gotten up from a nightmarish nap. She's wearing an oversized U of I sweatshirt and black fleece pants.

"Gretchen! What in the *world* are you wearing?"

"My pajamas, duh."

"But we're leaving for the Christmas Eve service in ten minutes!"

"I'm not going."

"Of course you're going."

"I told you, Mom. I don't feel good. I'm staying home."

Dad makes a sound in his throat, somewhere between a huff and a grunt.

Mom stands up and presses her lips to Gretchen's forehead. "You don't have a fever."

"My stomach hurts. And I've got a really bad headache."

I can't stop the snort that escapes through my nose. I was still awake when Gretchen, smelling like the dumpster behind a smoky bar, stumbled into my bedroom by mistake at two-thirty this morning.

"How long will it take you to be presentable?" Dad glowers over the top of his paper. "We need to leave in fifteen minutes, or we'll be stuck sitting in the front row."

"Didn't you hear me? I'm sick. I cannot sit through two hours of off-key Christmas carols while some snot-nosed brat pretends to be the Virgin Mary."

"Poor Gretchen," I say. "And here you thought you'd already met your church quota for the season, what with all that time you spent worshipping at the porcelain altar this morning."

"Shut up, Faith. Seriously, Mom." Gretchen plops down in a chair. "I really don't feel well."

Dad's eyebrows draw together. "Were you out drinking last night, Gretchen?"

"I was at a Christmas party. We had a few toasts. Nothing big."

"You're underage."

Gretchen waves off Dad's concerns. "I heard there's a stomach bug going around. I think maybe I caught it."

Mom's lips press together. "Maybe we should stay home."

"No," Gretchen is quick to say. "I don't want to ruin Christmas Eve for you guys. I'll stay home. You three go."

Mom moves to the kitchen, calling over her shoulder, "Why don't you go back upstairs, honey? I'll bring you a glass of ginger ale and some soda crackers, okay?"

"Thanks, Mom." But as soon as Mom turns her back, Gretchen gives me a feigned-innocence, eye-batting smile.

"Oh, right." I roll my eyes. "There's that mature college girl again."

"Girls, please. It's Christmas Eve." Dad snatches his coffee cup and follows Mom into the kitchen. "So are we going to church tonight or not?" His voice is tense.

"You and Faith can go if you want, I guess." Mom sounds resigned. Sad, even. "I'd better stay here with Gretchen. Make sure she's okay." A new soda bottle hisses open. "You could call your mother. Maybe she'd like to go with you."

Did I hear that right? Did Mom just suggest we take Grandma Maddie to church in her place? I meet my sister's eyes. "Whoa. Did you hear that?"

"Yeah," Gretchen whispers back. "Whoa."

We both lean in to better hear what's going on in the kitchen.

"Gretchen is hung over. She doesn't need a nursemaid."

Score one for Dad.

"There *is* a stomach virus going around, and you know how contagious those are. What if she gets dehydrated?"

Score two for Mom.

"Dehydration is just as likely, if not more so, from overindulgence of alcohol. If she can walk down here, she can get a glass of water and manage two hours without us."

Yay, Dad!

"And risk spreading a virus to the whole church? That's not right. She should stay home, but . . . I don't want my little girl home alone on Christmas Eve. Especially if she's under the weather." Mom pauses. Her voice drops into a sadder pitch. "Families should be together on Christmas. Why should we be in a sanctuary filled with people we barely even *like* when someone we *love* is at home, not only sick but alone?"

That's it, then. We have a winner. Mom doesn't want to go to Christmas Eve service any more than Gretchen does, but she doesn't want us to go without her either. And she certainly doesn't want us to pick spending the evening with Grandma Maddie over *her*.

I glance at my sister, who's biting her lip, probably wondering the same thing I am: Will Dad pick up on Mom's cues, or will he call Grandma and guarantee himself—all of us, really—an icy Christmas morning?

But for the quiet glug of soda crossing ice into a glass, the kitchen is silent.

My shoulders tense, and I share another wince with my sister.

"Sorry," she whispers. "But even if I wanted to go, there's not enough time to get ready now."

Too bad she didn't think about that before she went out and got hammered last night.

"You're right," Dad says, finally. "Families should be together on Christmas Eve. If you and Gretchen are staying home, we all stay home."

And that nixes my backup plan of asking if I can go to the service at Fellowship Community, too.

"Aww," Mom coos in a tone that sounds so much like Gretchen

it turns my stomach. "That is so sweet. Thanks, honey." I don't need to hear the little smack to know she kissed him, but I do.

Gross.

Not the kiss, the manipulation. Okay, the my-parents-are-kissing part, too. But the manipulation more.

Not that I've ever wondered where Gretchen learned to manipulate people, but seriously? Mom may be more subtle about it, but her motives are as transparent as a freshly cleaned window.

Dad's wingtip shoes move across the kitchen, toward the hall and his study. Obviously, Dad's definition of "together" means *under the same roof, no interaction necessary.*

Gretchen heads upstairs. Mom soon follows.

Silent night, indeed.

> *Faith:*
> **My sister is "sick."**
> **We're staying home.**

> *Noah:*
> **Come here! You can**
> **still make it in time.**

> *Faith:*
> **I wish. Parental veto.**

His next text is a pic of him, sad-faced, with a finger under one eye as if wiping a tear. I laugh but quickly snap a matching pic and send it to him.

With a sigh, I unzip my boots. Once back in my room, I change out of my dressy clothes and into comfy sweats. As I'm hanging my wool skirt up in my closet, my phone chimes, alerting me to a new text.

Noah:
SERVICE STARTING.
C U SOON. LUKE 2.

I do a double-take, wondering if I've accidentally received a text from someone named Luke. But no. It's Noah, sending a Bible reference, which is far from unusual. He often ends our nightly texting marathons with a Bible reference, but he must have been in a hurry with this text, because he generally reserves the caps lock for emphasis—and he almost always texts complete words, if not complete sentences—which puts him in the "keeper" column in my book. I know he's really busy tonight and texting me between things, which is sweet, so I don't mind. Also, he's *Noah*, and the fact that he texts me at all still kind of blows me away if I stop and think about it.

I reach for the little pink Bible I was given by my third-grade Sunday School teacher. Though it was sadly neglected in the intervening years, the past few weeks have often found it open on my desk instead of shelved in my bookcase.

I think back to my childhood, to the summer weeks spent at Vacation Bible School. Along with the other kids, I learned a song to help me memorize the books of the Bible. *Matthew, Mark . . . Luke!* I turn to chapter two and begin to read.

The Christmas Story. But a different telling than what Pastor Jack read at the nursing home. I smile. It's pretty cool Noah found a way to ensure that my Christmas Eve wouldn't be totally ruined by my sister's—and my mother's—selfishness.

But once he actually meets my family, will he even want to stick around?

*R*ehearsals for *The Sound of Music* are put on a two-week hold for the holidays. With Noah working a lot of extra hours covering shifts for his coworkers, and my family making our annual trek to visit my mom's side of the family in Omaha, I don't see him at all. Thanks to modern technology, however, not a day goes by that we don't talk, if only with our thumbs.

Still, I miss him. It's the oddest sort of loneliness, kind of like that mid-July feeling you get when you're not ready to go back to school yet, but you really miss seeing your friends all day. Except it's weirder because I also feel like I'm missing part of me. It doesn't make sense, but I don't know how else to explain it other than . . . I'm more "me"—or at least a more complete version—when I'm with him. But I'm not with him, so . . .

> **Noah:**
> **10, 9, 8, 7...**

> **Faith:**
> **4, 3, 2...**

Noah:
Happy New Year,
Madeleine Faith!

> **Faith:**
> **Happy New Year,**
> **Noah... I don't know**
> **your middle name!**

Noah:
Thomas. After my
dad.

> **Faith:**
> **Nice. Happy New Year,**
> **Noah Thomas!**

When Christmas break ends, life resumes at a frantic pitch. January speeds by.

Noah:
I get off at 3. Want
to hang out?

> **Faith:**
> **I wish. Speech after**
> **school + Dance Team**
> **practice tonight. Sorry.**

Noah:
Oh. Grab dinner
w/me before
rehearsal Friday?

Faith:
**Absolutely! Speech
practice, tho. Meet
@school @4:30?**

Noah:
**Yes! Finally! Seems
like forever.**

Faith:
**At least we've had
thumb speak.**

Noah:
**My thumbs salute
your thumbs**

Faith:
My fist bumps your fist

Noah:
**I'll see that fistbump
and raise you a
((hug)) on Friday.**

Faith:
Deal.

Noah is pacing beside a loudly purring Eliza when I come out of school.

"Why aren't you inside the car?" I call out. "It's freezing!"

He looks up, grins, and closes the distance between us. "I promised you a hug, didn't I?"

Before I can respond, he wraps his arms around me and lifts me off the ground, spinning two full circles. After the initial gasp, I laugh—three exhalations of varied pitches that free something I didn't even know was trapped inside, imparting nothing less than relief as he spins me one more time before setting me down and taking a step back.

"You, Madeleine Faith Prescott, are a sight for sore eyes."

"You, too." I'm grinning, the cheek-aching kind of grin. "It's been forever."

"Too long. Hungry?"

"Starving. Today's mystery meat selection did not appeal."

"Does cheese-free pizza sound good?"

"Sure." Cheese sounds better, but dairy before a rehearsal is a hard no.

We eat at a little pizza joint on the square in Leopold. They do mostly delivery, but there are a few wobbly tables. It's piping hot—much appreciated on this frigid January night—and so loaded with other toppings that I almost don't miss the cheese. He insists on paying. After fifteen seconds of useless argument, I let him.

Even bundled up as we are, it's a cold jaunt to rehearsal. Walking along the sidewalk just outside the Opera House, we amuse ourselves by trying to make fog shapes with our breath in the January air. We're terrible at it, and the laughter we share takes the edge off the tension I've felt since I looked at the schedule and saw which scene we're rehearsing tonight: our duet, "Sixteen Going on Seventeen."

We've done the blocking, our lines are memorized, and we've practiced the song several times with and without Dr. Hitchings's direction—even over the phone once or twice. Tonight, we'll put it all together.

And finally add in the end-of-scene kiss.

I'm nervous. So, so nervous.

This is the first rehearsal Dr. Hitchings scheduled for a Friday. Lucky for me, it was an away basketball game night, so I didn't have to perform with the Dance Team at halftime. We linger over our pizza but still arrive in time to see three other scenes, mostly featuring nuns.

I should say *Noah* watches three other scenes. But first, like the gentleman he is, he goes back out into the cold and retrieves my book bag from Eliza's backseat. Yes, it's Friday, and I have the rest of the weekend to do my homework, but I need something to focus on other than our upcoming kiss. Otherwise, the subtly fluttering butterflies in my middle might take over my brain.

My relationship with Noah is a strange incarnation of the friendzone. I can't deny I have romantic feelings toward him, but ever since the age-thing came up that day at the waterfall, we haven't spoken of dating, only of hanging out. The three months since we met have gone by quickly, but so . . . deeply. Somewhere on that timeline, I forgot that he's nineteen and I'm sixteen and we're the old best friends we've just met. Sometimes, our hands end up entwined. And ohmygosh, he gives the *best* hugs. But . . .

But tonight—on that stage, in this scene—I am going to kiss Noah Spencer.

It's just acting, I try to tell myself. *We're just actors, acting.*

Still, my heart is beating so fast, my breath can't quite keep up. Or maybe it's the cold air still imparting the almost-dizzy, can't-catch-my-breath feeling? Nah, we've been inside for a while now.

Every Noah-interaction leaves me crushing harder on him. What if this scene is our make-it-or-break-it moment? What if the execution of this kiss determines every future thing between us?

Acting. We're just acting.

Acting, acting, acting.

Breathe.

Maybe this kiss is simply the proverbial bandage we need to rip off and stash in the "be a professional!" acting bin. Maybe we need to leave the offstage reality of our relationship safely within the friendzone.

Except . . . I don't want to stay in the friendzone—or whatever this somewhat-romantic, hand-holding friendship thing is—with Noah. I think . . .

I think I've fallen for him.

No, I *know* I've fallen for him. Hard. Beyond crushing. Far beyond it. But I don't know what to do about that, especially within the framework of the scene—the kiss—we're about to perform.

The Abbess and Maria are working through the "Climb Every Mountain" song now. When Dr. Hitchings is satisfied, he dismisses them and calls out, "Rolf! Liesl! You're up!"

While the stage crew exchanges the last scene's props for ours, Dr. Hitchings sends us through a scale or two to warm up and has us sing our duet by the piano once before sending us up to the stage. There's no set yet, but the stage crew has provided a bicycle, a lamp post, and a park bench.

I can't remember the last time I had butterflies this crazed in my stomach. But they're not just in my stomach. They're fluttering around my chest, pressing the outer walls of my windpipe.

Breathe, Faith. Breathe from your diaphragm. Be a professional.

My silent pep talk takes me off the fluttery edge.

We get through the lines, hit our marks, but the scene feels stiff. Off. And I can't shake it. Noah sings. I react—

"More flirtatiousness, Liesl!" Dr. Hitchings hollers, and a moment later, "No, no, no! Stop."

The piano halts. Dr. Hitchings motions us downstage. He puts his hands on his hips, scowling up at Noah and then at me. "What happened?" He crosses his arms at his chest. "Are you kids having a spat or something?"

"No, sir," Noah says. I shake my head.

"Do you even *like* each other? At *all*?"

"Very much," Noah responds.

I nod, but my brain is an echo chamber, repeating Noah's answer.

"That's what I thought. But even if you reach a point where you are sworn enemies, your guts writhing with animosity toward each other, it dies,"—he slices a finger across his throat—"before you take the stage. It. Dies. Understand? The nanosecond you step up *there* . . . all else disappears. You." His points at me with such force I almost expect a sound. "Once you set foot on my stage, you cease to be Madeleine. You are Liesl. You don't ease into being some wishy-washy version of Liesl. You *are* Liesl. Instantaneously. And you?" He jabs his finger Noah's direction. "You cease being Noah. On this stage, you are seventeen, going on eighteen, and you are alone with a pretty girl you want to impress with your maturity and worldly wisdom. You are Rolf. Clear?"

"Yes, sir." Noah says, and I echo him.

Dr. Hitchings drops his arms and gives us one emphatic nod. "Now *show* me."

We return to our opening blocking marks.

"Show me cat and mouse, Liesl!" Dr. Hitchings calls. "Man versus minx, with just a touch of innocence hiding behind your desire to fully develop your inner minx-ness. Got it?"

My inner minx-ness. Um . . . sure. I think.

"Okay." I nod again, feeling a little bit like my head is on a spring. "Got it."

"Go get him." Dr. Hitchings flourishes a hand toward the piano. "From the top!"

My cheeks match my ears for heat. I'm so glad I wore my hair down tonight.

Top of the scene. Noah's lines. My lines. He sings. I sing. We dance, we dance, and then comes the first lift—oh! It's like flying! He's never lifted me this high before—a spin, another lift, dance, dance, lift, twirl out, back and . . .

It's time to kiss Noah.

Rolf. *Rolf!*

I reach up on my tiptoes . . . and plant my lips squarely on his lips.

He does not respond.

But that is the response expected from poor shocked Rolf.

I hold . . . hold . . . and then pull away, grinning: first at the boy I just kissed and then at the audience, but it's a forced smile.

As the script and direction requires, I let out a "Whee!" and then kick up my heels and flounce off the stage, leaving Noah—er, Rolf— dumbfounded, center stage, awaiting the lights out that won't actually happen until tech rehearsal, the week before the show opens.

I'm such an idiot. Such. An. Idiot! Why did I build up that kiss so much in my head?

Kiss? Ha! That wasn't a kiss. That was counting, with timed lip-contact and an audience. And it's hardly worthy of the smattering of applause coming from our cast members in the audience.

Inwardly cringing, I return to the stage for critique.

"Better," Dr. Hitchings says. "Still a little stiff. I want more. More! Again, from the top."

Deep breath in, out. *I am Liesl Von Trapp. I'm innocent, but I am no angel.*

When I open my eyes, I'm seeing Rolf, not Noah. When I kiss Rolf, I put my arms around his neck and press that kiss on him with gusto—as Liesl, not Faith.

"Now *that's* what I'm talking about!" Dr. Hitchings exclaims. "One more time!"

We reset. By the fourth time through, the rest of the cast has departed for the evening. The next "one more time" is literal, and this time, I'm confident we nailed it. The only people left in the audience are Dr. Hitchings, sitting in the front row, and his wife, on piano, but both are beaming.

We are dismissed, and my adrenaline—or whatever chemical causes breathless butterfly sensations—crashes. I'm exhausted. Elated. Embarrassed. Spent.

Noah needs to talk to Dr. Hitchings about next week's practice schedule. Not looking forward to introducing my backside to the thorough chill of Eliza's cracked leather upholstery, I find Noah's coat and dig the keys out of the pocket. For once, I'm the one being chivalrous. Eliza won't be fully warmed by the time he comes out, but at least she'll be nearer the door.

Outside the Opera House, I pace, blowing into my cupped gloves while waiting for Noah to finish talking with Dr. Hitchings inside—and for Eliza to warm up enough that the heat vents can blow something warmer than the frigid January air. Hearing Noah's laugh, I turn toward the Opera House. He's just outside the door, talking with the director and his wife as they lock up.

"Oh, you're still here, Madeleine?" Nancy Hitchings calls with a smile. "Were you waiting for *me*?"

Her tone tells me she's kidding. "Sorry, but no. I'm waiting for my carpool buddy. It's quite a commute from Kanton to Leopold, you know. Ride-sharing is a must."

"Indeed," Nancy laughs and pulls her coat tighter. "You should have warmed up the car for her, Noah! It's freezing out here!"

I point to Eliza, humming loudly at the curb. "No worries. I swiped his keys and brought the car up. But the seats were so cold that I thought I'd be warmer out here, walking around."

"You're probably right." Noah grimaces. "It takes a while for the old clunker's heat to kick in."

"I'm looking forward to a warm fire and a cup of tea when I get home." Nancy gives a "*brrrrr!*" and a full-body rhumba-dance shiver. "What do you say, Maestro? Shall we let these fine young actors take their leave of us?"

"We shall, indeed. Thanks for agreeing to a Friday night practice, kids. I know you would rather be at the movies or a ballgame or something."

Is he kidding? I'm doing theatre. With Noah Spencer. There is nowhere I'd rather be.

"I appreciate your dedication. And that you take direction so well," Dr. Hitchings adds. "Not everyone does, you know."

"No problem." Noah waves it off.

"You kids have a safe drive home now."

"Will do." When we reach the bottom steps, Noah puts his arm around my shoulders. "Sorry Eliza's such a cold-hearted beast."

"Aw, she's not so bad. I hope you don't mind about the key-swiping. I probably should have asked . . ."

"No, I'm grateful." He gives me a wide smile and tugs me to his side. "Practice went well tonight, don't you think?"

A hint of heat stings the cold tips of my ears. "Mm-hmm. After a while."

"Yeah. That first time through was a little . . . rough."

Kill. Me. Now. "Yeah."

I pause at the curb for Noah to open the car door and remind myself—again—that it wasn't me kissing Noah. It was Liesl kissing Rolf. But regardless of his arm around my shoulders or the way I fit so perfectly snuggled into his side, I'm not sure which way we're leaning on this narrow ledge between friendzone and romance.

But he likes me. Very much.

Noah wrenches the passenger door open, interrupting my

musings. As I climb in, he asks, "Are you in a hurry to get back home?"

"No. I do turn into a pumpkin at midnight, but as long as I make curfew, we're cool."

"Do you have a lot of homework this weekend?"

"I finished it right about the time Dr. Hitchings was trying to convince Darla that her Austrian accent wasn't necessary to the integrity of her character."

"Whatever that accent was, it wasn't Austrian." Noah laughs. "It sounded like a cross between Scottish and . . . I don't know . . . *Vietnamese?*"

"For real." I laugh through my grimace. "But, back to your question. No, I'm not in a hurry to get home. I mean, it's nine o'clock on Friday night."

With a cockeyed grin, he hums a few bars of a song.

"'Piano Man'?" I guess. He nods. "Wrong day. In the song, it's a *Saturday.*"

"You know me, always changing the lyrics to suit the moment." He winks and slams the car door. Eliza requires a firm hand.

"I can't be out too late tonight," he explains after he cranks the now-lukewarm heat. "I'm on the early shift tomorrow. But I'd like to show you something I helped Mac build a couple summers ago, if you're interested."

"Sure. A house?"

"Not remotely." Noah looks over and smiles. "Let me surprise you."

About three miles outside of Kanton, Noah turns onto a snow-packed gravel road. The county road crews have done an admirable job clearing a path, but Noah is careful to take it slow.

He points at a large Cape Cod style house. "That's where I live. There's a set of stairs just inside the garage that lead up to my apartment, so I can come and go as I please without bothering anyone."

Is he taking me to his—?

"Noah, I don't think we—" My words cut off when he doesn't turn into the driveway.

"What's wrong?"

"Never mind. Sorry. I thought you were going to take me to your apartment."

"Uh, no." He shakes his head. "That would be a really bad idea. Besides, this is much better. And we're almost there." Noah makes a slow, sharp right into what looks like a field entrance, but wide tire tracks and piles of snow to either side show it's been recently plowed.

"There's a stocked pond just down this lane. It's frozen now, of course, but since Mac likes to go ice fishing, he keeps the path cleared. There aren't any lights around, and the trees are still small, but the dock—that's what I helped build—is a great place to stargaze." The car hits a bump. "Sorry. It's not really a road."

"I'm a farm girl." I grin. "I can take it."

"A farm girl?" Noah laughs. "You are *so* not a farm girl. You live in Parre Hills, the only gated community within a ninety-mile radius."

"Okay, but it's kind of in the country, and my mom has a big garden, so it's almost the same thing."

"I'm not sure the thousand-acre, combine-driving FFA members would agree, but . . . whatever you say, Farm Girl." Noah chuckles and shifts the car into park. He pushes the overhead light on. "I'm glad you wore boots. We'll have to walk the rest of the way."

I turn sideways in my seat, press my feet against the door, and pull the door handle. The door wrenches open, almost hitting Noah as he comes around to my side of the car.

"Oh! Sorry!" I step onto the pathway's well-packed snow.

"You're stealing my chivalry."

I grasp his offered hand. "I can stage a do-over if it makes you feel better." Placing the back of my hand across my forehead, I adopt a breathy southern accent. "Oh, de-ah me, Mista Spensa. I do believe I feel a bit of a swoon comin' on."

I tip to the right and let myself fall. Noah will catch me.

He does. But then, with a grin, he lets go.

I gasp, drop a few more inches, and . . .

"Gotcha." Noah catches me again, this time in a ballroom-style dip.

His face is less than two inches away from mine, the position of our bodies straight out of the moment in an old movie when the hero is about to kiss the girl.

Please, please, let him kiss the girl!

The warmth of Noah's cinnamon-scented breath draws nearer, and then . . . he pulls me upright, clears his throat, and takes hold of my hand. "Let's go down to the pond."

I nod, but insecurity trills through my shallow breaths. "Okay."

It's good, what we have. I need to accept that our version of the friendzone is all Noah wants from me. It should be enough.

I want more.

But if he doesn't . . . I can accept that.

Eventually.

A thin top layer of snow has melted into ice. Our boots crunch through it. Above, the secretive stars whisper in winks of glitter over the white-covered ground. My breath fogs the air. My nose and cheeks are already cold, but warmth pulses through my gloved fingers, laced with his.

"Careful, now."

Noah leads me a few steps out onto the wide dock. A darker path—sand, I think—is sprinkled on the snow-covered dock, providing a less-slippery surface. A little further down, a bench awaits, closer to the edge.

"Our friendship has grown a lot over the past few weeks, don't you think?" In the clear night air, Noah's voice seems shockingly loud, even though he's speaking quietly.

I nod. "Mm-hmm."

"And tonight I . . . Well, I . . ." Noah places his hand on the small of my back and says, "Would you like to sit down?" He leads me to the bench.

I bend to sit, but when he says, "Wait." I straighten my legs.

Noah moves directly in front of me. "At practice tonight, I . . ." He turns his gaze up toward the stars, down to the snow, back toward the car—everywhere but at me. "What I mean is . . . the kiss. On stage."

My gut clenches. Here it comes. This is when he makes sure I understand we're only ever going to be friends and that our stage kiss was just acting. "What about it?"

"I can do better."

I blink. *What?*

"I thought the scene went pretty well by the end of practice," I say, feeling my forehead bunch in a frown beneath my stocking hat. "You looked surprised, every time. But . . . you're supposed to. Did you think Liesl came on too strong?"

"No, it's not that." Noah shakes his head. "You were perfect. Liesl's *supposed* to come on strong. The scene was great. Really. But . . . I just don't want you to think that's how I would kiss you, if *I* kissed you. Me, I mean. Not Rolf."

He takes a deep breath and lets it out slowly.

"That's not how I wanted our first kiss to go. I mean, on stage, with an audience . . . critiqued by a director?" He massages his temples with gloved fingers. "I knew it was coming, but I didn't think he'd actually make us kiss at rehearsal *tonight*. I wanted our first kiss to be . . . special. And . . . I wanted to be the one to initiate it. I'm sorry."

Our first kiss. I cannot contain my smile. This is not some "Let's keep it in the friendzone" speech.

It is exactly the opposite.

My heart soars, but when I note the insecurity in his expression, it turns over and melts like warm caramel.

"Noah." I place my mitten-encased hands on either side of his face and angle my gaze upward, meeting his eyes. "Liesl kissed Rolf, and Rolf responded exactly as he should have. But I've never kissed *you*. And you've never kissed *me*."

A smile quirks Noah's lips and chases the nervousness from his eyes. "So that's the way you want to play it, huh?"

"That's the way it is."

Noah covers my hands and curls his fingers around mine, pulling them down until my hands are wrapped within his, between us. "I know we've only known each other a couple of months, but I've never felt this way about anyone before. What's going on between you and me is bigger than friendship. This sounds incredibly cheesy, and I don't mean for it to be coming out that way, but . . . I think about you all the time. I really like you, Faith. I like you as . . . as more than a friend. I want us to be more than friends."

My throat is tight. Pressure builds behind my eyes, causing them to burn and fill. A whisper is all I can manage. "Me, too."

Noah lets go of my hands. His left hand rests at my waist. His right lifts, caresses the side of my face, and then trails softly to my chin. "Madeleine Faith Prescott," he says, using his thumb and forefinger to tilt my face upward, "may I kiss you?"

My eyes are already closed when I take a tiny step forward. "Yes."

Noah's left hand moves from the side of my waist to the small of my back, soon joined by his right. My hands circle his lower back, and . . .

Our lips touch. Our only audience, the stars.

His nose nestles next to mine. My eyelashes touch his cheeks. Soft and undemanding, our first true kiss is sweet and full of promise. It's romantic. *So* romantic. Perfection.

Ever so gently, he pulls away.

Noah rests his forehead against mine. The fog of our breaths mingles. I tilt my face and meet his lips again.

He pulls me closer—this kiss surer, deeper, and no less perfect than our first.

We are starlight on snow. The reflection of something already beautiful—absorbed, reflected, and remade into something . . . more.

And this kiss . . .

This kiss is everything I've needed to say . . . and longed to hear.

My mouth recognizes his smile just before his lips move to my forehead, leaving a soft kiss there, as well.

"My Madeleine Faith," he whispers. Touching my lips with his once more, he lifts his head and pulls me close until my head rests at the hollow of his shoulder, tucked in as if it was specifically engineered to fill that space.

"I don't want to mess this up," he whispers. "I feel like I could stand here and kiss you for hours, but I don't want us to become one of those couples whose relationship turns into a series of make-out sessions. This thing, this connection between us . . . the friendship aspect of our relationship alone is too valuable to let anything ruin it."

"I know." Comfort melts through my veins. A peaceful sweetness fills me with a sense of being desired . . . but also, strangely, *protected* from desire.

"The community theatre performance is less than a month away. Before you know it, we'll be all done with Rolf and Liesl and back to being Noah and Faith full time. We'll have time to go out on a *real* date. I'll come to your house, pick you up, take you out to dinner, a movie, maybe—"

"And you'll have to meet my parents."

"Of course."

"And suffer through them giving you the third degree."

"As they should."

"Oh, sure. You say that *now*. But that's only because you haven't met them yet."

Noah is a great, moral, upstanding sort of guy. But my parents are snobs. Do they even have the ability to see beyond their prejudice toward "artsy" people, to see that Noah is a good, solid guy? That his determination to follow his theatre dreams is admirable?

And there's his age to consider, of course . . .

"It'll be fine." Noah presses a kiss to my hair. "You'll see."

I hope he's right. Maybe he is. After all, he's a smart, talented, determined, and kind person. How could they *not* like him?

I swallow around a bitter thought that leaves the taste of premonition behind. *Because they are who they are, and I am who I am.* That reason alone is enough for them to justify disliking Noah Spencer.

A shiver runs across my shoulders.

"You're getting cold. Come on, it shouldn't take old Eliza too long to warm back up."

And courteous. He's so courteous. Surely, they'll see that.

If they'll just give him a chance.

Over the next few weeks, my name appears more and more frequently on the community theatre practice schedule. Even when I'm not at the theatre, Noah and those few sweet kisses we shared at the pond—not to mention a few more we've shared since—are on my mind. Too much on my mind, maybe, since I don't realize I've been neglecting my best friend until I ask her to sleep over one Saturday night and she is . . . surprised.

> *Jenna:*
> **Srsly?**

> > *Faith:*
> > **Duh. Let's pig out &
> > binge watch something
> > til we're stupid.**

> *Jenna:*
> **Yaaaaaaas.**

Jenna:
**Speaking of pigs,
will there be bacon?**

Jenna:
& chocolate?

Faith:
**LOL. I'll see what I can
do. But you know my
mom.**

Jenna:
**Grr. Fine. I'll bring
the bacon &
chocolate.**

Faith:
Enough for two?

Jenna:
**Depends on how
hungry I am.**

Faith:
LOL

At one end of the large family room in my basement, a bar/mini kitchen is well-stocked with healthy snacks—thanks, Mom—and Jenna's not-so-healthy additions. In no time at all, we've arranged a beautiful selection of boxed candy on the coffee table and melted butter to drizzle over Mom's healthy air-popped corn. We've microwaved enough boxed bacon to clog a year off our arterial life—

or so Mom says when she comes down and sees the pile on the plate.

Jenna sticks her head out of the movie closet of my large basement family room. "Action, comedy, romance, or . . . the boys?"

"You have to ask?"

"We're still vowed to silence about our secret love for boy band deliciousness, right?"

"Yep."

"Sweet. Girls' night! *Finally*."

A few moments later, Jenna comes out of the closet holding the two DVDs we both own but would probably not admit to still watching with any of our other friends.

"*This Is Us* or *Where We Are?*" she asks, holding one DVD in each hand. "Or, should we spend the next two hours buffering through YouTube, watching the video diaries from their adorably awkward fetus days?"

"It's all good, so I don't care." Behind the family room's built-in bar, I pop open a can of soda and divide it between two glasses of ice. "You pick."

"Hmm. I don't feel like fighting the buffering spinner thingy tonight. Let's watch this one." Jenna kisses the DVD case holding *One Direction: This Is Us.*

Ignoring the sofa's intended use, we sit instead on the floor, leaning our backs against it. As the opening sequence begins, Jenna reaches into the bowl and takes a handful of popcorn. I do the same.

"So . . ." Jenna shoots a glance toward the empty staircase and then gives me a sly smile. "Noah's a pretty good kisser, huh?"

With a handful of popcorn halfway to my mouth, I freeze. "How did you—?"

"I knew it! I can't believe he finally kissed you and you didn't tell me!"

"Shh!" My eyes dart toward the stairs. "Don't let my mom hear you!"

"Okay, okay." Jenna laughs but keeps her voice low. "This is huge! I need details! It was totally romantic, wasn't it?"

I nod.

Jenna squeals. "I knew it! Deets, girl. Spill 'em."

My smile is probably wide enough to carry sunshine to the next county. I glance at the stairs again and lean in. "We were at a pond, out in the country, under the stars." A shiver travels across my shoulders at what is officially the best memory of my life so far. "It was *totally* romantic. He asked my permission first, of course—"

"Of course he did." Grinning, Jenna rolls her eyes, and I know she's hanging on my every word when she prompts, "And then . . . ?"

"His hand was on my face—it was so sweet, the way he kind of held my chin with his thumb and forefinger—and then he put his arms around me and . . . he kissed me." I can't stop the sigh.

"Awwww." Jenna sighs, too, but a moment later, she frowns. "That is so unfair. The first time Cole kissed me, he missed and got my nose. I was just getting over a cold, and it was all red and chapped. I was mortified."

"I remember."

"So . . . Noah's probably, um, pretty experienced, huh?"

"With girls?" I tilt my head. "I don't think so. Not the way you mean, anyway."

"No roaming hands?"

"No." I shake my head. "Not his style."

But the way Jenna asked makes me wonder . . .

"Does Cole have wandering hands?"

She looks toward the stairs again. "Yeah. Sometimes."

"Are you guys, um, you know . . . ?"

"No! I mean, I think he probably wants to." Jenna shakes her head. "When we started dating, I told him it wasn't going to happen.

But sometimes, when we're making out, I wonder if it's really that big of a deal."

"It *is* a big deal," I say, and I believe it. "You only get one first time."

"I know." She shakes her head. "And I know if we do it once, we'll do it a dozen times and probably end up having a huge fight someday, and then he'll mouth off to his friends, tell them I'm some sort of slut, and then everyone will talk about me the way they used to talk about your sis—" She cringes. "Sorry."

"It's okay." I know Gretchen has a bad reputation, and I don't doubt its accuracy. But she's still my sister, and it makes me angry and sad that she's so reckless, which is part of the reason I'm determined to live differently beneath her shadow.

"But, Jen . . . if Cole starts being a jerk about it, you just give me the word, and I'll bash in his kneecaps. Or his man parts. You know, whichever seems like a better idea at the time."

"Right back atcha. So you might want to warn your song and dance man. Oh. Shh! Louis solo alert!" She grabs the remote and turns up the volume.

"But seriously, Jenna, if Cole—"

"Shh!" She smacks my leg. "Hush. Forget Cole. Forget Noah." She gestures toward the TV with both hands. "All other boys cease to exist when Louis Tomlinson is singing."

I quiet as commanded, because although Louis is singing now—like the pirate version of an angel, I might add—I know that Harry is about to do a vocal riff, and he totally kills it on those.

On the carpet beside me, my phone vibrates.

Noah:
I'm on break.
Missing your smile.

Faith:
melts

Noah:
That was the goal.
Hope you're having
a good time with
Jenna.

Faith:
Yep. We have bacon &
chocolate.

Noah:
Sweet.

Noah:
...and salty.

Faith:
Cute. Your humor is
well-cured.

Faith:
I can't believe I said
that.

Faith:
My brain-to-thumb
connection is fried. I
blame the bacon.

Noah:
**I thought it was
funny.**

"No boys!" Jenna presses pause on the remote, grabs my phone, and scoots away so I can't grab it. "I take that back. Boys, yes. But only unattainable British boy band boys."

Jenna types something into my phone. Waits. It buzzes. She types something else, grins, and hands it back to me.

Faith:
**This is Jenna. We're
having a girls-only
night. Go away.**

Faith:
**Except for realz, no
boys aloud. (still Jenna,
btw)**

Noah:
**But I'm being very
quiet.**

Faith:
???

Noah:
**You said 'no boys
ALOUD'**

Noah:
**I think you meant:
"allowed"**

Faith:
**No wonder she likes
you. Nerd.**

Noah:
I like her, too.

I quickly text back.

Faith:
**Me again. Faith. I
should probably sign
off.**

Noah:
**Break is almost over,
anyway. Have a
good night with
Jenna.**

Noah:
**…but I'm still
missing your smile.**

Faith:
Right back atcha.

"Oh, geez. Your face. *Staaahp*. What did he say now?" Jenna holds out her palm. "Lemme see."

"Don't worry. We're finished." Still grinning like a crazy-for-Noah fool, I give her my phone. "Only unattainable British boy band boys for the rest of the night."

"About time!"

Jenna and I have been best friends since third grade, and although we have less and less in common as the years go by, we will always have "our boys."

"It never gets old, does it?"

"Nope. Never." Jenna grins.

We watch the movie in silence for a while, occasionally singing along. I'm used to Jenna's pitch issues. I actually find them kind of endearing.

"So . . . about Noah," she says when one of our lesser-favorite songs comes on. "Would you say you've finally found your own personal Harry Styles? Or is he more like Niall? Or Liam, maybe? Liam seems like he would make an excellent boyfriend. Please don't say he's a Louis, though. I don't want to have to fight you. Louis is mine."

"I wouldn't dare." I laugh, but the singers I'd held up as my romantic ideals of awesomeness in middle school fall strangely short when compared to Noah Spencer.

"He's like all four of them combined, only . . . better. He may even have a little bit of Zayn's soulful—"

"Oh, barf. So he's perfect." Jenna's tone is dry. She pantomimes being sick and then wiggles her eyebrows. "At least he's a good kisser."

I grin. "He is that. Now shut up and watch the movie."

"You get to kiss him on stage, right? At the thing in Leopold?"

"Yeah. Now shush already."

"I am so buying a ticket to that stupid musical."

That stops me short. "Really? But you *hate* musicals!"

"You hate volleyball, but you still come to my games."

"I don't hate volleyball."

"Liar."

"You're right. I hate volleyball. You'll really come?"

"Of course I'll come! How many times does a girl get a chance to see her best friend make out with a guy in front of her parents?"

"Don't remind me." I groan. "Dad's on call at the hospital all that weekend, but my mom is going to opening night." I wrinkle my nose. "I was secretly hoping they were going to be out of town."

"Because of the kiss?"

"No. Okay, a little, I guess," I admit when she arches one eyebrow and gives me *that look*. "But mainly it's because I'm always so nervous when they're in the audience."

"Why?"

"Because I can't do anything right. My mom's never been in a play in her life, but she's the expert on everything I'm doing wrong."

"Come on, Faith. I've heard her tell you how good you are."

"And every single time it's followed with a, '*but next time you should try to . . .*'" I grab a handful of popcorn. "It's not just that, though. I'm nervous about her meeting Noah."

"Why? He seems like a good guy. Hey!" She points at the TV. "Niall's looking at us. He is looking at us!"

It's what we imagined when we were younger, every time one of the guys looked at the camera. But even the happy sight of Niall singing directly to me—er, the camera—can't completely ease my tension about opening night and what will come after.

Eventually, Noah will have to meet my parents.

Backstage, I'm one scene away from the shrill whistle that will call Liesl von Trapp forth for her debut on the remodeled Leopold Opera House stage. Somewhere, likely near the back, my mom is watching, probably keeping a mental list of every perceived fault in the performance, if only to assuage her boredom.

Energy is high, zinging through the atmosphere so thickly that it's almost a tangible thing, at least backstage. It's a packed house, and the audience seems very responsive so far, which makes our job as performers much easier. Still, I'm sure Mom will find something someone is doing wrong, even though the only role she's ever played in a theatrical production is as a chauffeur, driving me to and from rehearsals and performances before I got my license.

In my stomach, butterflies multiply, and some grow claws as they always do this close to taking the stage. I take a deep breath, square my shoulders like the good little von Trapp child that I am about to become, and . . .

A faint waft of cinnamon cracks through the competing scents of hot lights, lingering sawdust, and set paint. As gentle fingers graze the inside of my forearm, sliding down to lace with mine in that sweet, now-familiar Noah-way, a friendlier, heart-shaped butterfly joins its stage-born brothers and sisters.

I turn a smile up at him, but I can feel its wobble.

His gaze is warm. Centering. I take a deep breath in . . . and out. Who knew cinnamon had such calming properties?

Noah squeezes my hand. "You've got this, Madeleine Faith."

I tiptoe-lean to place a well-blotted kiss on his freshly shaven, set-sprayed jaw then double check to make sure no lipstick was left behind. "Thanks."

Noah stays beside me, silent, his hand in mine. About two minutes before my entrance, he gives my hand a squeeze and releases it.

"Break a leg, Liesl," he whispers, reminding me of the mental shift I need to make, and then presses a tender but bolstering kiss to my hair—which can't be pleasant, because the makeup crew practically shellacked it with hairspray.

"Right back atcha, Rolf." He won't go on for a bit yet, but I'm saying it now anyway.

He gives me a little wink and backs away, giving me room to pass by him on my way to my entrance point, stage left.

At the interior edge of the curtain, I bounce a few times on the balls of my feet and do a neck roll left, then right. It's almost time for my entrance.

Right on cue, my jaw tightens and my mouth dries, a familiar sensation that generally follows the appearance of those illusory butterflies. But I don't fear this particular incarnation of stage fright. I *welcome* the feeling now, because I suddenly remember that those butterflies are working on my behalf. They're simply condensing the magic, *safeguarding* it . . . until the moment when I step into the lights and they give it back to me.

It's an incomparable thrill, this pre-performance high. I feel like

I could faint or cry or throw up or laugh hysterically or spontaneously combust, but . . . wow! I love this feeling. It's *such* a rush!

This. This is what I want. This is how I want to live. This is . . . me, being fully, unequivocally *alive.*

The whistle shrills. Captain von Trapp, calling his children to meet the new governess.

I.

Am.

Liesl.

I'm beaming as I take the stage for the curtain call. My body is buzzing, like the moths darting through illuminated dust motes under the stage lights. I curtsey . . . and swoop to the side, joining the other von Trapp children who came on together before me, to make room for Captain von Trapp and then Maria.

After the final bows, the houselights come up, and we exit the stage to line up and greet the audience in the lobby.

Standing between Dr. Miller—we're offstage now, so he's not my "Father" anymore—and the boy who plays Friedrich von Trapp, I smile at the audience members as they file through. But there's one person who does not file through as expected. She beelines for me.

Mom.

She offers me a plastic-wrapped mixed bouquet and one of the most disingenuous smiles I've seen since Kaitlyn Roscoe introduced herself to me.

About a million degrees of heat travel up my neck as I take the flowers, seeing she has a program in her other hand.

The program that lists "Liesl" as being played by *Madeleine Faith Prescott*.

"Thanks for coming, Mom. And for the flowers."

"You're welcome . . . *Madeleine*."

Uh-oh.

I flinch as her jaw twitches and eyes narrow. I'm a little surprised the corners of her fake smile don't crack under the weight of that ice.

"The building is not quite as fancy as I expected from your description, but it is a surprisingly extravagant facility for this size of a community."

I swallow. "Did you enjoy the show?"

"It was fine. The nuns were a little shrill at times but . . . not terrible. It was nice enough, overall. Good job."

High praise indeed, from the formidable Janet Prescott, C.P.A.

"Thank you."

"You'll be home by midnight?"

I nod. "Of course."

"Okay, then. It's been a long day. Be careful driving home."

"You, too."

She exits without speaking to any of my castmates, not that I expected her to. When she's gone, the tension in my shoulders loosens with the knowledge that she won't be coming to either of the other two performances this weekend.

Until I remember she still has that program . . . and that I'll need to tread lightly tomorrow to wipe the "Madeleine" part of it from her mind.

Saturday's matinee experiences a few bumps, as I've learned is often the case with the second performance of such a limited run. When one of the nuns forgets her entrance and slips on stage late, it's no big deal, but when Gretl, the youngest von Trapp child, forgets to deliver a pivotal line and has to be prompted, it's a breath-stealing twenty seconds or so—eternity, when you're on stage. Finally, she delivers the line, and as it must, the show goes on.

Afterward, Grandma Maddie filters down the line of performers in the lobby. Unlike Mom, she starts at the top of the receiving line and works her way down, giving out "Nice job" and "Well done" accolades as she goes.

"Madeleine Faith!" She exclaims and wraps me in a giant hug. "You were superb! Oh, my! Simply perfection." She turns to Dr. Miller, ignoring the fact that he's talking to someone else. "This is my granddaughter, you know. Isn't she wonderful?"

"She is," he says, smiling at me first and then Grandma. "We're very glad Madeleine decided to join us this year."

"Thanks, Dr. Miller." I was anxious around him at first, knowing his daughter had been vying for the same role, but he's actually a very kind man and not at all what I expected after experiencing Leopold Loyalty firsthand on audition day.

"Madeleine is my namesake," Grandma continues. "But she's the one who's going to make our name famous. This girl is going to be the toast of Broadway someday. Mark my words."

"I don't doubt it," Dr. Miller says, offering both of us another genuine smile before turning to greet the next person in line.

"Sorry I didn't make it to opening night," Grandma says, "but since your mother was coming, I thought it might be better if I . . ." She shrugs.

I get it. And she's right. Especially considering the way my name reads in the program.

"But I'll be back tonight!" Grandma gives me another breath-stealing hug. "Oh, honey. You were just wonderful. Wonderful! Ack! I'm holding up the line. See you tonight, sweetie!"

As promised, she returns a few hours later for the evening

performance, which turns out to be, at least in my opinion, the best of the three. At the curtain call, when I notice the person sitting beside her, my already-wide smile enters cheek-aching territory.

"Ryan!" In the lobby, I step into my brother's hug. "I didn't know you were coming!"

"I wanted to surprise you." He gives me an extra squeeze and steps back. "That was awesome, Faith. Really. Great show." He leans in. "And I don't think I'm biased by saying you were the best part. This musical theatre thing you've got going on? It's good." His eyes are warm, his gaze serious. Honest. "You're really, really good, Faith. You *belong* up there, on the stage. Don't let anybody tell you differently. Got it?"

There's no question as to whom his "anybody" refers. "Got it."

Ryan's words soak into places of my brain that feel parched and make them float. He's always been a wonderful big brother, but his responsibilities rarely give him time to come visit these days. I miss him. The fact that he would come to Leopold, for me, makes my day. Especially considering the cold shoulder he'll likely receive from Mom for coming with Grandma Maddie.

Or not. The parameters for cold-shouldering have always been markedly different for the non-artsy, not-named-after-their-grandmother Prescott children.

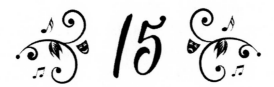

It's Sunday, the morning after that final show of *The Sound of Music*, and my mind is still happily buzzing with the last vestiges of the performance high I've been riding all week. I'm all smiles when I join Dad—and Ryan, who stayed the night—at the breakfast table.

Mom's absent this morning. Last night, when she found out Ryan went to the show with Grandma Maddie, she claimed a migraine and went to bed early. This morning, she fixed breakfast for Dad—only Dad—and then went for a run.

I've no doubt she'll have it out of her system when she gets back, though. I mean, it's *Ryan*. Not even Mom can stay angry at him for long.

"Listen to this, Dad." Across the top of *The Sommerton Journal*, Ryan winks at me. "*Under the direction of Dr. Jeremiah Hitchings, the Leopold Community Theatre christened the newly restored Leopold Opera House with a standing-room-only performance of* Rodgers and Hammerstein's The Sound of Music. It goes on, blah, blah, blah." Ryan clears his throat. "But here's the good part: *The high point of the first act was when Leopold Community Theatre newcomers Madeleine Prescott, in the role of Liesl von Trapp, and Noah Spencer, as rookie Nazi recruit Rolf, flirted their way through the most convincing portrayal of 'Sixteen Going On Seventeen' this reviewer has ever seen."* Ryan tilts the page toward his father. "Look, Dad. There's even a picture of our little star, right there!"

Dad lowers the medical journal he's reading and takes the paper from Ryan's outstretched hand.

He smiles at the photo taken during our duet. Tilting his head back a bit to peer through his bifocals, he reads the caption aloud. "*Madeleine Prescott . . .* Madeleine?" Dad arches an eyebrow at me. "Your mother's not going to like *that*."

"She already saw it in the program." I'm surprised he hasn't heard about it.

Dad sighs, shakes his head, and looks back to the paper, reading the photo's caption aloud. "*Madeleine Prescott and Noah Spencer wowed the crowd with their flirtatious duet during the Leopold Community Theatre's opening night production of* The Sound of Music." He pauses. His mouth moves silently as he re-reads the caption. "Noah Spencer. I know that name." His brow furrows as he studies the picture. "Why do I know that name?"

"I've been riding with him to Leopold for musical practice for about two months, Dad. I talk about him all the time." I roll my eyes and give my brother a look that silently conveys the *duh* I'm thinking.

Ryan chuckles.

"And he's . . ." Dad re-reads the caption. "Sixteen? Seventeen? He looks older than that."

"No. He's nineteen. The *song* was 'Sixteen Going on Seventeen.'"

Ryan shoots me a strange look. I mouth, "What?" to him, but he just frowns.

"Nineteen?" Dad pulls the picture closer. "That fits a little better. But you say he's still in *high school*?" Censure overlays Dad's words as he slides the paper back to Ryan.

"No, Dad. Noah is a student at the community college. And he works two jobs, besides. He's saving up to transfer to a theatre school in England next fall."

"A *theatre* school." Dad makes a face as if he's just smelled rotten garbage. "Well, *that's* practical."

Knife, meet chest. "It's not just any theatre program, Dad. It's the London Academy of Musical Theatre. It's one of the most well-respected—"

"Right. Right." Dad wipes a hand through the air between us as if he's erasing the content of the conversation from his memory and then picks up the medical journal again, only to pause, lowering it. "So if this Noah character is a student at the community college, what is he doing in a high school play?"

"Da-*aad*." I groan. "It wasn't a high school play. It was Leopold's community theatre." I enunciate each syllable, "Com-mu-ni-ty. As in, all ages."

"And it was really good, Dad," Ryan interjects. "Our little Faith has some serious talent. You should have seen her. She was awesome."

"If all those late night practices end up affecting Faith's grade point average, it won't be so *awesome*." Dad lifts his journal.

"Aw, c'mon, Dad." Ryan winks at me, and some of the tension in my shoulders loosens. "You know how important it is for Faith to have volunteer community involvement on her college applications."

"True," Dad concedes without looking up. "But she has to keep her grades up if she wants to get into a good school."

"My grades are fine." I clench my teeth. "I learned my lesson when you and mom made me quit ballet last year."

Ryan places his hand on my arm and squeezes, reminding me to practice restraint.

"Faith's a responsible kid, Dad. Give her a little bit of credit. Oh! That reminds me. I have next weekend off, and I wanted to run something by you."

"Two weekends off in a row? For a resident?" Dad lowers the magazine again. "How did you manage that?"

"New month. And the luck of the draw, I guess." Ryan shrugs. "Danielle and I are going to Des Moines and—"

"More wedding plans?"

"Oh, probably a little of that, but it's not the main thing. Danielle's mom got a bunch of tickets to go see *Les Misérables* at the Civic Center."

"*Les Misérables?*" My voice rises about three octaves over the course of those syllables.

He shoots me another wink. "We thought maybe we could take Faith with us this time."

With an undignified squeal, I jump out of my chair, practically knocking Ryan from his as I tackle him with a hug.

Ryan gives me a squeeze. "What do you say, Dad? If Faith can drive up to Iowa City early Saturday morning, she can ride with us to Des Moines. We'll go to the show Saturday night and stay overnight at Danielle's mom's house. We'll head home Sunday after lunch."

"I'll be at a conference in Phoenix next weekend," Dad says without looking up from his reading. "Check with your mother. See what she says."

"Thanks, Dad!" I squeal again and hug Ryan a second time. "You're the best brother ever!"

Ryan grunts from the pressure of my hug. "Yes, I am. I'll even help you clear the table." He lifts his eyebrows and nods toward the kitchen.

I start gathering the dishes, and Ryan takes what I can't carry. In the kitchen, I turn on the water and start rinsing.

Ryan takes a plate from me and loads it into the dishwasher. "So tell me about this Noah Spencer," he says in a low voice. "I have a feeling there's a little more going on than what you're telling Mom and Dad."

"I'm working up to it. You know how they are." I, too, keep my voice low. I glance toward the breakfast room. "Did you see Dad's face when I told him Noah is transferring to a *theatre* program?"

"Yeah." Ryan nods. "So they're still giving you a rough time about wanting to major in musical theatre, huh?"

"Can you call it 'giving me a rough time' if they don't even take it seriously?"

He sighs and loads another dish when I hand it to him. "And you say Noah's a freshman in college? That's a little old for you, isn't it?"

"No, it's not. We have a lot in common. And, um, he's not a freshman." I hand my brother a glass. "He's in his second year."

"I see." Ryan is quiet as he loads another two dishes. "And I take it you're a . . . couple?"

"Mm-hmm."

"I know Dad's fairly oblivious, but Mom knows you're dating him, right?"

"Um, no. Not yet. Like I said, I'm working up to it."

"But you *are* going to tell them soon, right?"

"I'll have to. I mean, we haven't really *dated*-dated yet. We've been too busy. Noah works a lot, and since he took time off for musical practices, there wasn't a lot of other time available. We rode together a lot. Hung out on breaks. You know." I shrug. "But now the musical is over. He wants to do the whole chivalry thing, you know? Come in, meet the parents." I pantomime a shiver. "It's a little scary. Mom and Dad can be so—"

"Oh, come on. They're not that bad."

"Oh yeah? Remember when Gretchen went out with that boy from Sommerton who was planning to go to tech school for computer programming rather than a four-year school?"

"No."

"Oh, yeah. You didn't come home much that year." I shut off the water and lower my voice to a whisper. "My point is that Mom and Dad are total snobs when it comes to that stuff. And Noah wants to be an actor. An *actor*, Ry! What if they say something really rude and hurt his feelings?"

"I don't think the acting thing is going to be as big a deal as the age thing."

It's not something I think about anymore when I'm with Noah, but . . . "The age thing?" *Gulp.*

"Yes, Faith. The age thing. You're only halfway through high school."

"So you think I'm too immature?"

"I didn't say that." Ryan arches an eyebrow. "*Usually,* I would say you're a lot more mature than other kids your age."

I catch his meaning. The tone of my last comment was a tad petulant.

"But life experience informs a person's natural maturity level. Face it, Faith. Noah might've played a teenager in *The Sound of Music*—and he did a great job—but in real life, Noah Spencer is an adult."

"Nineteen is still a teenager."

"And," Ryan says, crossing his arms, "regardless of how mature you think you are, you're still a minor." He sighs. "Grab the dish soap."

I fill the reservoir and replace the soap under the sink as Ryan closes the dishwasher door and starts the cycle.

"So," he says, leaning against the counter, "are things getting, uh, serious between you two?"

"Yeah."

A line forms between his eyes, just under the one creasing his forehead. "How serious?"

"Chill, bro," I laugh. "It's not like we're talking about getting married or anything. Geez."

"Well, are you being, you know, um . . ." He gives a deep, staccato grunt. "I mean, he doesn't pressure you to, well, engage in—"

Clearing his throat, Ryan curls his fingers around my elbow, steers me out of the kitchen, down the short hall, and into the laundry room, where he shuts the door.

"Faith." He turns the full force of his frown on me. "Are you sexually active?"

"*What?*" My mouth drops open. "No!" I hiss, wrinkling up my nose. "I cannot *believe* you just asked me that."

It's then I notice that, peeking out from beneath his russet-brown hair, Ryan's ears have taken on a deep shade of red. If I wasn't so embarrassed myself, I might laugh.

"Are you blushing, *Doctor* Prescott?" To cover up my discomfort, I focus on his. "Don't they teach you how to talk about this sort of stuff in med school?"

"Shut up. You're my baby sister. It's different." Smiling lopsidedly, he lets out a huff of air. "But just so we're clear . . . you're not having sex?"

"No-oo! Absolutely not. Noah's not like that, Ry. And neither am I. He's a good guy. In fact, some of the girls in Noah's church choir are worried that *I'm* going to corrupt *him*."

"You?" Ryan's eyebrows lift and then narrow. "Seriously?"

"I know, right?"

"I want to meet him."

"Today?"

"No. I have to head back home in a couple hours. But why not next weekend? I have tickets to *Les Mis*, remember? I figured you'd want to bring Jenna, but I guess if you'd rather bring Noah . . ."

"Really?" When he nods, I throw my arms around his neck and plant a kiss on his cheek. "I love-love-love you, Ryan!"

"I love you too, you little goofball. But it's not set in stone yet. I want you to get the okay from Mom and Dad first."

"*You* ask them. But wait until Mom's over being mad at you."

"And here I thought you were so mature."

"Oh, fine. I'll ask." I bite my lip. "But you come with me. For moral support."

"Fine." He chuckles. "For moral support. But remember, Noah still has to pass the big brother test."

"He will. I promise."

"I won't be easy on him."

"You're going to love him, Ry. You'll see." A grin stretches my cheeks enough to make them ache . . . then falls. "But if Mom's still mad at—"

"Pfft," Ryan says, waving his hand in a dismissive gesture. "I wouldn't worry about it. She burns hot but fizzles out just as fast. As long as neither of us mentions Grandma's name, she'll act like it never happened. You'll see."

Hair still wet from her post-run shower, Mom sits at the kitchen table opposite Ryan and me, sipping her coffee as she digests our request. True to Ryan's prediction, she's calm, rational, and unaware of the tension that has me digging my fingernails into the underside of my chair.

"And you'll be home by what time Sunday night?"

I glance at Ryan.

"We'll aim to get back to Iowa City by three," he says. "That way Faith and her friend can be back in Kanton between four and five. Will that work?"

"Let me check the calendar. Hang on. I put my phone on the charger." Mom rises from her chair and leaves the room.

"My 'friend'?" I whisper at Ryan. "Nice."

"Don't be too happy, kiddo. If Noah doesn't pass the big brother test, that's all he's ever going to be."

"And if he passes?"

Ryan leans back in his chair and crosses his arms. "Then I'll expect you to come clean with Mom and Dad immediately. Deal?"

"Deal."

"It looks like the weekend is free." Mom leans against the door frame. "But I'm not sure it would hurt you to have a weekend to rest, Faith. You've been running like mad all winter."

"Mom, it's *Les Misérables*."

"Fatigue is a serious thing. I don't want you to end up getting sick."

"I'll get to bed early this week, okay?"

Mom purses her lips, glances at Ryan. "You or Danielle will do all the driving in Des Moines, right?"

"Right."

"Good." She takes her place at the table and another sip of coffee. "Will you ask Jenna to go with?"

"Nah," I try to sound casual. "I was thinking of asking Noah. You know, the guy who played Rolf? *Les Mis* is one of his favorite musicals."

The way Mom locks eyes with me, I have to pull out every acting skill I have not to crack under the pressure and bloom into a full-on blush. After a few intense moments that feel like an hour, Mom's gaze turns back to Ryan.

"And the sleeping arrangements in Des Moines will be . . . ?"

"The bonus room over the garage has a futon and a pull-out sofa which will work for me and Noah. Danielle and Faith can share her old room."

Mom's lips press together, but she nods. "Okay. But no funny business, Faith. We don't even know this boy. Who are his parents?"

"His parents are missionaries. They live overseas."

"Why doesn't he live with his parents?"

"Because he doesn't want to be a missionary."

"Well, that's sensible, at least."

Which is less sensible in Mom's eyes: being a missionary or being an actor?

The only sound in the room is the ticking clock, the sound of which I can't recall having ever noticed before. Now, it seems obnoxiously loud as I wait for the target of my mom's stare to become anything but me.

"Faith will be well-chaperoned, Mom. Don't worry." Ryan—my hero—swoops in to break the tension. "So, can she come with us, or what?"

Mom's eyes move back to me for another eternal moment. Finally, her gaze returns to Ryan. "I suppose. I trust you, Ryan. You, at least, have a good head on your shoulders."

I grit my teeth. The implication is clear: Ryan is the mature, responsible, and dependable first-born son. Me, on the other hand? The dramatic, music-loving, artsy child? Not so much.

But maybe that's not what she means. With a little effort, I relax my jaw. Maybe Mom is just worried I'll get worn down and end up with the flu or something. She did, after all, just give me permission to go to *Les Misérables*.

And not only that, she gave me permission to go with Noah.

On our way to meet up with Ryan and Danielle in Iowa City, Noah repeatedly reassures me that he can handle my brother's test. If I wasn't gripping the steering wheel so tightly, my hands would tremble. But the anxiousness of that short drive has nothing on the moment of our arrival.

Ryan and Danielle are out the door before we've fully exited the car. We're not halfway up the sidewalk when they meet us.

Noah greets Ryan with a handshake.

"Faith," Ryan says, "Noah and I are going to head back inside for a sec. A little pre-road-trip chat."

"We'll go start the car," Danielle says, and before I can object, she takes my arm and leads me to Ryan's SUV.

Danielle tries to make small talk. And I respond, I think. But I'm shaking a little, at least on the inside, and I'm not sure my answers make sense, since I don't fully comprehend words at this point.

"It'll be okay," she says and reaches to the backseat to put her hand on my knee, probably just to make sure I realize she's talking. Wise move. "It's Ryan, remember? King of the Softies?"

"But he's— And I don't want Noah to be—"

"Noah's a good guy, right?"

"Yeah. He is. But . . . the big brother thing . . ."

Finally, after eternity has come and gone and come back around, my doctor brother and my actor boyfriend emerge, smiling.

They're both smiling.

I can breathe.

Ryan slides behind the wheel. Meeting my eyes in the rearview mirror, he gives a slow nod. "He passed," he whispers before Noah is fully in the car.

One growly teddy-bear-of-a-brother down, two fire-breathing, fine-arts-mocking parents to go.

It takes a little over two hours to reach the Des Moines Civic Center. Ryan parks in the parking garage, and after a relaxed dinner at a nearby restaurant, we walk the short distance to the venue to find our seats.

Even though I've seen the film numerous times, I am absolutely enraptured by the passion of the live performance. From the overture's opening note to the tear-jerking, triumphant end, I experience an unparalleled range of emotion that has me grinning and laughing one moment and taking Noah's offered tissue the next.

Noah squeezes my hand as we follow Ryan and Danielle out of the Civic Center. "I don't need to ask if you liked it, but . . . what was your favorite part?"

"I loved it all." Awe infects my words. "So much." No bit of film could ever convey the poignancy felt from that stage. "I can't believe how emotional it was when Javert jumped off the bridge. I hated him for what he did to Jean Valjean, but in that moment, I felt sorry for him. And it looked so real! And when Eponine died in Marius's arms! Oh!" I grip Noah's arm, coming to a dead stop on the sidewalk. "And then, when Fantine's ghost sang to Jean Valjean . . . ? *Gah!* I'm so glad you thought to bring tissues!"

"I had a feeling you might need them. A benefit of having seen it before, I suppose." Noah smiles. "Seeing you see it for the first time was just . . . cool. It brought back the wonder. I think my reaction was the same the first time. I've seen it on stage three times now, and the movie several times, of course. But it never gets old. Thanks for inviting me."

"Who else would I ask?" I wrinkle my nose, imagining Jenna's boredom. "Besides, Ryan wanted to meet you."

"Your brother's pretty cool. I wasn't sure what to expect. You made it sound like I was in for a modern version of the Spanish Inquisition."

"Was it horrible?" My voice almost squeaks on the last word.

"Uncomfortable, yes. Horrible, no. I'm a pretty straightforward guy, and I don't have anything to hide about, well, about the things he asked me about." He pauses, and a dry chuckle exits through his little cringe. "I'm not gonna lie. It got pretty personal, pretty fast."

Considering Ryan grilled me about sex last weekend, I can only imagine the sort of questions he posed to Noah.

"I am so sorry. Consider me mortified on your behalf."

"He really cares about you, Faith. Sure, it was a little awkward—okay, a lot awkward, there for a bit. And I'm not sure he believed me about . . . everything, but I survived, and he let me come with, so . . ."

"Ryan has no patience or use for liars, and he can smell a lie a mile away. He told me you passed his test. Trust me, he believes you about . . . whatever. Everything."

"Good. The subject of purity is very important to me. And I've talked about it before, with friends, in youth group, and stuff, so I've given it a lot of thought over the years. But it's a lot different when you're put on the spot by your girlfriend's big brother."

I try not to react visibly to the fact that he just referred to me as his girlfriend. He's never said it aloud before. Not to me. "I bet."

"Yeah." He chuckles. "Enough about that. I'm over it." Noah gently tugs my hand. "Wait. The 'Don't Walk' light just came on."

Ryan and Danielle have already crossed the intersection and are nearing the parking ramp. They look back at us, and Danielle sends us a little wave. I point at the light, and she gives a thumbs-up.

"I like your brother." Noah's breath fogs the chilly night air. "As soon as he came out of the apartment building in Iowa City, even before you said anything, I knew that had to be him. I'm pretty sure he talked to me after the final show last weekend, but I didn't put it together that he was your brother. Now, I don't know how I missed it. You two look so much alike. Same big brown eyes, same cinnamon-colored hair. I would never guess Gretchen could be your sister."

"We take after our dad's side of the family. Gretchen is more like Mom, all blonde and bombshell-y. Gretchen could walk onto a cover shoot for *People Magazine,* and everyone would think she belonged there."

"Yeah, you're probably right." He nods. "Gretchen is really pretty, I guess. If you're into that blonde, bombshell-y sort of look." He shoots me a cockeyed grin. "I'm not, by the way."

Warmth surges through me.

"I have a thing for brunettes. One in particular." He groans. "Wow. That was maybe the cheesiest thing I've said today. But seriously, that bombshell thing is so . . . I dunno. Not my thing. Your beauty goes deeper. What's inside your head and your heart comes through with more clarity. Your beauty is intelligent and natural. Does that make sense?"

"Thanks. But Gretchen knows how to work the helpless blonde angle pretty well."

"Boy, does she. I went to high school with her, remember?"

"Yeah. But she's smarter than you think. She can actually get pretty deep sometimes."

"Oh, I know she's smart. Gretchen was the salutatorian of our class, after all. But I always wondered what she would have been like if she would have used her powers for good instead of . . . well, whatever she used them for."

"Yeah, really." I laugh, shaking my head. "Every once in a while we see glimpses, so there is hope, I guess. Hey, the light is blinking." As it changes, we leave the curb. "So, enough about my sister. Tell me, what was *your* favorite part of *Les Mis?*"

"I know it's dorky, but I love the scene when the priest lies about Jean Valjean stealing the silver and then gives him *more* silver. I think it's a great portrayal of the way God gives people second chances." Noah takes a breath. His smile drops a few degrees. "And speaking of second chances, I need to—"

"Speed it up, you lollygaggers!" Danielle calls back. "It's chilly out here!"

"What were you going to say?"

"Later," Noah whispers as we reach the parking ramp's elevator where Ryan and Danielle are waiting. "We'll talk about it later."

"So are you guys ready to head back to my mom's," Danielle asks, "or do you want to go grab a bite somewhere?"

"I could handle a snack," Ryan offers.

"You can *always* handle a snack. Your stomach is a black hole." Danielle lightly punches his gut. "I was asking Noah and Faith."

"I'm open to whatever you guys want," Noah says. "Faith?"

"I was too excited to eat much for supper." Even though the music still rings in my ears and my heart, hunger isn't too far behind it. "Let's go eat."

"Awesome." Ryan grins and pulls the car keys from his pocket. "So, Faith, did you like the live show as much as you liked the movie?"

"*Did I?*" I let out a little squeal. "I loved it! I never knew just how *passionate* the story would be in person. Thanks, Ryan. Thanks, Danielle. And thanks, Danielle's Mom, wherever you are!"

"Brenda." Danielle laughs, shaking her head. "Her name is Brenda."

I throw my arms open and angle my face toward the cement ceiling. "Thank you, Gracious Brenda, mother of my future sister-in-law, for your magnanimous gift of theatre awesomeness!" My voice echoes through the parking ramp.

"See?" Ryan grins at his fiancée. "All the world *is* a stage for my little sister."

"But seriously, those seats your mom scored were awesome, Danielle. I think I actually felt somebody's sweat fling on me!" I'm almost embarrassed by my voice, which is in a higher range than normal and sounds nearly as giddy as I feel.

"Eww." Danielle wrinkles her nose. "I'll be sure to tell my mom how much you appreciated the flinging sweat. I, for one, would've rather been back a few more rows. Mom won the tickets in a contest at work, but she was already scheduled to be out of town this week, so she offered them to me. My only worry was that your mom wouldn't let you come with us."

I make an almost-snort sound in my throat. "I was lucky. If I had asked her myself, I'm sure she would have said no. But since *Ryan* asked, it was a shoe-in. He's the favorite." I shrug and come close to rolling my eyes. "Except, of course, when Gretchen's around."

Danielle glances over her shoulder from the front passenger seat. "Hang in there, kiddo. Your mom's a tough cookie. But you're a strong one. You'll survive."

We drive to a bar and grill close to Danielle's mother's house. While snacking on an appetizer platter, we discuss the upcoming wedding.

"Ryan's parents think we're crazy to get married before he finishes his residency," Danielle explains to Noah, "but we don't want to wait that long. Besides, I have a good job. It's not like we'll starve."

"Yes, you're very sensible." I nod. "Mom and Dad love that about you. They tell everyone about your M.B.A."

"I know. It's a little weird."

"So what are your college plans, Noah?" Ryan asks.

Noah glances at me and then back to Ryan. "If you would have asked me a week ago, I wouldn't have been able to give you a confident answer. But I finally got my acceptance letter this week, and it looks like I'll be heading to the London Academy of Musical Theatre."

"Oh, right. I think Faith mentioned something about that."

"You got in?" My voice is smaller than it should be.

"Yeah." Noah nods but doesn't meet my eyes. "I got in."

"When do you leave?"

"August tenth."

A sudden burning sensation shoots through the bridge of my nose, stealing my ability to form a coherent thought. I need to say *something*. This is big news. This is what he wants. This is the beginning of his dream coming true. I should be supportive. I should be happy for him. And I *am*, but—

Say something! My brain screams.

"Congratulations, Noah. That's—" I swallow. "That's awesome." The spinach dip sours in my stomach. "Um, which program?"

Noah finally meets my eyes. "The three-year program."

Under the table, he reaches for my hand and gives it a firm squeeze that seems to say, "*I'm sorry.*"

"I got the letter yesterday. Apparently someone dropped out, and I was next in line."

I can't believe he didn't call me. Or at least text me. This is huge. Life-changing. For both of us.

And I'm finding out about it . . . like this? He could have told me. He *should* have told me.

I try to pull my hand away, but Noah doesn't let me.

"I wanted to tell you right away, but I didn't know how. I didn't want to ruin this trip for you. I'm sorry."

I'm being stupid. Selfish. I should be happy for him. "No, no. It's fine." I force a smile. "I'm happy for you. Really."

I am, I argue against the crumbling sensation in my chest. *I am happy for him.*

But I'm devastated for me.

I try to smile, but I fear the attempt isn't all that convincing.

"Congratulations, Noah," Ryan says, clearing his throat around the awkwardness that's descended on our table. "I take it that's a pretty good program, huh?"

"It is."

"Have you ever been across the pond?"

"If you mean England, no. Unless you count a couple of airport layovers when I was a kid," Noah says. "But I've been overseas more than I've been stateside. My parents are missionaries. We lived in Eastern Europe for most of my childhood."

"Missionaries. Right. I think Faith might have mentioned that. How do your parents feel about you pursuing a life in the theatre? That's a far cry from the mission field."

"I'm sure they would have liked for me to share their calling, but they understand that I don't," Noah says. "Dad and Mom run a fine arts camp for kids—that's where I caught the theatre bug in the first place. They've said there'll always be a place for me on the camp staff, if I'm interested in joining them, but they also know that choosing a job outside of vocational ministry isn't going to negate my faith." The corner of Noah's mouth lifts. "Besides, I'm an adult, and it's my life to live. They get that."

There's a subtle change to Ryan's expression when Noah says, "*I'm an adult.*" When he glances my way, however, I look down at my plate.

It's true. Technically, Noah is an adult.

I am not.

"You seem pretty grounded." Ryan leans back and rests his arm on the booth's ledge, behind Danielle. An ornery smile flicks at the corners of his mouth. "Especially for only being nineteen. Not many kids your age could make it through the Ryan Prescott Boyfriend Screening Process." He laughs, adding, "Then again, who am I kidding? I know very few guys *my* age who could take it! In fact, I'm not sure I'd even be here right now if Danielle's brother had done that to me."

"You're terrible." I give him a stern but fake scowl, even though I want to hug him for taking the conversation away from the dangerous direction it was headed.

"But I'm thorough." He winks at me and then grins at Noah. "You passed the test for now, but . . ." He shrugs. "We'll see."

"In other words, if I hurt your little sister, you'll hunt me down and break my kneecaps, right?"

"More like skin you alive and experiment with vivisection," Ryan says. "Keep in mind, I'm a doctor. I have the tools and the skills to do it, too."

"That is, hands down, the most disgusting thing you have ever said." Danielle swats Ryan's arm. "And I had to listen to your account of a bowel obstruction surgery last week, so that's saying a lot."

"People eating food here." I shudder. "Enough with the nasty medical stuff."

"Well, at least I know where I stand," Noah says, grinning at Ryan.

The conversation turns, but I have a hard time concentrating against the refrain of *he's leaving, he's leaving, he's leaving* pounding against my heart.

The week after returning from *Les Misérables* finds Noah swamped, working around his midterm exams. We have phone contact, of course, but it's not the same. Luckily, my own teachers pile on enough end-of-the-quarter homework to keep me busy while we're apart.

I'm elbows-deep in a Physics assignment—literally, since I'm lying on my stomach on the living room floor with papers all around me and my textbook open. Mom and Dad are at some medical symposium or something, and Gretchen is home for spring break, keeping watch over the house.

In other words, me.

We've been doing our best to ignore each other, but when she plants herself in my direct line of sight and expels that huffy *look at me!* breath, I oblige.

"What."

Her purse is slung over her shoulder, and she's holding a small bunch of grapes in her hand. "I'm running into town to get some ice. You need to have this mess cleaned up by the time I get back, got it?" She pops a grape into her mouth.

"Why? And it's not a mess, it's homework."

"I don't care what it is, get rid of it. You need to clear out tonight. I'm having some friends over."

"It's Tuesday."

"So? I'm on spring break, baby. Every day is Saturday!"

"I still have Western Civ homework after this and an English Lit test on Thursday. I need to study. Can't you and your friends go somewhere else?"

"Nobody else's parents are out of town." Gretchen sorts through the collection of books on the table. "*Fahrenheit 451*. I remember that one. Very depressing." She sets it aside and then picks up my little pink Bible. "Hey, that's mine!" She opens it to the presentation page. "Oh. Guess not. I used to have one just like this. I got it from my Sunday School teacher, I think."

Gretchen tosses it on top of my open Physics textbook. I let out a huff and move it to the side.

"Mom said you were getting religion all of a sudden. You're doing a Bible study on Wednesday nights or something?"

I nod. "At Fellowship Community Church."

"Why? Never mind. Don't care." Gretchen shrugs. "Mom thinks it's a phase. Like when I dyed that blue streak in my hair for Homecoming school spirit."

"It's not a phase." Could this family *be* any more messed up?

"Whatever. Look, you need to get your stuff cleared out, okay? My friends are gonna be here soon."

"But I need to study!"

"And you can. Anywhere but here. I could be drinking daiquiris in Cancun right now, but Mom decided you needed some adult supervision while she and Dad are gone. Apparently, you have a new *friend* she's worried about. A boy." Gretchen crosses her arms and gives me a wicked half-smile. "And she wants me to keep all the bad boys away from sweet little Faithy-waithy."

"Then stop inviting your creepy friends over. Problem solved."

"Well aren't we getting sassy!" She sits down, cross-legged, almost on top of my open textbook. "So who's this new boy she's so worried about?"

"Noah Spencer. But she doesn't need to worry. He's one of the good ones."

"Noah *Spencer*?" Gretchen's eyes go wide, and she freezes, holding a grape two inches from her lips. "You don't mean *the* Noah Spencer? The one who was in *my* class?"

"Yes. And he is totally respectable. Ask anyone."

Gretchen laughs, eats the grape, and pulls another that quickly disappears into her mouth, even though she's still laughing.

"First of all, stop eating those before you choke. Secondly, what's so funny?"

"Other than Mom being worried you're going to get knocked up by Noah Spencer?" She snorts. "Noah is the polar opposite of a 'bad boy.' At least he was back in high school. Totally nice guy. Polite, almost to a fault. When he moved here, all us girls thought he was pretty hot stuff, you know? He's super cute."

As if I hadn't noticed?

"But what with the drama queen thing and the fact that he turned pretty much all of us down when we asked him out, a lot of us just assumed he was gay. Except he was *soooo* religious. But, whatever. Stranger things have climbed out of the closet than a preacher's kid who likes show tunes."

"Oh, so if a guy's not into you, he's automatically gay?"

She purses her lips sideways, looking up at the ceiling as if checking an internal database. "Yep. Pretty much."

"Well, he's not."

"You would know, apparently." Gretchen arches an eyebrow and pops another grape into her mouth. "But I never would have taken Noah for a cradle robber."

I clench my teeth so hard it shoots pain up into my cheekbones. "He's not a cradle robber."

"Whatever." My sister leans forward, gives me a big grin, and then bites down on a grape without closing her lips. Juice squirts me right in the eye and leaves a path across my textbook.

"Knock it off!" I pull my hand across the page.

Gretchen sing-songs, "Sorr-rry," and then looks at her phone.

I sigh. "What time are your friends coming?"

"In about an hour, probably. So pack up, little girl. Like I said, I don't care where you go. Just *go away*."

Gretchen digs around in her purse. "A-ha!" She holds up a small foil square and then tosses it on the floor, beside my Physics book. "Play with Noah Spencer if you must, but play it safe, you hear?"

I gape at the shiny little square. "Is that a—?"

Mother of . . . she did *not* just casually toss a *condom* out in Mom's living room.

Yes, she did.

"I can't believe you just . . . That is so nasty."

"No, it's practical and *smart*. You don't want to wind up with some disease, do you? Or pregnant?" Gretchen picks up the condom, reaches across me and my stuff, and tosses it into the open book bag just beyond arm's reach. "I get it. Noah's a good guy. But you can't even count on the good ones to be prepared. We girls have to look out for each other."

"I don't want that thing! I am not . . . doing that."

"You keep saying that, kid." Gretchen's voice softens. "But it doesn't hurt to be prepared, just in case you change your mind."

"But I—"

"You don't need to get so defensive. I'm just trying to look out for my little sister."

The tips of my ears heat, and I make a mental note to get rid of the condom the first chance I get.

"I'm out." Gretchen slings her purse over her shoulder, and the softness of a moment ago is swept away. "Be gone when I come back, 'kay?" She bats her eyes.

I slam my textbook shut, grumbling, "As if I'd actually *want* to be here with you and your creepy friends." But she's already sashaying out of the room.

After shoving the books into my bag, I grab my car keys and a light jacket. On my way out the door, I call Jenna and suggest a combination study session/dinner trip to The Smoked Salt Grille in Sommerton.

Hey, if I have to study elsewhere, I might as well see my favorite waiter, right?

"I dare you to order the barbequed ribs," Jenna teases me after Noah takes our drink order.

"Are you kidding me? What a mess!"

"A *delicious* mess. Come on, Faith! We could split an order."

"No way." I arch an eyebrow at her. "You wouldn't eat ribs if *Cole* was our waiter."

"True. A barbeque sauce goatee is not exactly attractive." Jenna plays with the end of her long blonde ponytail as she gazes at the menu. "So what are you going to get?"

"I don't know."

"Well, maybe if you studied the menu a little bit more than you studied the waiter, you'd be ready when he comes back." Jenna sighs so melodramatically a stranger might mistake *her* for the wannabe Broadway star instead of me. "I should have known you were just using me to see Noah."

"They have big booths here." I tap my pencil against her *Fahrenheit 451* study guide. "We can spread our stuff out and study while we eat." Still, I grin. Caught. "Getting to see Noah is a bonus, of course."

"I'm glad you think so."

I didn't notice Noah's approach from behind, but from the smirk on Jenna's face, she saw him coming. I try to kick her under the table.

"Missed." She grins. "Best keep those sports skills on the stage, Ace."

Noah places a large Mountain Dew in front of Jenna, but before setting my iced tea down, he reaches for the salt and sprinkles a light coating on my beverage napkin.

"You remembered!"

"At The Smoked Salt Grille, we aim to please. Jenna?" Noah offers to salt her napkin as well.

"No thanks. Salt is meant to season food, not paper products."

This argument is as old as our friendship. My brother taught me the trick when I was five. "It helps the napkin not stick to the bottom of the glass."

"I know," Jenna concedes—a rare thing, indeed, "but it looks dumb, and I've got my rep to think about. I'll let my napkin stay sticky and save the salt for my French fries, thank you very much."

Noah tosses me a wink. "Are you ladies ready to order?"

"Yep." Jenna nods. "Faith wants the baby back ribs."

"No, I don't." I kick Jenna under the table. This time, I don't miss.

"Ow! Okay, okay. Faith is still deciding, but I want the baby back ribs. And a box for the leftovers." She sticks her tongue out at me.

By the time Noah has gone through Jenna's choices of side dishes, I've picked a sandwich off the menu.

"All right, ladies, I should be out with your food in a few minutes."

Jenna watches over my shoulder as Noah walks away. "He's pretty cute."

"Mm-hmm."

"Good shoulders. Nice butt."

"All true."

"Have you told your parents you're going out?"

"We haven't actually 'gone out' yet."

"What about all those trips up to the waterfall?"

"They don't count. I mean, it's not like we're going on a date. He doesn't pick me up or drop me off. My dog comes with me. Not a date."

Jenna's look is dubious. "You have picnics, right? And you discuss acting stuff and Jesus stuff and hopes and dreams stuff—just guessing here . . ."

I nod.

"And I know he holds your hand and you hug and kiss and—"

"You make it sound like we're just going up there to make out! It's not like that at all."

"I *know*." Jenna takes a sip of her soda. "That's what makes it such a romantic stinking date!"

"It *is* romantic, but I still say it isn't a date." I grin, but . . . she has a point. Still . . . "We're hanging out. We haven't gone out, like on a real date, yet."

"Real-schmeal." Jenna rolls her eyes. "Do you know how many girls would kill to have the sorts of dates you and Noah have? Dates where a guy just wants to talk—and listen to you talk—about stuff you care about instead of just wanting to get into your . . ." Jenna breaks off with a scowl. "Well, a lot of girls would love to be in your," she makes air quotes, "not-a-real-date shoes, Faith Prescott."

I stare at my friend. "Do I need to kick Cole in his man parts?"

"What?" Jenna sputters, choking a few coughs of Mountain

Dew. "Not really. Not yet. But he's not exactly romantic, you know?" She sighs. "Cole never wants to just talk anymore. It's just all about the kissing. All the time. Honestly, I'm getting a little tired of having to take concealer with me when we go out."

"Concealer? Why?"

"To hide the evidence of chin burn, m'dear."

I laugh. "Chin *what*?"

"Chin burn. You know, it's like carpet burn from a guy's stubbly chin rubbing against yours for an extended period. Cole's a hairy guy. I mean, he's been shaving since seventh grade or something. He's got a good start on a five o'clock shadow by two in the afternoon. By nine or ten, it's like rubbing sandpaper on my skin. Translate that into a twenty-minute make-out session, and I practically need face camo before I go home."

Noah often has stubble, but I've never . . . "How come I never have that happen when Noah kisses me?"

"If I had to guess, it's probably because kissing isn't recreation for you guys like it is for Cole and me."

"Recreational kissing." I laugh. "Is that a new sport?"

"If it was, Cole and I would win the state title. Maybe the nationals. *ESPN* would be all over us." She snort-laughs. "While we're all over each other."

"Gross. Remind me to change the channel that day."

"Like you'd ever watch *ESPN* on purpose, anyway." Jenna snorts again. "But seriously, the way you describe kissing is totally different, kind of foreign to me. For you guys, it seems like it's more like . . . like the punctuation at the end of a sentence. For us, it's more like the whole paragraph. Chapter. Most of the book, actually. Probably."

She laughs, and so do I.

"But you get it, right? Cole and I kiss because we like kissing.

You and Noah kiss because you're just being in the moment or something." Jenna picks up her glass. The napkin sticks to the bottom.

I laugh. "Serves you right."

"I don't care if every drink I ever order sticks to my napkin. I will still think you're a freak for salting yours." Jenna peels the napkin off the bottom of her cup. "What were we talking about before we got sidetracked with the kissing stuff?"

"I have no idea. Studying for our *Fahrenheit* test?"

"No . . ." Jenna fiddles with her straw. "But that's probably a good idea. Quiz me."

I look over my notes and start in with some questions.

"This is boring," Jenna moans after about fifteen minutes of studying. "And you never did say why you haven't told your parents about Noah yet. Didn't Ryan make you promise to tell them as soon as you got back from Des Moines?"

"Yeah." At Jenna's look, my defenses rise. "I'll tell them. I will. Soon. But it's different with my parents. You know how they are. I have to wait for just the right moment. Ryan gets that." Although, in truth, he probably assumes I've found that moment by now.

"Yeah, yeah, yeah. Now, hush. Mr. Perfect is on his way over here with my baby back ribs, and I intend to give them my full attention."

ow that Noah knows he's going to London in August, he's working more, saving as much money as he can. We're able to meet up and hang out now and then, but it's most often a last-minute, spontaneous event.

Noah:
**Teacher in-service
today, right?**

Faith:
Yep. 1pm dismissal.

Noah:
**My 1:15 class got
canceled! Coffee at
Grady's Grind?**

Faith:
**Sweet! I can be there by
1:30, no prob.**

Noah:
**Look for the nerd
drinking the out-of-
season cinnamon
latte.**

           Faith:
           I like that cute nerd.

Noah:
**He kinda likes you,
too.**

Noah:
**Except minus the
"kinda"**

It's tax season, so my mother is working long hours, including most Saturdays. I know I promised my brother I would tell Mom and Dad about Noah, but during tax season? Mom's highest stress season of the year? Umm . . . no thank you.

I still haven't told them when Ryan and Danielle drive down for lunch on Easter Sunday.

After lunch, while Dad lightly snores in his recliner, supposedly watching a tennis match on TV, Ryan and I play chess in a corner of the living room. Danielle and Mom share the couch and are flipping through bridal magazines. Gretchen is spending the long weekend with her new boyfriend's family in Chicago.

"Checkmate." Ryan says and then lowers his voice. "Have you told them yet?"

"Um, no. Not yet. It hasn't come up."

"It hasn't come *up?*" His tone holds a warning. "I thought better of you than that. Of Noah. He knows he has to meet them."

"I know, Ry. But I've barely seen Noah lately, and we agreed it would be super weird for him to come down to meet them when I'm not home."

"He can't be that busy."

"He's had to work extra shifts every weekend to make up for all the people who covered for him during *The Sound of Music* and the trip to Des Moines. We talk every day. But it's not like I've been sneaking around or hiding anything from Mom and Dad. We haven't even gone out on a real date yet, so it hasn't been an issue."

"You promised me, Faith."

"I know. I'm sorry. But you know how they are. And it's tax season, too." My voice is barely above a murmur. "I have to pick just the right moment."

"The longer you put it off, the harder it's going to be."

"I know."

I close my eyes and take a deep breath. No time like the present, right?

"Fine." I turn. "Mom?" I call across the room. "Dad?"

Dad snorts awake and looks at me, blinking rapidly.

"Hey, guys, I'm dating Noah Spencer now, okay? Just thought you should know."

"You're going out? On Easter Sunday?" Dad un-reclines. "While Danielle and Ryan are here?"

"I'm not going out on a date today. I'm dat-*ing*. You know. 'Going Steady.' Like the song in *Bye, Bye Birdie.*"

I sing the refrain of the song.

"That's cute." Danielle grins. "I don't think I've heard that one."

"We did it my freshman year," I say, silently thanking her for changing the topic. "I was only in the chorus, though."

"Noah." Mom sets her magazine in her lap. "He's the one who went with you to Des Moines, right?"

"Right." Oh well. Nice try though, Danielle.

"And now you're dating him?"

I nod.

"So why haven't *we* met him yet?"

"Because we haven't actually gone out on a date yet. Like I said, he works on the weekends. We haven't gone anywhere together since we went to Des Moines."

"Doesn't sound too steady to me." Dad leans back in the recliner and closes his eyes. "But you know the rules. We have to meet a boy before you go out with him."

"I know."

"He was the Nazi in that community theatre thing, right?" Mom's tone implies he may not have been acting.

"Yeah. He played Rolf."

"You kissed him in that play."

"My character, Liesl, kissed his character, Rolf. It's called acting." I almost roll my eyes . . . and then mentally kick myself for nearly giving in to the impulse. My tone was bad enough.

"Faith," Ryan warns under his breath.

"If you're kissing a boy, we need to meet him." Dad shifts again. His eyes pop open. "Noah Spencer. I thought you said he was studying drama in England or some crazy thing. What's he doing kissing you in Iowa when he's supposed to be in England?"

"He's transferring to a school in London in the fall." My mouth goes dry. "He's still here for a few more months."

"So he goes to high school in Leopold, right?" Mom's eyes narrow. "But you said he's *transferring* to London, which usually means . . ."

"He's enrolled at the community college right now," I supply. "And he works two jobs."

I'm selling it too hard. *Shut up, Faith!*

Mom tilts her head. "How old is this boy?"

"Nineteen."

"He's a freshman, then? At the . . . community college?"

"Uh . . ." I squirm. "No. He graduated with Gretchen."

Mom makes a sound caught somewhere between a gasp and a grunt. "He was in *Gretchen's* class?"

I nod.

"Are you hearing this, Joseph?"

"Mm-hmm . . ."

She turns her gaze on Ryan. "And you encouraged this? Did you know how old this Noah Spencer was when you agreed to take him on an overnight trip with your baby sister?"

"Yes, I did. That's why I wanted to meet him. But he's a good guy. They're really cute together."

"*Cute?*" The word clicks with a cold, staccato *T*. "Cute? My little girl is dating a college sophomore, and you think it's *cute?*"

Blood pounds at my temples, thrusting heat through my skin. "I'm not a little girl anymore, Mom. I'm almost seventeen."

"Your birthday isn't until October. You are *not* 'almost seventeen.'" Mom turns her gaze on Ryan again. "Tell me, Ryan. What reasons might a twenty-year-old man have for chasing after a young girl like Faith?"

"He's nineteen," I say through gritted teeth.

"Well, he can't be nineteen for much longer if he graduated with Gretchen. She's been twenty for several months now."

"Noah *is* still nineteen, right?" Ryan asks me, frowning. I don't think he cares, but he is a stickler for having his facts straight.

I nod. "Until almost the middle of September."

"There you have it. Noah is still nineteen for several months. If you're going to nitpick Faith's age, Mom, you have to nitpick his age the same direction."

After nearly ten years out from under our parents' roof, Ryan isn't as easily cowed by Mom's intimidation tactics as I am.

He leans back in his chair and crosses his arms. "Believe me, Mom. Dad. Noah Spencer is a solid guy. I really don't think you need to worry about him."

A vein twitches in Mom's neck. Her lips press together as she pulls off her reading glasses. "Nineteen is still too old for Faith. End of discussion."

"He's a nice kid, Mom," Ryan repeats. "I'll vouch for him. Heck, I'll vouch for both of them. Faith's a pretty dang good kid, too."

Ryan is the best. The. Best.

"I said, *end of discussion.*" Mom puts her glasses back on and picks up the magazine. "Faith, you are not to date this Noah character. Period."

"You haven't even met him!"

"And there is no reason for me to meet him since you are not going to be dating him."

My chest squeezes as if my heart has collapsed in on itself. Even so, I hate the whine in my voice when I plead my case to my father. "Dad? Come on. If you'd just meet him, talk to him, you'd see that Noah is a—"

"You heard your mother."

"Now," Mom re-opens her magazine, "I intend to put this behind me and enjoy the rest of a rare afternoon with my son and his future wife." Her words are clipped. "Faith, I think you could benefit from some time alone in your room. I know *I* could benefit from you having some time alone in your room. Go."

That's it, then. After shooting a quick, silent plea toward my brother, I rise and do as commanded. As I make for the stairs, each breath seems to suck the atmosphere further into a black hole.

"Faith has a good head on her shoulders." Ryan's angry voice breaks the thick silence. "Why are you so much harder on her than you were on me and Gretchen?"

Go, Ryan! Out of sight, I pause on the stairs. I've never heard anyone speak to my mother in that tone.

"Every child is different. Faith isn't like you or Gretchen. Faith is . . . sometimes I don't even know where she came from."

Gee, thanks, Mom.

"But then I remember exactly where her artistic, dramatic, musician tendencies come from, and I refuse to let her travel that destructive path."

"Faith is not Aunt Becca."

My hands clench into fists. I hate it when Mom compares me to her sister.

My mother loves structure and predictability. She adores columns and numbers that add up to an expected outcome—and she prefers it when the people around her behave that way as well. Her sister is exactly the opposite. A free spirit who thrives on chaos—most of which she creates with her own questionable life choices—Aunt Becca is, in a word, *fun*. She's really easy to like . . . but it's not quite as easy to respect her. We see her rarely, even less since she and her struggling band of middle-aged alternative rockers moved from Chicago to Denver—a move that came soon after the legalization of marijuana in Colorado.

"The tendencies are there, Ryan," Mom continues. "If my parents had set clearer expectations and had been firmer with Becca, she might actually be a productive member of society now."

"Maybe you should start paddling Faith with a big ol' King James Bible, then. Isn't that how Grandpa Hoffman punished Becca for her godless ways?"

"I am not like my parents, especially in that regard, and you well know it."

Not like your parents? That makes two of us.

"And that's another thing," Mom says, sounding exasperated. "This Noah character, he's too religious. I mean, his parents are missionaries off in Africa, or some crazy thing."

"I believe he said Eastern Europe. But why does it matter?"

"It's not normal. And you know what they say about preachers' kids. Wild. Morally rebellious. Do you really want your baby sister dating the son of a preacher?"

"Wow, Mom. I had no idea you bought into so many stereotypes. Shouldn't we want Faith to be with someone with high moral standards?"

"There are high moral standards . . . and then there are people who only give lip service to their high moral standards."

"True, but Noah doesn't strike me as that type. He's genuine. Solid."

"Did you know that Faith has started going to Bible studies at that Fellowship Community Church?"

"She mentioned it."

"Those people are fanatics. I've heard they put their hands in the air when they sing."

"So does Beyoncé. What's your point?"

I can only imagine the deadly scowl Mom must be giving Ryan in the pause before she says, "You *know* what I mean."

"Unfortunately. But what I also know is that you're setting impossible and unfair standards for Faith that you didn't place on me or Gretchen. Faith's a good kid, Mom. Trust her enough to loosen the cord and let her grow up."

"When you've raised three children, Ryan, I'll consider asking you for parenting advice. Until then, you would do well to keep it to yourself. And if I find out you've encouraged Faith to disobey me, I'll . . ."

The threat hangs in the air.

Until Ryan laughs.

Oh, crap. I cringe. Laughing at Mom while she's in this state of mind isn't going to help my cause.

"You'll what, Mom?" He laughs again. "Ground me?"

Mom exhales loudly. "Look, I know you and Faith have a special bond. But step back from the situation. For just a few minutes, see if you can set aside that she's your baby sister. Maybe then you'll see where Faith's involvement with this Noah character could lead."

"They're both good kids. If you would just meet him—"

"Ryan, if Faith gets pregnant, and this boy heads off to acting classes or whatever, is your little apartment big enough to hold you, your new wife, and Faith and her baby? Because if that happens, she's not staying here."

Whoa. I cover my mouth to keep my shock from coming out as sound. How can Mom think I would—?

And even if I did, she would disown me? Kick me out?

Will she also provide me a sweatshirt with a big red "A" on the chest, my own personal scarlet letter, as a parting gift?

"C'mon, Mom. Faith is too smart for that. And Noah isn't that sort of guy. Believe me, I questioned him pretty harshly."

"Oh, please. What would you *expect* him to say to a girl's big brother? Besides, if he's studying to be an actor, how can you know if he was telling the truth or just putting on a good show?"

The insult against Noah balls my hands into fists and heats my scalp. I have to strain to hear Mom's now softer voice over the blood pulsing in my ears.

"But even if he is a *good guy*, as you say"—I can almost see the air quotes she probably used to further express the sarcastic tone of her voice—"you know how it goes in the heat of the moment. And this is *Faith* we're talking about, remember? She's ruled by her emotions. Always has been. It's dangerous. Although, I suppose that's one of the things that makes her so good at drama."

The miniscule compliment is hidden inside the much larger, conversation-encompassing insult, but it grabs my ears. *Mom thinks I'm a good actress.*

I creep down a few steps to hear them better.

"Faith is a teenager, and teens are unpredictable. If you don't believe me, believe what science says about all those young, raging hormones, racing around their brains and bodies, seeking a life to destroy."

"Pretty sure 'science' wouldn't frame it quite like that."

Watch it, bro. We're on thin ice here.

"I had to watch it happen to my sister. I refuse to see that happen to one of my kids. You watch the news. Every other day some actor or musician ends up overdosing, committing suicide, or being arrested for . . . whatever. Artistic types are emotional and unpredictable. They're flighty, fickle souls. And few of them come to a good end. Why would you want to encourage that for her? You didn't know Becca when she was sixteen, but trust me. She wasn't that different from Faith."

Even though Mom's voice is tighter, sadder now, I'm seeing red—and it has nothing to do with that imaginary "A" she seems to think I'll soon deserve.

How can she compare me to Aunt Becca? Yes, we're both musical, I guess. But my personality is about as much like Becca's as Ryan's is like Dad's.

Which is not at all.

"Becca was smart, beautiful, and talented," Mom says, with an oddly hard sort of wistfulness in her voice. "A real force of nature, my sister. She could have been so successful. She could have gone to college, maybe become a music teacher, at least. Instead, she invested all her potential in a boy with a guitar and a dream, neither of which panned out. You won't let yourself see it, but it's there. Faith is so much like Becca it's . . . it's scary."

"She's not," Ryan insists.

"She *is*. I've never understood either one of them. Knowing Faith, she probably thinks she's *in love* with this Noah Spencer, but when he turns on the charm and smooth-talks her into the back seat of his car, will she have the presence of mind to take precautions? Or will she just follow whatever passionate whim shows up at the moment and end up waiting tables at some dive so she can buy diapers and formula?"

"Janet." Dad clears his throat and enters the conversation, surprising me. "Faith may be artistic like Becca, but she's not a flake. Ryan's right. Faith has a good head on her shoulders."

Thanks, Dad. My heart lifts just a little.

"You didn't have to clean up the messes Becca left behind, Joseph." Mom's voice is hard again. "I did. If we don't keep Faith on a tight leash, she'll take us down the same path."

"Mom," Ryan's voice is soft, "you're making a bigger deal out of this than it is."

The spring in the couch pops, like it does when someone stands who's been sitting where Mom was sitting. I pull my head back out of sight and creep a few steps higher.

"I think it's time for coffee," Mom says. "I'm going to go make a fresh pot."

That's it, then. The subject is closed. Not that it was ever truly open, regardless of Ryan's efforts.

I race up the stairs so I won't be caught eavesdropping. With each step, a sense of doom climbs higher, starting in my stomach until it becomes lodged in my throat—hard, like a rubber ball. Once Janet Prescott makes up her mind about something—or some*one*—there is no changing it.

I can't date Noah.

Spikes dig into the soft tissues of my throat, weakening my knees as I close my bedroom door. I barely make it to my bed before the rest of my hope and strength is siphoned away.

Clutching a pillow to my chest, I turn toward the window and stare, unseeing, at the rainy Easter sky. Tears march a steady but silent cadence down my face.

In a matter of a few months, Noah Spencer has melted into my soul. I know by the way he treats me—from the words he texts to the looks we share across a table or a room—the essence of me has taken residence just as deeply inside him.

A cry rises within my chest, daring me to let it move beyond the mass of pain blocking its release. I lift my fist to my lips and bite my index finger to keep from letting the sound escape. I stay like that.

I stay.

I wait, my heart chanting his name.

When the choking suffocation finally subsides, I pull my fist away. My finger throbs where I had been biting it. I look down.

There is something resolute, something *heartening* about those indentations on my skin.

I examine the slight curve of the red line, a curve perfected by professional orthodontia.

Four years ago, there would have been a different, more irregular shape, made by teeth that jutted this way and that. My teeth didn't align overnight. It took time, the application of due force, and, if Mom's exclamation over the bills was any indication, great cost.

Great cost.

I sit up straighter. Outside my window, the trees come into focus, backlit by the slow descent of the sun, mostly hidden by rainclouds.

Maybe my path to Noah won't align overnight. That doesn't mean it won't ever align. I can be patient—I don't have to ask myself if it's worth it. Noah's soul reflects mine, and mine his. He is the mirror of my heart.

Our time together is limited. Winning the right to be with him for the next few months is worth anything I will suffer along the way, or after.

Yes, when Noah leaves for London, I'll have to figure out how to navigate life without him near, but now, while he's still close . . .

I will not—*cannot*—give him up. It would be like cutting out my heart. Somehow, *somehow*, I will make my parents see the beautiful soul inside Noah Spencer. Because if they see him for who he truly is, maybe they'll finally see . . . me.

But how?

I reach for my phone.

Noah will know what to do.

"I don't know what to do."

Noah's quiet proclamation strikes my heart with a dull, helpless thud that matches the bleak temperature of this early spring afternoon.

Regardless of the cold, however, track season is in full swing, and I'm here to watch Jenna run.

The fact that I can see Noah here without raising suspicion is, of course, a bonus.

As runners from several high schools shiver in shorts and nylon track suits, Noah and I view the races from the lonely top row of the metal bleachers. A caveat to the privacy offered by our choice of seating is that we also catch a fair bit of wind. Wrapped about our shoulders, a tartan wool blanket, pulled from the trunk of my car, offers a little warmth. My gaze lifts, as if I might find the answer to our dilemma above. Clouds rush over the gray April sky, driven by a brisk wind. If the answer's there, I sure don't see it. It's been two weeks since Mom made her "no Noah" ruling, and nothing has budged her resolve.

"They won't talk to me on the phone," Noah says. "I tried writing a letter, but—"

"I saw it in the trash. Unopened." I sigh. "You probably should have left off the return address."

"Oh. Right. I didn't think of that."

"I opened it and tried to make her read it, but she ripped it in half and took it right back to the trashcan."

A loud pop signifies the start of the next race. I jump. So does he.

"I went to your mom's office, but after the front desk guy called her to announce me, he kicked me out and threatened to call security if I came back."

"I know. She told me about that. I'm sorry."

"The guy looked a little scared of me. It was freaky. Did she tell you what she said to him? I mean . . . never mind. Maybe I don't want to know."

"I wouldn't worry about it. I think he's new. She—" I sigh. "She goes through a lot of assistants. His reaction probably had nothing to do with you and more to do with the toxins that dripped off his marching orders."

"Oh."

My eyes are on the runners, but even though I easily identify Jenna sprinting toward the first hurdle of her race, my mind barely notes the grace with which she sails over the first, second, and third hurdles. The crowd cheers, and I half-heartedly applaud my friend before turning back to Noah.

"What about your boss's wife, Dr. MacIntosh? She works at the hospital. Maybe she could talk to my dad at work. Put in a good word for you."

"I already thought of that. No dice." Noah shakes his head. "Amanda tried to talk to your dad after a staff meeting, but he shut her down."

Beneath the blanket, I link my arm through Noah's. He weaves his fingers through mine.

"Don't give up." I squeeze his hand. "There has to be a way. I mean, they're still letting me go to your church on Wednesday nights, right?"

"About that." Noah lets out a long breath. "I guess your mom called the church to make sure your Bible study was for high school girls only. And that I wasn't involved."

"Unfreakingbelievable." Except it is, unfortunately, too believable, since it's my mom. "But I should have known. Like she'd believe I could be in the same building as you and not have to rip my clothes off."

"Well, she must have been pretty convincing, because Pastor Luke—he's the youth pastor—"

"Yeah, I know."

"He cornered me last Sunday and asked . . . Well, he wanted to make sure that we weren't, um, doing anything like that."

Noah's ears are pink, and I suspect it isn't all from the wind. How could anyone think he's the sort of guy who would . . .

But that's the problem. My parents don't know him.

"I haven't done anything to deserve this. I'm one of the good girls."

"Don't take this the wrong way, but do you think your mom is harder on you because she's trying to make up for letting Gretchen get away with so much in high school?"

"You assume my mom would admit Gretchen was anything other than perfect." I pick at a loose thread on the blanket. "No, it's not that. My mom is one hundred percent blind when it comes to the Golden Child. Gretchen probably could have told Mom every single thing she was doing, in graphic detail, and it wouldn't have mattered. Mom's double standard is infuriating, but it's nothing new. This isn't about Gretchen. Honestly, I don't even think it's about you being too old or too religious or whatever. It's about me being too artsy. Because artsy people can't be trusted."

"Which is a strike against me, too."

"True. That one sticks, you show-tune-loving freak of nature." I give him a sideways grin and elbow his ribs.

He grants me a smile, but it doesn't reach his eyes.

"At least we can still hang out at stuff like this," I say. "They can't keep you from coming to a public sporting event."

His sigh is too big, too deep to be good. "It still feels kind of sneaky. Don't you think?" He frowns. "I want to be with you, but I don't want to be dishonest about it."

A twinge in my jaw agrees with him, but my heart does not. "We're not hiding. We're not sneaking. We're in plain sight. There's nothing wrong with you coming to a track meet."

"I don't even *like* track. I didn't come to a single meet when I was a student. But now, all of a sudden, I'm the team's biggest fan?" He gestures toward the Kanton team. "I don't think I even *know* any of these kids. I mean—"

"*Kids?*" My defenses rise. Jenna is one of only a handful of sophomores good enough to run varsity. Most of the athletes on the field are a year or two older than me, which makes them only a year or two younger than Noah.

"You know what I mean." Noah sighs. "Faith, I've been praying about this. About us. Mac and Amanda MacIntosh are praying for us. They both think, and I agree, that it's high time I meet your parents, whether they want to meet me or not."

"But they *won't* meet you. They won't even consider it."

"So far." Noah pauses as another race begins. "Your parents think you're going to Jenna's Friday night, right?"

"I *am* going to Jenna's Friday night."

"Right." Noah shifts in his seat. "But then you and Jenna are planning to meet up with me later."

"So?"

"How about, instead, you and Jenna go to the movies on your own. And I . . ." Noah pauses, inhales, and then exhales hard through pursed lips. "I'll go to your house."

"Are you *nuts*?"

The horror I feel must match my face because Noah laughs. "What are they gonna do, Faith? Sic the dog on me?"

"Who knows? I wouldn't put anything past my mother anymore. I don't want you to get hurt."

"You think Janey would hurt me?"

"It's not that. Janey wouldn't hurt you. She knows you. And I don't mean physically. It's my *mom*." I groan. "She's just mean. And—and *paranoid*. And it didn't help, having Aunt Becca call last week, asking for money. Whenever she calls, Mom gives me the evil eye for days after."

"Why do *you* get the evil eye?"

I explain about the way Aunt Becca is and how strict, yet hypocritical my mom's parents are.

"Is that why your mom is so anti-church?"

"She's not anti-church. She's anti too *much* church. But, yeah. It's probably because of the way she was raised and the way Becca experiments with different faiths. Mom believes religion is dangerous unless taken in very small doses."

"And she has the proof to back it up," Noah nods. "That's sad."

"Yeah. But I don't know why I have to be punished for my aunt's mistakes." I scowl down at the track. "This past week, Mom's really gone mental on me. I have to account for every minute of every day. If I come home from school a little late, she checks the mileage on my car. It's so not fair. She's totally convinced that you're some pervert, looking to steal my virtue."

"They just want to protect you. And that's why I have to go down there. I want to protect you, too. I think I can get them to see that."

Noah's words warm me more than the wool blanket, but they can't chase away the butterflies flitting around in my stomach. The thought of him showing up at our door, unexpected . . .

"I don't want you to have to face her alone."

"You do it all the time. And besides, I don't intend to go alone. Not really."

"Who's going with you?"

He points up.

"Oh. Right."

"I'm going to pray hard. Mac and Amanda will pray, too." Noah squeezes my hand, and the warmth in his eyes intensifies. "Will you pray about it with me? Can you trust God to take care of . . . us?"

"I'll try."

It isn't an idle promise. Being around Noah, listening to him pray, praying with him . . . Prayer is becoming my default mode these days.

Want to scream at Mom? Pray. Want to tell your parents every rotten thing your older sister has ever done—or at least the ones you know about? Pray. Want to grab a pint of ice cream and devour all your toxic feelings?

I'm still working on that one. There is never enough ice cream in our house.

Noah lets go of my hand and puts his arm around my shoulders.

I swallow. Hard. What if God wants Noah and me apart before he leaves for London? What if my mom, even in her caustic way, is walking more in God's will than we are?

No. That can't be right. She's walking a path paved in stubborn prejudice and arrogant ignorance. And if I've learned anything about Jesus these past months, it's that arrogance and bigotry aren't his style.

Noah squeezes my hand. Bows his head. I scoot closer to his side and close my eyes.

Lord, we really need your help. Please, God. Please break through my mother's stubborn heart. Make her see Noah for who he really is. Please. I'll read my Bible every day. I'll memorize two new verses every week. I know it's stupid to bargain with the Creator of the Universe, but I can't seem to help myself. *Please, God. Please, just let me be with Noah.*

Over the next few days, I pray more than I've ever prayed in my life. I think I may even be praying, in a silent, wordless way, as I walk out of the movie with Jenna Friday night.

Or maybe I'm just thinking.

Worrying.

About Noah meeting my parents.

"Did he text you yet?" Jenna asks.

"Umm . . . I'm too scared to check."

"Give it over."

I squeeze my eyes shut, pull my phone from my back pocket, and hold it out to her.

"Oh. Um . . . Yeah. He . . . did."

I open my eyes. She's wincing. "It's . . . not good." She turns the screen toward me.

It's only four words.

Four words that pretty much cave in my world.

Noah:
I'm sorry. I tried.

My heart sinks into an abyss. I cut the night short, arriving home at 10:30 instead of my midnight curfew.

"It would seem you had a little communication problem with your boyfriend, Faith."

I jump. Mom was waiting for me, just beyond the door. "What?"

"Give me your phone and your keys."

"Why?"

"Because you told me you were going to the movies with Jenna."

"I *did* go to the movies with Jenna."

"And . . . ?"

"And what? We ate popcorn?" I hold out my hands. "After the movie, we went to Pizza Hut and gorged ourselves on breadsticks. Then I came home."

"And when did you meet up with that Noah Spencer?"

"I didn't."

"You expect me to believe that? He came here to pick you up."

"No, he didn't." I cross my arms. "Noah came here to talk to *you*. He knew I was with Jenna."

"I don't believe you."

"Why should I be surprised?" I throw up my hands and try to move past her, but she holds out an arm to block my way. I let out a huff. "Seriously? Call Jenna. Ask her."

"I'm not an idiot. I know how these things work. I'm sure you and that Noah arranged this whole thing *with* Jenna. He just forgot where he was supposed to pick you up."

"That's stupid. If we were trying to keep it from you, why would he come *here* to pick me up?" I hate how guilty that makes me sound. Especially since, other than the pick-up location, that *had* been our original plan for tonight.

I shake my head to send those thoughts on their way. Our plans changed.

"I knew he was coming here to talk to you. That's why I gave him my code for the gate."

Mom's lips press together. She holds out her hands. "Keys. Phone. Now."

"Urrrgh!" Frustration growls through my teeth.

"Hand them over. Now."

"Fine." I slap my keys into her hand and then pull my phone from my pocket and do the same, glad I had the forethought to delete all my text threads while Jenna and I were waiting for our breadsticks.

"You're grounded."

There's no point in arguing. "For how long?"

"This time next week, we'll reevaluate. If you can watch your attitude, maybe that will be long enough. If you can't, the term will be extended." Mom pockets my keys. "You'll be riding the bus to school next week. I'll have Gretchen come down to keep an eye on you while your dad and I are in Chicago next weekend. If you toe the line, you may get some of your privileges reinstated when we return. In the meantime, you can plan to spend tomorrow cleaning out the garden shed."

"Great. Am I excused now?"

"Yes. But I suggest you watch the sarcasm, young lady."

Other than making a landline call to Jenna after Mom and Dad are asleep that night, asking her to text Noah and let him know I'm phoneless, I keep Mom's restrictions to the letter for the prescribed week. No phone. No computer use, other than that needed for closely monitored homework time. No friends. No mouthing off.

When Gretchen arrives Friday afternoon, I'm actually relieved to see my sister.

"You know the rules," Mom warns me as she and Dad get ready to leave.

Mom turns to Gretchen. Smiles. The difference in her expression is marked enough to nauseate anyone not on its receiving end. I never am.

"Thanks for coming, sweetie. I know you probably have better things to do than keep an eye on your little sister, but I really appreciate it. I hope Justin doesn't mind giving you up for the weekend. He's such a nice young man."

"Yeah, he's great. And it's no problem, Mom." Gretchen puts an arm around my shoulders. I do my best to keep from rolling my eyes. "We're going to have some girl time. I thought maybe tonight we'd give each other pedicures and find a movie to stream or something."

"Sounds good. We'll be back around four or five on Sunday."

They leave. I slump into a chair.

"Wanna order pizza?" Gretchen asks. "We can pick out a movie while we're waiting for it to be delivered."

"You were serious?"

"Uh, *yeah*." She says it like we always pal around on the weekends she's home.

Honestly, I'm a little freaked out right now.

Gretchen surprises me and sticks to the verbalized plan. After the pizza is delivered, we gather our pedicure supplies and head to the family room in the basement.

"Mermaid Scales?" I read the bottom of a bottle of iridescent blue/green nail polish. "This one's kind of pretty."

"Yeah. I like it. Hey, do you still have those nail pen things Mom put in your stocking last Christmas?"

"Umm . . . I think so." I rummage through the plastic bin where I store my nail polish supply. "Here. I've got hot pink, black, and . . . white."

"Okay, start the movie. And don't tell mom we had nail polish in a room with carpet. She'll kill us both."

"No kidding."

Who is this girl? I can't remember the last time Gretchen was actually nice to me, but tonight there's a tenuous camaraderie between us. It's so rare that I enjoy my sister's company or that she even considers mine an option, that I'm not sure how to respond to her casual openness. I'm cautious, but eventually I relax. For whatever reason, at least for tonight, Gretchen is . . . nice.

We eat junk food, give each other pedicures, and watch movies until the wee hours. It's almost like being with a friend.

The sectional sofa is big enough that both of us can sleep comfortably without getting in each other's way, which we do, at last, and stay there until almost eleven Saturday morning. We might have kept on snoozing into the afternoon if not for the incessantly loud vibration of Gretchen's phone on the glass-top coffee table.

From Gretchen's tone, I know she's talking to a guy. Probably her new boyfriend, Justin. When she starts giving directions to the house, I head upstairs. "Sister time" is apparently over.

I hurry through my shower and normal routine, hoping to keep the peace with Gretchen by clearing out of the bathroom we share by the time she's off the phone.

Grabbing my makeup bag, I head to my room, wrapped in a towel. Gretchen is waiting for me there.

"Justin's coming over this afternoon."

"I figured." I nod, wondering if last night's sister-bonding will continue into the new day.

"So . . . I was thinking," she says with the hint of a smile, but it's a last-night-Gretchen smile instead of the usual *I'll-eat-you-for-breakfast*, Cheshire cat grin. "I know Mom's been kind of rough on you lately."

She does? Most of the time, she barely acknowledges my existence until I'm in her way.

"I had lunch with Ryan and Danielle last week, and they kind of filled me in."

Ah.

"Since she left me in charge, I thought maybe . . . maybe you'd like to hang out with Noah tonight."

I blink. "Really?"

"Yes, really. I'm the adult in charge, right?"

"Ri-ight." Yes, Mom put her in charge, but I assume she did it because she knows the joy Gretchen usually gains by making my life miserable—which allies them in the anti-Faith cause.

"But Mom said—"

"That I'm in charge." Gretchen crosses her arms.

True, but I'm pretty sure Mom would revoke Gretchen's authority if she knew the two of us are getting along and that me hanging out with Noah is suddenly on the table.

But she doesn't know.

And Mom did, after all, leave Gretchen in charge, so who am I to question the adult in authority?

"I'm in charge," Gretchen asserts again, "and I'm giving you permission to go see your boyfriend. Not here, of course. Justin's going to be here, and that would be . . . weird. But I'm sure you two can figure something out." Gretchen frowns. Her brows drew together. "Just don't do anything stupid that will get us both in trouble, okay?"

"I won't. I promise."

I'm going to see Noah.

I'm going.

To see.

Noah!

My grin is so wide it almost hurts my cheeks. Impulsively, I wrap my towel-dried arms around my sister and hug her tight. "Thank you so much!"

"Stahhhp." Gretchen laughs and shakes her head. I plant a big kiss on her cheek. "Enough! Go call him."

With a squeal, I spin around to get my phone off my desk, only to stop before I'm halfway there. "I can't call him. Mom took my phone, and . . . I'm pretty sure she keeps a close eye on the numbers that show up on the landline bill."

"She does. Use mine." Gretchen holds it out. "Just set it on my dresser when you're done. I'm gonna go get in the shower."

Noah is probably at work, so I send a text.

> **Gretchen:**
> **I have permission to see you tonight. Are you busy?-Faith**

He always checks his phone on his break, so I know he'll text back. The waiting could very well kill me. I set Gretchen's phone in plain sight on my vanity table while I dry my hair and get dressed.

A date. I'm going on a date with Noah.

Maybe.

If he doesn't have other plans.

I bite my lip as I look in the mirror. Could he have other plans?

I decide to curl my hair. It's fairly straight naturally, and my normal routine is to give it just a few swipes of the straightener to keep it sleek, but curls might be a nice change.

Plus, they take five-ever to do on my thick hair, so it'll help pass the time.

I pull the seldom-used curling wand from the drawer of my

vanity table, plug it in, and begin the long process of glamorizing my "cinnamon" head.

Just as I'm unwinding the last curl from the wand, the screen of Gretchen's phone lights up.

> **Noah:**
> **Ok, FAITH. What's**
> **my favorite kind of**
> **tea?**

What?

Ohhh . . . he's suspicious because the text came from Gretchen's number. I've got this.

> **Gretchen:**
> **Cinnamon. Like the**
> **color of my hair. (See?**
> **Me. Faith.)**

> **Noah:**
> **Whew! Had to be**
> **sure, tho. Pick you**
> **up at six?**

My hands shake in anticipation as I type back.

> **Gretchen:**
> **See you then. -Faith**

I take Gretchen's phone to her room, as requested.

"Nice curls. When I finish drying my hair, can you do that on me?"

"Sure."

"Did you hear back from Noah?"

"Yeah. He's picking me up at six."

"Cool. Hey, Justin should be here in an hour or so, I think. Will it creep you out if he stays over tonight?"

Umm, yeah. "In the guest room?"

"Sure. Yeah. The guest room. In the basement," Gretchen says, nodding. But from her hesitation, it's safe to assume Justin will not be in the guest room alone.

"What time do I have to be home?"

"Just stick to the normal curfew, I guess," she says and then laughs. "Which means, whenever you want."

"It might have meant that for you," I say, arching an eyebrow, "but if I'm home even one second past midnight, I get grounded."

"Seriously?" She blinks. "Wow, Mom and Dad sure are getting strict in their old age. Okay, let's just say . . . I won't be mad if you miss curfew, but don't stay out so late that I get worried, okay?"

I give her a salute. "Aye-aye, Cap'n."

Since Gretchen's hair is shorter and has a bit of natural wave, it doesn't take as long to do her curls as it did mine, but she's still finishing her makeup when Justin arrives.

Wearing a blue oxford over a white t-shirt, designer jeans, and deck shoes, Justin looks like just the sort of insufferable yacht-club type my mom would assume to be the perfect man.

Yep, that seals it. With Justin at her side, Gretchen's reign as the favorite daughter is secure.

He's nice enough, I suppose. Handsome, too, if a girl is into preppy guys who like to walk by mirrors and check themselves out. Justin comes from a wealthy family and is pursuing a respectable career, planning to join his grandfather's law firm when he finishes school. He's exactly the sort of guy Mom and Dad would pick for me, if given the chance.

And nothing like the one I've picked for myself.

As the afternoon wears on, I decide I don't like him. At all. The way he looks at Gretchen, you'd think she's some sort of medal he's won based on his own awesomeness. It's kind of sickening, to be honest, and makes me want to go upstairs and burn all her bras in protest. Regardless of how she acts like an airhead—clearly for Justin's benefit—Gretchen is not an idiot. How can she like a guy like him?

I mean, sure, I suppose it must be nice to date a guy our parents approve of, but if their approval comes from such surface ideals as wealth and specific professional ambitions, I'm not interested in earning it.

Not that I ever will.

By five forty-five, I've had enough. Excusing myself to wait for Noah outside, I sit in Mom's favorite Adirondack chair on the front porch.

The evening sky has taken on a bit of gold and lavender, harkening twilight. It's peaceful, and I don't mind the slight chill if it keeps me out of the *Gretchen-hearts-Justin* snugglesphere. Within five minutes, my ears detect the approach of Noah's car, and I stand, willing my hands not to shake. It seems like forever since I've seen him.

I wrestle Eliza's door open and slip into the passenger seat before Noah has a chance to get out of the car. He may not have come to a complete stop, actually.

"Hey." My voice is breathless, and my cheeks are tight from what is probably a ridiculously goofy smile.

"Hey yourself," he says, smiling. His eyes widen as he gets a good look at me. "Wow. Your hair is . . . wow."

"Thanks." A little heat rises to the surface of my cheeks. "I curled it. Too much?"

"No. It's just—it's . . . wow. It's really beautiful. You're beautiful." He laughs and shakes his head. "Sorry. I sound like an idiot. I was so jazzed about coming here, I was practically shaking, and then you get in my car, looking all, like . . . *wow*. It's a lot to take in, considering I was beginning to wonder if I'd ever see you again."

I wince. "Yeah, I was wondering that, too. How bad was it, with my mom last week?"

"There wasn't time for it to go bad. When she opened the door, I said, 'Hello, Mrs. Prescott. I'm Noah Spencer.' And, just like that, she slammed the door in my face. Not a word. Not a chance."

That was all he got for his effort? A door slammed in his face? How could she treat him like that? She treats vacuum cleaner salespeople better. "I'm sorry."

"It's not your fault." He shrugs. "So . . . you're ungrounded now?"

"Technically. I don't have my phone or keys back yet. Mom said a week. That would be over today, but . . . she must have forgotten." I bite my lip.

"Should we go inside so I can meet your parents?"

"They went to Chicago and left Gretchen in charge."

"Ah." His eyebrows lift, and his lips round. "Oh."

Noah flexes his fingers on the steering wheel. "Faith, I . . ." He drops his chin close to his chest and rests his right elbow on the armrest between us.

I reach for his hand. After a moment of hesitation, he gives my fingers a light squeeze.

"Okay, then." He lifts his head and gives my fingers one more squeeze before letting them go to put the car in reverse. "Let's go."

oah is quiet. Too quiet. As we near the Parre Hills gates to exit, I ask if he minds if I turn on the radio.

"Why? You hate music."

His smile loosens a knot in my throat. I laugh and dial up the volume. It's "Hey There Delilah" by the Plain White T's.

"Ugh." He groans. "This song again?"

"How can you not like this song? I know it's been around forever, but it's such a catchy little tune."

"I guess." His forehead creases with . . . not exasperation exactly, but something close to it. "But it's been playing all the *time* this week. No kidding. Like, every time I turn the radio on, there it is. It's like the DJs dug it out of the vault and then decided to stick it back into the rotation every couple of hours or so, just to mess with me."

I would laugh, but he actually sounds peeved. By a song. How weird is that? "You hate it that much?"

"No." The frustration in his voice melts on the melody of a smile. "I like it a lot, actually. This song always makes me think of you."

"Really?" My heart soars.

"Yeah." Noah puts both hands on the wheel. "And what it's going to be like after I leave."

. . . and falls. "Oh."

"No, don't be sad. Listen to the words." Noah starts to sing along with the chorus but then stops suddenly. "You know how I change the words of songs sometimes?"

"Mm-hmm. You're a total hack."

"Yes, I am." He grins. "Well, for this one, I change the name from 'Delilah' to 'Madeleine.' And later in the bridge, when it talks about 'a thousand miles'?"

I nod.

"I change it to *four* thousand miles and, well . . ." He turns a warm, half-smile my way. "It's you and me. Our story. Or it will be, in any case."

Noah sings along with the next verse, improvising changes to the wording as the melody progresses.

It's an upbeat, happy tune. I've sung along with it on the radio for years without really thinking about the words. But tonight, especially listening to Noah's subtle lyric changes, the song almost breaks my heart.

Almost.

But sweetly.

As the tune reaches its final chorus, I add in the harmony. The lyrics of this song carry a promise, a promise that warms the ever-present *Noah-is-leaving* shaped ache in my soul.

"Noah?"

"Hmm?"

"I think you've officially found *our song.*"

"Our song." There's a strange softness in his echo, almost as if he has a sore throat, but I know better.

The song ends, replaced with a commercial for an auto parts

store. Noah dials the volume down. "So, where would you like to go?"

"I don't know. Have you eaten?"

"No. I was planning on taking you out. Or . . ." Noah pauses. "Did you eat dinner already?"

"No. What sounds good?"

"Anything but pizza. I've been eating leftover pizza all week."

"We could just drive through somewhere, grab sandwiches. Have a picnic?"

"A picnic?" Noah laughs. "Sure, why not. Where?"

"How about a park or something? If we're going into Sommerton anyway to get the food, we could go to that park on the north side of town. The one with the duck pond and the fountain. It's April, so they should have the picnic tables out by now."

"It might get a little chilly tonight. Maybe we should eat in and then pick up some coffees to go or something before we go to the park."

After eating sub sandwiches in a mostly deserted fast food restaurant—thankfully, I don't know any of the patrons, which means they won't recognize me and report back to Mom—we head to the drive-thru lane at Grady's Grind. Ten minutes later, we're walking a tree-lined, paved pathway to the picturesque duck pond, frothy coffees in hand.

"Let's go away from the trees so we can see the stars," he suggests, guiding me to a bench.

Noah's arm wraps around my shoulders. I snuggle into his side. Comfortable silence envelopes us as we gaze across the still water to the tiny island where recently-returned geese gather for the night.

"Faith," he begins in a voice just above a whisper, "your parents don't know you're with me, do they?"

"No," I admit the omission that's been riding me all night. And most of the afternoon, really. But . . . "This was Gretchen's idea. And since they left her in charge . . ."

Noah is silent for a few moments, but I feel tension building between us, and I don't know how to make it disperse.

Finally, he exhales a long, slow breath, but a sense of dread washes over me when that sigh is followed by, "We need to talk."

Noah pulls his arm from my shoulders, and the temperature seems to drop a few extra degrees.

"This sneaking around and lying to your parents . . . it's not right."

"But Gretchen—"

"Gretchen's approval is only adding a more palatable layer to the lie." Noah's look sends a twinge of guilt through my heart.

"I know," I whisper. I don't know why I tried to justify it. "And I guess I lied to you, too, when I texted that I had permission to see you. You probably thought that permission was from Mom and Dad."

He looks down at his hands, now clasped in his lap. "I hoped. But *I* would be lying if I said I didn't suspect there was more to your text than what it said. I mean . . . you sent it from Gretchen's phone. That's why I waited so long to reply. I wondered if the message really was from you or if your mom and your sister were setting some kind of trap." He shakes his head. "We've gotten ourselves in a pretty tangled web, haven't we?"

I scoot away, lifting my knee sideways on the bench so I can face him. "I'm sorry. I should have explained. But I was afraid that if I did, you wouldn't . . ."

I let my voice trail off. My gaze swerves out over the pond. I can't meet his eyes.

"You thought I wouldn't agree to see you."

"Exactly. And . . . you would have been right to stay away." I look down at my hands for a minute and then meet his eyes again. "Noah, you're so . . . *good*. Don't get me wrong, I love that about you. I do. You always know the right thing to do, and you always do it, even when it's the hardest possible thing to do."

"No, I don't."

"Yes, you do. Like going to see my parents last week. That was the right thing to do, but it took a lot of guts."

He shrugs.

"I can be brave, and I can be good. But I'm not bravely good, you know? At least not consistently, like you."

"Faith, I'm not—"

"You *are*. But just hear me out, okay? The thought of being with you makes me want to be brave, to stand against my parents and their prejudice. I want to prove how wrong they are about you. And about me, too." My hands fist, my fingernails digging into the soft flesh of my palm. "But I don't know how to do it, because when it comes to being good—at least my parents' definition of the word—I'm hopeless."

"You're not hopeless. And you're being much too easy on me."

"There you are again, being good." I bump his shoulder with mine. "But regardless of how we got to be together tonight, if this is being bad or disobedient or rebellious or whatever . . . it seems pretty justifiable to me."

I take a breath. "My mom's behavior toward you isn't remotely justifiable. I can't even—I mean, it's not like we're drinking or doing drugs or having sex—which, by the way, is what she's *really* worried about. When we're together, we talk about music and theatre and— and *God*, of all things! You're my best friend and . . . and a mentor, even, in a lot of ways. You get me like no one else ever has. Like they never will. Of *course* I want to spend time with you! Why can't she see that? Why are we the ones who are wrong, when our only offense is wanting to see each other?"

Noah envelopes my hand in his, gently rubbing his thumb across the skin between my thumb and forefinger. "It's not what we're doing or not doing," he says finally. "It's *how* we're not doing it. According to your parents, I'm not welcome at your house or in your life. You're not supposed to be dating me, but here we are. On a date."

Noah puts his hand on my chin and turns my face. "No matter what Gretchen says you can do tonight, we're doing exactly what your parents said we *can't*."

A curl blows across my face. Noah tucks it behind my ear. "Yes, your mom and dad left Gretchen in charge, and Gretchen gave you permission to go out with me. But—and I'm just guessing here—I assume neither one of you is going to tell your parents about tonight, are you?"

A fast breath, just shy of a snort, expels from my nose. "Not likely."

"I didn't think so." Noah's smile is warm, but sad, too. And something about it sets off warning bells of panic in my brain.

"There are words I haven't said to you because I've always considered them sacred. And this is probably the worst possible moment to let them loose, but the thing is . . ." He swallows. "I love you, Madeleine Faith. I've never said that to a girl before, not romantically. And I never wanted to, until you."

My breath catches as much on the tears shining in his eyes as the words.

"I love you, too."

"I know you do. Even without the words, I think we've both known it for a while."

I nod. But the words are awfully nice to hear. And say.

"And that's why this is so difficult."

My breath freezes on the slap of conclusion that punctuates that statement, even though he's still speaking.

"Love is brave, Faith, but it rejoices in the truth. And what we're doing, regardless of how we rationalize it, is dishonest."

"I know." I swallow around the cold-spiked lump in my throat. Meeting like this is the same as lying. And lying, even by skirting around the truth, is wrong. "I'm sorry. It's my fault. My lie. And I dragged you into it tonight. I'm sorry."

My apology, my regret at causing his discomfort, is sincere. But inside, I squirm around the argument that pits my heart against my spirit. "But my parents are passing judgment on you, Noah! That's wrong, too, isn't it? They don't even *know* you. They won't even give you a *chance*."

"You're right." Noah looks out across the night-blackened water. "That's where I get conflicted, too."

He lets go of my hand, stands, and sticks both hands in the front pocket of his sweatshirt. "I'm not used to being cast as the villain, but ever since your mother slammed that door in my face and then grounded you because of it, well, it feels like I'm the bad guy." He rocks back on his heels. "But I feel like I'm a victim, too. And I hate that feeling even more."

"I'm sorry." How many times will I say that tonight? And every time, it's truer than the time before. "You don't deserve this."

"It's not your fault." Noah sits back down on the bench. "It's a moral dilemma and a spiritual dilemma, and I don't know the right answer. Sometimes I'm not even sure what the question is." His next sound is more of a growl. "Why would God bring us together—and, just so we're clear, I *do* believe he brought us together—and then let your parents rip us apart based on . . . well, *nothing*? Nothing that can be substantiated by fact, anyway. I've prayed and prayed. I've sought wise counsel. I want . . ."

Noah trails off with a sigh.

"Maybe that's the whole issue," he says, finally. "Maybe I'm blinded from the right answer by what I want."

"I've been praying, too. I've been scouring my little pink Bible every night." I bite my lip. "This is going to sound weird, okay? But every time I go to God, looking for answers, I feel this . . . this expectation. It's almost like God is telling me to just hold on. Like, everything is going to be okay . . . but not yet."

"Not yet?"

"Maybe I'm reading into it. I don't know. It's just a . . . a feeling. I know I haven't been reading the Bible or praying, not seriously at least, as long as you have, but I don't know how else to describe it. I just feel like God is saying, 'hold on.' But I'm not even sure what that means. It could go either way."

"I see what you're saying." He nods. "Do we 'hold on' by doing as your parents wish, not seeing each other until they give us the thumbs up? Or do we 'hold on' and keep doing what we're doing, going against them, trusting that God will show them the truth about me—about us—in the meantime?"

"Exactly! And I have no idea which one it is."

"Me neither." He puts his hands on his thighs and rubs them to his knees and back a few times, hard. "Sometimes I wonder if maybe I'm telling God what I want him to do more than I'm asking him what I should do. But the one thing I *do* know is that I—"

Noah's voice chokes up. He clears his throat, and his hand finds mine again.

"I know I love you, Madeleine Faith. I *love* you. And I love knowing that you love me, too." He takes a breath and squeezes my hand. "I love *us*. If God is telling you—no, telling us—to hold on, well, that's something worth holding on to, isn't it? Even if we don't exactly know what it means."

I can't speak, but I don't need to. When I scoot to Noah's side, he puts his arm around me and pulls me even closer than before. The posture feels right. Good.

We fit together. We make sense when nothing else does.

Why can't Mom just give us a chance?

"But at the same time, I question it."

What?

Noah takes a deep breath in through his nose and exhales just as slowly. "These last few months, I've spent a lot more time thinking about *you* than thinking about *God.*"

"That's a little ironic." I expel a tiny snort. "Before I met you, I barely gave God any thought at all. Now I actually listen to the words of the hymns at church. I pay attention to the sermon instead of doodling all over the program. Well, most of the time, anyway. I'm even in a Bible study now, thanks to you, and I've learned so much from it. Well, I *was* in a Bible study." I let a little growl-sound escape. "But since Mom doesn't want me hanging out with people from your church anymore, I guess that's over. At least for—"

"About that," Noah interrupts. "Sorry. I kind of saw that one coming. I hope you don't mind, but I did a little digging for you, and it turns out that the youth group at First Church of Kanton sponsors a girls' Bible study on Saturday mornings. About three girls go, I guess, so it's not as big as what you're used to, but it's something."

"Really?" I've never heard anything about it. Then again, when your family only attends church on religious holidays, you kind of fall out of the loop. "Maybe I'll check it out."

I can't see how Mom could object. It's our family church. And— bonus!—that Noah Spencer character doesn't go there.

"Most guys would rather have me study their fantasy football league charts than the Bible. You've taught me so much. You're such a good example of what a Christian should be. I wish they understood that."

My words are meant to encourage, but a fresh tension stiffens his frame.

"A good example would not cause you to sin by meeting you behind your parents' backs. That's not much of an example, Faith."

"Noah—"

"The Bible says to honor your parents. Obey your parents. And I'm leading you into disobedience just by showing up."

"You didn't know—"

"I suspected. And when I found out, it wasn't like I turned the car around and took you home, was it?"

I tilt my gaze to the sky. "No offense, God, but being a Christian sure makes it hard to be a human being. This totally bites."

"Yes, it does." Noah laughs, and his posture relaxes.

"I bet this is one of those times you wish you had a direct line to Heaven like everybody seems to think a missionary's kid should, huh?"

"You know it. But the truth of it is that we're the only people who know what we have and haven't done. I know that I love you, and I want to honor your love for me. And God knows that, too."

"I wish he'd set a bush on fire or something and tell my mom."

"Me, too. Sometimes I think the best thing would be for us to keep our distance until your parents agree to meet me. Maybe it would be easier, maybe there would be less opportunity to sin, if we stopped seeing each other."

"But Noah, I—We . . ." Panic constricts my chest, halting my airflow.

Noah squeezes my shoulder. "The Bible says Christians should avoid even the *appearance* of sin. Sneaking around behind your parents' backs implies we have something to hide, even if we're not doing what people might *assume* we're doing."

A cold, heavy lump forms in my stomach. I try to swallow, but there's no moisture in my mouth.

He just said he loves me. Surely he won't—

"Noah." His name exits my lips on a hoarse whisper. "Are you . . . breaking up with me?"

Noah is quiet. With each passing second, the lump in my throat grows, until my neck aches from the pressure of it.

Finally, he squeezes my shoulder. "No." He leans over and kisses my hair. "I thought I could. I probably *should*. But I can't."

"Oh." A bit of the pressure releases, but I can't shake the tightness in my chest. "Good. You scared me." I swallow. "Having you so far away is going to be hard enough next fall, but not having you at all when you're so close would be—"

I can't finish the sentence, can't allow myself to imagine the emptiness that would consume me with Noah near, but inaccessible. I've had short tastes of it, and it is a bitter, sour thing.

"I have an idea," he says. "It's a long shot, but it might solve our problem. What would you think of us trying to build a deeper friendship, but without—without the, um . . . romantic stuff?"

My mind whirs in confusion. He just said he couldn't break up with me, but . . . ? "Are you saying you just want to be friends?"

"Yes, but . . . No." He shakes his head and closes his eyes. "But, ultimately, *yes*. Your parents don't want you to be romantically involved with me, right? So if we can agree to take out the element of romance, we can still be together *and* still honor your parents."

I ponder that. "So what you're saying is, you think that if my mom and dad see that we can be friends without being romantic for a while, then maybe later we could, um, add the romance back in?"

Noah nods. "Yeah. Maybe. After they've gotten to know me as your friend. After we've played by their rules."

I try to imagine being with Noah and not holding his hand, not letting myself snuggle into his side, like I'm sitting right now. "How do we even do that?"

"Um, well, I guess I hadn't thought that far. No kissing, for sure."

I like it when Noah kisses me. I like it a lot. But we aren't like Jenna and Cole, who consider it the gold-medal event of every date. "Okay."

"We should probably stop the hand-holding, too."

"So snuggling like this would be out?"

"Right."

And yet he makes no move to release me.

I smile at that. "Can we do that? I mean, when I'm near you, I just want to be, well, closer to you."

"Uh, yeah. Exactly. I think that's what your parents are afraid of."

It takes me a second to catch his meaning. "Oh. Right." Can he feel the heat of my cheek through his sweatshirt? "So when would this whole 'just friends' thing need to start?"

"Soon." Noah stands up and holds out his hand. "Dance with me?"

"Here?" My head spins. "Dancing is pretty romantic, Noah."

"So we'll stop being romantic later."

"But there isn't any music."

"I guess we'll just have to create some, then." Noah stands and pulls me to my feet, into his arms. "After all, we've finally identified our song. I think we ought to use it at least once. This may be our last chance."

As we go into May, keeping romance out of my relationship with Noah turns out to be much easier than I expected.

Probably because Noah's final exams, his two jobs, and my mother, who is determined to occupy every spare instant of my time, leave us literally no time to get together.

At least my phone is back in my possession.

Spring cleaning has always been my mom's post-tax-season project. Usually, we all steer clear of her single-minded drive toward restoring order and spotless dignity to our home—which wasn't messy to start with. This year, however, spring cleaning has become a mother-daughter activity, taking hours after school most days and nearly every waking hour of my weekends.

It's hard, but I help without complaint. I even volunteer for some of the worst jobs, hoping my attitude and maturity will be noticed . . . and that it will soften Mom's heart toward me and, eventually, Noah. After three weeks of being a cheerful, obedient, and dutiful daughter, who only communicates with my friend Noah by electronic means—I still can barely believe she relented and allowed even that—I finally build up the nerve to broach the subject one Saturday.

"You've probably figured out that Noah and I decided we should just be friends."

Of the seemingly thousands of spring cleaning projects Mom is checking off a multi-page spreadsheet, today finds us cleaning and alphabetizing the bookshelves in Dad's study.

"You know," I continue when she doesn't look up, keeping my tone casual, "nothing romantic or anything. Just friends."

My mom actually snorts. "Right."

"No, seriously. We agreed that we're not going to hold hands, or kiss, or anything like that. We just want to be able to hang out. To talk. To sing together. Really. Total friendzone."

"But you don't want to be in the friendzone, as you say, with Noah Spencer." Something just shy of tenderness floats across the study on Mom's voice when she chuckles. "I'm not quite so old that I don't remember what it was like to be a teenager. Having a crush on a boy can seem pretty serious at your age. And this Noah fellow? Well, he's a looker."

"True." I nod. "But I have lots of guy friends who are cute."

"Noah is more mature than the boys your age. That ups his attractiveness, I'd wager. And that's why I don't want you dating him." The tenderness is gone, but there is no animosity in Mom's voice.

If she can stay neutral, so can I.

"I know. I understand that. Noah does, too. That's why we decided to just be friends." I grab a book from the pile on the floor, look at the spine, and slide it into position on a freshly dusted shelf. "Besides, he's leaving for London in just a few—"

"He really is leaving, then?" Mom brightens. "When?"

"In August. August tenth, I think." I know. That date was seared into my brain the first time I heard it. It still stings.

"Oh. Not until the end of the summer, then."

"Right. People who date in high school usually break up when one of them goes off to college, anyway, so it would be silly to try to keep a romantic relationship going with an ocean between us for three years. Being friends makes more sense."

Silly isn't exactly the word Noah and I had used in our discussions of long-distance relationships. The word *painful* was mentioned. *Excruciating*, a time or two. But *silly* is a word Mom might better appreciate.

"Three years, huh? At *drama* school?"

"Yes. The London Academy of Musical Theatre."

"Well!" Mom twirls her dust rag in the air. "La-dee-*dah*."

Inwardly, I bristle. Outwardly, I pretend her antics are amusing. "As friends, we can still keep in touch by chatting online and stuff." I pick up another book. "No pressure. And if we want to date other people, no problem. Because we're just friends."

My heart lurches over the idea of all the older, more sophisticated girls Noah will meet in London, girls whose parents are more open-minded, maybe even *supportive* of his theatre aspirations.

"But even with all the technology at our disposal," I continue, swallowing down everything in me that wants to contradict these facts with my hope, "there are time zones to navigate, and he'll be making new friends in London." I shrug, but the weight of my own words is like lead on my shoulders. "Once he's gone, the reality is that we—" I gulp, glad my back is to her as I dust this shelf a second time. "We probably won't talk much."

"I don't know, Faith." Mom sighs. "He seems too old to even be your friend. It's . . . well, I don't know. It's a little weird, isn't it?"

No. "Maybe." *No, no, aaaannnd no.* "But we're already friends. Real life isn't like the internet, where you can just 'unfriend' someone and that's that." I bite my tongue to keep from arguing the age issue. Again. "And the romance part ended weeks ago. *Weeks.*

210

You've seen my texts." Every night, the minute she gets home from work, I have to hand her my phone. "You've read my emails. We're friends. The romance part is . . . done."

"I have every right to read your texts and emails. I'm your mother."

"I'm not saying that you don't." I work to keep my voice even. "Actually, I'm glad you've read them, because it proves to you that Noah and I can just be friends."

"You've shown a remarkable sense of restraint these past few weeks, Faith. You may not think I've noticed, but I have. You've been helpful around the house without complaint. And I've seen in your eyes how you've battled to keep your mouth shut when you've wanted to argue."

A small noise squeaks in my throat, but I don't say a word.

Mom holds up her hand. "I know that sounds like a criticism, but it's a compliment. I'm saying you've shown me some maturity."

"Oh. Um . . . thank you."

Mom stares at me for a long moment, and I sense our conversation is about to change direction. I only hope it moves in the direction I desire.

"If you're with Noah," Mom says slowly, "I expect you to be out in the open, not cuddled up on the sofa in somebody's dark basement."

"Okay." My heartbeat jolts . . . and then takes off like a racehorse. Mom's going to let me see Noah? In person?

"And absolutely no funny business."

"None."

Mom turns to slide a freshly dusted book onto the shelf. "And I don't want him here."

"What?" I turn away from the book shelf with the book still in my hand. "You don't even want to meet him?"

"I'm giving you a little latitude, Faith. Not an endorsement. Please don't let me down."

Right. Okay. "I won't."

"You're on a very short leash."

"Got it. But I think he'd like to meet you."

"These are my terms for allowing you to continue this *friendship*. Take it or leave it."

I nod. Swallow. I'll take it.

It takes two more hours to finish the project in the study. After lunch, Mom announces we're finished cleaning for the day because she has a hair appointment in Sommerton.

"Mom?" I ask tentatively, not wanting to seem too eager. "Can I call Noah and see if he wants to hang out?"

Mom sighs. "I suppose. Just remember my terms. You are friends only. No funny business."

It's a nice day, so we decide to meet at the waterfall. Out in the open. Just like Mom said. For once, I beat him there and wait near the waterfall's ledge, but facing the trail. When Noah rounds the corner, it's all I can do not to run and throw myself in his arms.

But I can't. That would be romantic. And wonderful.

It's harder than I thought it would be. For both of us, I think. A simple touch of the hand, Noah's arm around my shoulders, a hug . . . affection is so natural, so comfortable between us. It takes a conscious effort to avoid it.

We walk up and down the creek bank until our shoes are wet and muddied. When we return to the waterfall, we rinse our shoes in the creek and then sit on a dry spot on the upper level of the waterfall's ledge to soak up the sun.

It's a gorgeous day. Wildflowers have sprung up all over the woods. The trees and grasses have greened up. Spring at the waterfall is a world of beauty unto itself.

I point at the bank behind Noah. "Do you know what those flowers are called?"

He leans back for a closer look. "Uhh . . . no."

"They're called Dutchman's breeches. You see how the blossoms are formed? They look like a pair of billowy knickers turned upside-down."

"Billowy knickers?" Noah laughs and wrinkles his nose. "That sounds like something straight out of *Jane Eyre* or one of those other works of classic literature Ms. Whetstein tortured me with in high school."

"Torture? I read *Jane Eyre* in Honors English last year. I loved it."

"Really?" He makes a comically horrified face. "I had to read it again for a lit class this spring. Trust me. It was torture."

I bring my open palm across the water, splashing it toward him, but only a few drops actually touch his clothes. "How dare you disparage the reputation of my Jane!"

"*Your* Jane?" He blinks and looks up the creek where my dog is exploring. "Nuh-uh. Your dog is not named after *Jane Eyre*."

"You have a problem with that?" I purse my lips and scowl . . . but then laugh. "No, I'm kidding. She's not named after anything, really. When she was a puppy, 'Janey' just seemed to fit her personality."

"Ah." Noah jumps up and pulls a handful of the little white flowers from where they grow. He bows, offering the bouquet to me.

"Perhaps my lady would accept this small token, with my apologies for failing to appreciate the tedious literature of which she is so enamored, even though she did not name her canine companion after said literary heroine."

"Excellent highbrow accent, Mr. Spencer. And because your accent is so excellent, I shall choose to ignore that you referred to

Jane Eyre as torture." I take the flowers. "Apology accepted. Except . . ." I bite my lip. "I, uh, don't think you're supposed to pick flowers in a nature preserve."

"Oops." Noah's eyes widen. "I forgot about that."

"You're such a rebel, you lawbreaker, you. Not to mention that giving a girl flowers is usually considered romantic, and we're not doing that sort of thing anymore."

"Right again. Forgive my lapse."

"Done." I lift the bouquet and examine the stems. "It looks like you got a few of them by the roots, so maybe we can replant those. These," I say, sorting the flowers and tossing the bad ones into the stream, "are goners. I'm not sure how Dutchman's breeches are seeded, but let's just pretend they're going to circle-of-life it and become a new patch further downstream, shall we?"

"I shall hope for that outcome. In the meantime, how shall I express my gratitude for your help in hiding the evidence of my careless misdeed?"

I love that he's kept the accent, so I match it with the one developed during hours spent watching *Masterpiece* on PBS. "I believe any young man who unlawfully picks wildflowers must have his good name protected by a quick-thinking young lady of his acquaintance."

"By all means." Noah doffs an imaginary top hat. "Proceed."

I move to the bank and look at the muddy clay. "Er, this could get messy." I drop the accent.

"Let me. I'm the one who broke the law, after all. You can't see it, but my hands are already dirty. Just like Lady MacBeth's, except with pollen instead of blood."

"I must have missed the memo. I didn't realize it was classical literature day."

"You started it."

"No, I started with Dutchman's breeches. Botany, not books." I set the flowers in Noah's open hand. "You're the one who mentioned *Jane Eyre* and then adopted the accent and put on that dashing cravat and top hat."

"I'm so absent-minded. I don't even remember tying my cravat on this morning. But I'm gratified you find it dashing."

"Indeed."

Noah grins, adjusts the imaginary cravat at his neck, and then digs around in the dirt, placing the fragile stems back into the earth and then gently patting the mud back in place.

"Hey," he reaches toward a nearby cluster of undisturbed Dutchman's breeches. "Look back here!" He pushes the flowers to one side—carefully this time. "Check it out. It's a little cave!" He reaches forward.

"Stop! You don't know what's in there!" I yank him back. "There could be a snake or a black widow spider or a rat or something."

"You're right. Hang on." He rinses his hands in the stream, dries them on his jeans, and then pulls out his phone. "Flashlight app."

He angles the light toward the hole in the bank. "There are a couple of webs, but . . ."

I shudder when he ignores the fact that something alive made those webs at some point and sticks his hand inside the miniature cave.

"Seems to be critter-free. I guess the creepy crawlies got tired of living in the Dutchman's pocket."

"The what?"

"Oh, come on. This little miniature cave is in back of the Dutchman's breeches, right? Therefore, it *must* be his pocket."

"You're weird."

"My mom would say clever."

"Because she's your mom, and your mom is nice."

215

He laughs. "You've never even *met* my mom."

"Then we're even. But I imagine your mom as being very nice."

"She is, actually." He smiles. "I think you two would get along really well."

I turn my attention back to the little cave so I don't dwell on the differences between our mothers. "Do you think anyone else has ever discovered this little pocket? Apart from rodents and spiders, I mean."

"Hard to say." Noah shrugs and lets the flowers fall back into place. "But . . . maybe it's just been waiting for us to find it. Maybe it's ours."

"Ours? You mean like this is 'my' waterfall?"

"Yeah. We could leave each other notes and stuff here when we can't get together." He winks. "Nothing romantic, of course."

"Never that! But stuff would get wet, wouldn't it? And honestly, I'm not sure I want to stick my hand in there and root around."

"You're right. Besides, leaving papers in there would be like littering, sort of. And I've already broken the law once today."

"And I'm your accomplice." I nod and examine my fingernails, which are a little dirty from sorting the muddy flower stems. "I need to wash off the evidence."

Over by the stream, I stick my open hands in the water, palms down, and watch the play of sunshine, shadow, and water cast lines on my skin. "The water's still pretty cold. I thought after the last week it would've warmed up."

Noah crouches beside me and puts his hand in the water. "It is cold." His hand slides beneath mine and my fingers curl down, weaving through his. "Better?"

"Better." But it's not the water temperature I'm thinking about now.

"Good. After all, how can one keep warm alone?"

"Is that Shakespeare?"

"No, King Solomon. It's from *Ecclesiastes*. Revised Noah Version. And . . ." A strange, strangled sort of laugh exits his lips. "And it's really inappropriate, considering . . ." He clears his throat. "But it came to mind."

"Are you *blushing*?"

"Probably."

"Over a Bible verse?"

"Look it up when you get home, and you'll know why. That's all I'm saying."

"Your ears are seriously pink! But you said *Ecclesiastes*, right? I thought Solomon wrote all his embarrassing lovey-dovey stuff in *Song of Songs*."

Noah gives a comic groan. "So did I."

I've never seen him so flushed. I want to laugh, but I practice mercy instead and change the subject. "So, were you serious about leaving notes in . . ." I squint, trying to remember what Noah called the miniature cave, "in the Dutchman's pocket?"

"Sure, why not?" He gives my fingers a squeeze. "It could be like our personal mailbox. We could find an old jar or something to keep the notes from getting wet or lost. Or taken by giant snake-eating spider-rats." He grins and bumps his shoulder against mine.

"You just had to go there, didn't you?" Minus the creepy-crawlies, it's kind of a cool idea, though. Sweet. Whimsical. Like Noah. "Our own personal mailbox. I like it."

Light and water dance over our joined hands, but regardless of how romantic it looks—*feels . . . is*—I can't let myself dwell on those thoughts and the danger they present.

As friends, Noah and I can be together.

We can't be anything more.

Not yet.

With a hard swallow, I untwine my fingers from their happy underwater home and then rise and shake the water from my hand. "We probably shouldn't—"

"I'm sorry." He stands, wiping his hand on his jeans. "I wish I could say that was a totally unromantic hand hold, but it would be a lie." He meets my eyes. "It won't happen again. Okay, it might. But I'm sorry. Sort of." His frown deepens. He winces a little. "Actually, I'm not sorry at all. I know that's not what I'm supposed to say. I know we need to stick to the plan, but it's so . . ."

He trails off, but silent strings of words fill the space between us like a reprise of all we said that night at the duck pond when we agreed to enter the friendzone.

"There's going to be a learning curve," I say finally. "But if we stick to the plan, there's hope."

Noah swallows, nods. "So we hold on. Without actually holding on."

"Yeah." I melt beneath the love in his crooked smile. "We hold on."

What other choice do we have?

Soon after our yes-we-can-just-be-friends—*er, mostly. We're trying*—meeting at the waterfall, Noah finishes his classes at the community college, earning his associate degree. The pleasant weather keeps him busy with outdoor construction jobs, and between my voice lessons, show choir rehearsals for final concerts, and Mom's annoyingly creative chore lists, finding time we can spend together is difficult.

When we *are* together, it's most often at the waterfall. Even when our schedules don't align to allow us to meet in person, it's still a place of connection, via our personal mailbox. We text, we chat, we utilize the various smartphone apps available to us, and we leave things for the other one to find in the Dutchman's pocket. At first, I was pretty squeamish about reaching in there to retrieve the glass jar Noah provided, but I'm getting over it.

There are no more heart or hug emojis in our texts. No kisses when we meet . . . or part. Sometimes we accidentally hold hands, but when we realize it's happened, we stop. There are no long hugs or arms around my shoulders.

And, wow. I miss all of that.

Still, I know we're probably crossing a few romantic lines. People who are "just friends" don't leave each other secret notes in hidden places. At least not after about fifth grade. And although I know Noah is my friend—the deepest, truest, most wonderful friend I've ever known—my heart still holds him as something more. And those rare occasions when we do get together, my heart silently sings a ballad worthy of the stage.

It's been a warm week, but this particular day dawns with a slight chill. A foggy, late-May mist hangs the promise of rain in the air, but I'm meeting Noah at the waterfall today. The weather's gloom can't dampen my anticipation.

He isn't as carefree.

"Noah?"

"Hmm?"

"You've been awfully quiet this afternoon. Is something wrong?"

"Yeah." He takes a deep breath. "I think a lot of things are wrong."

"Like . . . ?"

Noah squeezes my hand and then sets it in my lap. As usual, I don't recall the moment our fingers entwined. Had I reached for him? Had he reached for me? Does it matter? From his frown, I assume it does.

"Sorry." I swallow around a pang of guilt. "It's . . . it's hard to remember."

"No, I'm sorry. I shouldn't have suggested we come here. We have to stop meeting here."

"Why?"

"Your mom's conditions were that we needed to be out in the open, right?"

"You can't get more open than this. It's a nature preserve. A public area."

"True, but we never see other *people* here, so I'm pretty sure it's not quite what your mom had in mind."

Noah picks up a small stick and rolls it between his palms. "When you left the house this afternoon, did you tell your parents where you were going?"

"Yes."

Noah nods, looking down at the water below our dangling feet. He clears his throat. "Did you tell them that I was going to be here?"

"No."

The disappointment in his glance burns through me, revealing . . . guilt.

I close my eyes against the press of tears. I could have told them. I should have told them.

But what if they'd said no?

So I didn't.

On purpose.

Putting it in those stark terms, even if only to myself, paints the lacking parts of my character in bolder strokes I can't ignore.

"I guess I only told them a part of the truth." As I let out a long breath, my temper flares. Not toward him or even my parents. I'm angry—spitting-mad angry—at myself. "Which means I may as well have been telling a lie."

"Faith, don't—"

"I lied, Noah."

A tremor moves through my frame, leaving me feeling heavier. What have I done? What will this do to . . . us?

Admitting—no, *owning*—that I lied makes me feel dirty. Ugly. Hopeless. But I know what the Bible says about sin. I know what I need to do to rid myself of the weight of its shame.

"I-I should go home and—and confess." My voice breaks. I feel my face crumpling, so I bury my face in my hands, unwilling to let Noah see my full-on ugly cry.

"Faith, look at me."

"No. I can't." My body shakes. I'm cold, more inside than out. "You deserve someone who . . . someone better." I push to my feet, averting my face. "I should go."

Without getting up, Noah reaches for me. His fingers wrap gently around my wrist. "Now just hold on, Faith."

"*Hold on?*" The words volley back to him in a higher pitch than is dignified.

"Yes," he says, understanding in an instant what brought about my reaction. "Hold on."

I risk a glance his way. His smile is weak but true.

"We'll go together."

"Together." I shake my head. "Are you *nuts?* Mom said we could be friends, but I still can't bring you to the house."

"It's time." Noah rises to one knee, facing me. "You're not the only one who needs to confess. To repent."

His grip on my wrist slides down to my hand.

It crosses my mind that this is a posture I've dreamed about for our future—our *way-in-the-future* future. But in my dreams, he doesn't ask, "Will you pray with me?" And he doesn't follow it by clarifying, "This is not a romantic hand-hold, by the way," just before bowing his head.

I kneel, facing Noah, and join my other hand with his.

"Father God," he begins, "we want to do the right thing, but we keep messing up. We want you to be the biggest part of us, of our friendship, and whatever else it is and could be. Forgive me, Lord, for continuing to deceive Faith's parents—"

"No." My head shoots up, interrupting his prayer. "You can't take the blame for this, Noah. It was me. I'm the one who didn't tell the whole truth." I look up at the gloomy sky. "Scratch what he just said, God. It's my fault. Just me. I'm the one who needs forgiving."

"Hey," Noah says softly. "I knew your mom's rules, but I wanted to be alone here with you more than I wanted to please God by hanging out with you around a bunch of other people."

"More than you wanted to please my *mother*, you mean."

"No, I mean God. Coming here today was my idea. Putting things in the Dutchman's pocket was my idea. I'm as much at fault for being romantic as you are, if not more. I'm guilty, Faith. My need, my appeal for forgiveness is just as necessary as yours."

He closes his eyes. "Lord, you know our hearts. You know I love Madeleine Faith Prescott as much more than a friend. You know I don't want to cause her pain or hardship—and I certainly don't want to cause her to sin—but I keep doing exactly that." His intake of breath hitches, and his voice falls to a whisper. "Forgive me, Lord."

His earnest regret, his disappointment in himself—in us—is almost a tangible thing. It stains the air between us with a raw hope that I recognize, strangely, as the truest expression of his love I've yet experienced.

"Forgive me," he whispers. "Forgive us. We want to honor you, to follow the rules that will let us be true to the love we know is real, but we really stink at following through with the promises we've made. Please help us to make things right and to be stronger in the future." With each sentence, each earnest request, his voice gains strength. "Fill us with your peace, Lord. And if it's your will, please soften Mrs. Prescott's heart toward us. And Dr. Prescott's, too."

A strange, sizzling knowledge moves up my arms and across my shoulders, even as tears wet my cheeks. In this moment, more than any in my experience, I sense the presence of God with us, almost apart from time, as Noah prays.

"Help us to trust that your timing is perfect, even when it doesn't seem fast enough for us. Help us to flee from the temptation to deceive others. Help us shine the light of truth to Faith's family, to our friends, and to the world by honoring you." Noah squeezes my hands. "Lord, we love you. We trust you to protect and defend the love you've allowed to grow between us." He takes a deep breath. "May we walk through each moment, cognizant that you are beside us, before us, behind us, and working through us. May your will be done in our lives and in our relationship, as it is in Heaven. In the precious name of Jesus Christ, we pray. Amen."

To add to his prayer would be superfluous. Noah said everything I should have said to God, everything I longed to say to God, for me. All that's required of me is my agreement.

My "amen" is little more than a whisper, but holy prickles alight on my skin, acknowledging the cry of my heart—our hearts.

Still holding my hands, Noah stands. Once I'm on my feet, he drops them.

"Now, Madeleine Faith, my dearest friend in the world, I think it's time we hike to your house." He gives a slight frown. "Or should we go get my car and drive down there?"

And just like that, the tingles disappear, replaced with a sinking dread that pulls hope from the base of my brain, one tendril at a time.

"Let's get your car," I say with a sigh. "You might need a quick getaway if things go bad."

When we arrive at my house, however, Mom is out running errands. Though I know it's only a temporary stall, I breathe a sigh of relief. Her absence secures Noah's entry into the house.

Dad frowns when we walk into the living room but stands when Noah crosses the room and offers his hand.

"Dr. Prescott." He shakes my dad's hand. "I'm Noah Spencer. I know you weren't expecting to see me today, but if you have a moment, I need to speak with you."

Dad invites Noah to sit, albeit reluctantly, and listens to our apology for meeting in a way that violated my agreement with Mom and, by extension, him as well.

We take turns speaking, but Noah does most of the talking, which is good, since his calm delivery comes across better than my rambling apologies.

"I appreciate you coming to speak with me," Dad says, finally, but his frown is still in place. "But unless there's something you're not telling me about the, uh, extent of your relationship . . ."

We both shake our heads.

"We've told you everything, Dad."

"Then I'm not really sure why you both seem so upset about having gone hiking together." He looks at me. "It sounds like your mother was pretty specific in her requirements, and she never said you couldn't go to the waterfall, so I don't have an issue with it. But she also said you weren't to bring Noah here. You did, and I'm afraid that's not going to sit well with her."

"But you understand why we thought it was necessary, don't you, sir?"

"Can't say that I—" Dad is interrupted by the ringing phone. "Can you grab that, Faith?"

I do. And that's when everything falls apart.

"Faith, I told you I didn't want that boy at our house."

"Mom? How did you—?"

"Put your father on the phone."

Panic grips my chest. "It's Mom." I hold out the phone to my dad. "She wants to talk to you."

Once he says hello, Dad doesn't utter another word for a good minute. Finally, he says, "Okay," and hits the end button on the handset, expelling a long sigh. "Faith, your mother is in the garage. I guess she recognized Noah's car from the last time he was here."

Dad stands up. "I'm afraid you're going to have to leave, Noah.

Janet says she will not come in the house until you're gone."

"She won't—" Noah blinks. "She won't even talk to me?"

Dad shakes his head. "I think it would be best if you go now." He holds out his hand awkwardly. "I'll pass on what you said, but . . . I wouldn't hold your breath for an invitation to come back. Once Janet makes up her mind, there's no changing it."

Noah shakes Dad's offered hand, his face wreathed in puzzlement. "What about you? Do you understand now that I truly care for your daughter? That I want to do the right thing by her and by you, as her parents?"

"Er, well . . . I suppose you, uh, made the effort to, er . . ." Dad hems and haws, not really saying anything.

"Okay, I get it." Noah's eyes narrow, and his tone darkens. "Will you at least admit that I'm not the big bad wolf your wife seems to think I am?"

"Well, I, uh, think that is, perhaps a little bit, uh—"

When it becomes clear Dad doesn't know how to respond, something shifts in Noah's expression. It's a subtle change, one I doubt my dad notices, but in that moment, I know that a good portion of the respect Noah has tried to show my Dad has vaporized.

"Mr. Prescott, sir," he says, standing a little taller, "you've heard the truth from us today. Faith and I—"

The phone rings again. Dad reaches for the handset and looks at the caller I.D. but doesn't answer the call. "Faith, your mother is waiting. I think it's time you show your friend out."

I put a hand on Noah's arm. "Come on."

Noah stares at my dad for another few seconds. His brow furrows on an exhale. He shakes his head and then lets me lead him down the hall.

"Noah, I-I'm sorry."

"You have to put up with this all the time. You have nothing to be sorry about." His jaw moves, grinding his teeth. "I don't think I have ever been so, so—"

"Angry? Frustrated? Hurt? Disgusted?" I supply words reflecting my own emotions.

"Yeah. All that and then some." He presses the balls of his hands on the sides of his head. "She won't even come in the house? What am I, a leper?"

"Actor, leper, musician . . . It's all the same to her. Take your pick." My words exit through teeth air can barely fit between. I am so angry right now. So. Angry.

"I think I finally understand the term *righteous indignation*." He drops his hands. "Yes, we messed up. But we recognized it, and we did the right thing. We confessed. We apologized. We tried to make it right." He winces. "Well, until I got snarky with your dad."

"You call that snarky?" My laugh is short, tight. "You barely glared at him."

"Okay, okay." The corner of his mouth twitches. "But you have to admit, I wasn't one hundred percent respectful there at the end. Not to mention that I'm still in the house." His half-grin disappears. "But I just don't get it. How do they justify—? I mean, we came clean. We apologized. We laid it all out there. And in return, we get this . . . this total disregard from your mom."

"I know. She's acting like a four-year-old."

"I wasn't going to say it, but . . . yeah. Kind of. And what's with your dad? He acts like he's some sort of supplicant to her whims."

"I don't know. He's always been that way." I shrug. "It's how their relationship operates."

"That's messed up."

I nod. "Dad avoids conflict by letting her have her way."

"She won't even *meet* me." He shakes his head.

Noah gives a growl of frustration. His arms shake from the force of his hands, fisting at his sides.

Our gazes lock for a charged moment. I see the internal battle waging behind Noah's eyes—a battle I suspect is mirrored in my own.

His breath comes faster, and his lips press together. He looks up at the ceiling and then down to the floor. And then, with one final glance down the hall, likely aimed further, toward my parents, a short, uncharacteristically belligerent phrase breaks from between his lips.

"Screw it."

A silent glance is our split second agreement. He pulls me to him.

The crush of his lips is a culmination of longing, vexation, and hope . . . all bathed in fire, igniting a sense of destiny within the beautiful mystery of who we are, together, alongside the deepest dreams of what we could become someday.

There is strength in this kiss. Passion, with honor. It's almost as if the power of this one concentrated moment of connection is the key to thwarting every threat against all we know to be true between us.

I cling to Noah—*my Noah*—returning his kiss, matching every flame of his desperate, passionate frustration and his full, unquenchable love with my own.

"Just *friends?*"

Mom's voice drops like a sheet of ice between us. We break apart, breathless.

"You expect me to walk in on something like *that* and believe, for even one second, that you two have been behaving as 'just friends' for the past few weeks?"

No-no-no-no-no-no! I grip Noah's hand, trying to catch my breath, slow my pulse, and cool my cheeks while panic screams inside my brain.

"If you're finished mauling your *friend*, Mr. Spencer, you can remove yourself from my property."

Noah's breath is as ragged as mine. "I'm sorry," he whispers and squeezes my hand. "I shouldn't have . . . Faith, I'm so sorry."

The sincerity, the anguish in his eyes melts me—frees me.

"Don't be," I whisper back. "I'm not."

She is wrong about us. Even about that kiss, regardless of its heat. She is wrong to treat Noah like this.

My muscles tremble. Not from the kiss, not from the adrenaline of being caught in such an inopportune moment with the boy I love. No, this trembling is the release of a soul-deep anger, one caused by a grievous wrong. This must be what Noah meant by righteous indignation.

"I said, *get out*," my mother growls.

I ignore her. Placing a hand to my heart, I spread my fingers apart and then clasp them into a fist. Pressing that fist over Noah's heart, I open my hand. "Love never fails."

"It always hopes," he whispers back, nodding. "Always perseveres."

With one hand on the doorknob, Noah pauses, turns, and meets the cold fury in my mother's eyes. "I doubt you will believe me, Mrs. Prescott, but I have never and *will* never mean any harm toward your daughter. I hope someday you'll see that."

"*Get. Out.*" The pitch of Mom's voice rises with each word. It's almost painful. "Get out of my house!"

Meeting my eyes one last time, Noah presses a kiss in my hair and goes out the door.

It's a good thing we decided to drive here from the waterfall. Even though it's the end of May, Noah would suffer a cold hike back through the nature preserve with that much ice clinging to his ears.

Mom is talking—shouting, really—but her words are senseless

syllables, dulled in my ears. Turning my back on her verbal tirade, I press my hand to my throat, watching out the sidelight window until Noah's car is out of sight. When I finally turn to face her, she is silent, her lips a thin line, her face a purple shade of red.

She's shaking. In a movement so fast it makes me jump, she pivots and storms off, but as she passes the side table, she expels a curse word I've only heard her use during major sporting events, and slams her hand across an eye-level shelf, taking an object from it with the same force she probably used as a volleyball star, spiking the kill.

The hand-blown vase, a Christmas gift from Aunt Becca, flies off its shelf, shattering against the closed door to Dad's study.

Mouth open, I'm frozen. So is she, for a moment.

"Janet?" Dad calls from the living room.

"It's nothing," she hollers back. "Everything's fine."

No. No, it's not. My throat is dry. I can barely swallow. My gaze is riveted on the fractured evidence of a moment of violent rage.

"Clean that up," Mom tosses the cold words over her shoulders. "When you've made certain you've found every last sliver, go to your room. Don't even think about coming downstairs again until morning."

It's spring, but the bitter winds of a hard winter could not be colder than the silent promises sweeping toward me on my mother's glare.

The first week of June brings final exams for me and an unexpected, slight relaxation to the house arrest I've been under since Mom walked in on Noah and me kissing. If one considers getting to study for finals with Jenna—but only if Jenna's mom is there— a "relaxation" of my mother's attitude toward me.

Sadly, I do.

Just as I have every school day since that fate-sealing kiss, I ride the bus to school. When classes are dismissed, Jenna and I are picked up, per Mom's conditions, by Jenna's mother.

"Hi, sweetie. Hi, Faith." Mrs. Slade smiles as I climb into the middle row seat of her minivan. "Did you girls have a good day?"

Jenna groans. "The Geometry final was brutal."

Since I'm on the AP track, I took the class last year, but I nod, knowing how Jenna has struggled all year. "Thanks for picking us up."

"No problem." Mrs. Slade meets my eyes in the rearview mirror. "And you're staying for supper, right?"

"Yeah, if that's okay. Mom said she'd pick me up at eight."

"Good, good. That will give you guys plenty of time to study.

And after tomorrow, you'll officially be juniors."

"Finally!" Jenna gives me a high five. "We'll be upperclassmen at last!"

"I cleared off the dining room table so you two can spread out your stuff in there." Inside the house, Mrs. Slade hangs her keys on a peg by the door. "Oh! I made cookies this afternoon. I'll bring you guys a plate of them in a couple minutes."

Jenna plops her book bag on the wood table with a sound that would send my mom scurrying for the scratch repair, if we were at my house. "What should we do first? History?"

"Sounds good. I made flashcards with battle dates on one side and the name and place on the other."

"Of course you did." Jenna rolls her eyes but grins. "And you probably color coded them, too, didn't you?"

"No. Well, I wrote the names of the battles the Union won in blue pen and the Confederate wins in pencil, so they're gray."

"Nerd."

I unzip my bag and root around. "Of course they're at the bottom. Hang on." I pull my books out, one by one, and stack them neatly on the table. The cards are in the bottom, and they've all come loose from last night's neatly rubber-banded stack. I grab one handful then another . . .

"Oh, give it here." Jenna yanks my bag out of my hands, turns it upside down, and shakes it, dumping the flashcards and the rest of the bag's contents, including several pens, a bunch of random sticky notes, a few hairbands, a necklace I'd thought I'd lost, and . . .

Oh. No.

Right on top—because it must have fallen to the bottom of my bag all those months ago—is a little foil square.

"Here are the cookies, girls. I hope you like oatmeal chocolate chip, Faith. I didn't—" Mrs. Slade goes silent. Her eyes widen. "Oh my heavens. Is that a . . ."

The look on her face is nothing less than shock, coated with a few shades of betrayal with a heavy dose of *I'm so disappointed in you* thrown in.

"It's not mine." I sound like a little kid caught eating paste. My denial is true, but even I hear its false ring.

How could I have forgotten that was in my bag? And for so long?

"Really," I say, desperate for them to believe me. "I'm not just saying that. It's *not* mine. It's Gretchen's. She gave it to me, I mean."

Both Jenna's and her mother's eyebrows rise.

"Not because I wanted it! I didn't *ask* for it or anything! Gretchen was . . . Well, she was being Gretchen. I was going to throw it away a long time ago, but I guess I just forgot about it."

Jenna doesn't blush easily, but her cheeks are twin flames, matching her mom's. If the floor could open up and swallow me right now, that would be *grand*.

Mrs. Slade opens her mouth and closes it several times before she finally sits down in the chair next to me.

"Faith, honey, I know you've been seeing one boy exclusively for quite a while now. And I know he's older and probably more experienced—"

"He's not like that. We haven't done . . . anything like that. We wouldn't."

She nods, but it's clear she doesn't believe me.

"Your mother is concerned. She asked me to keep an eye out, but I didn't think . . ." She sighs. "You and Jenna have been friends for so long. Sometimes I forget you're not little girls anymore." She clears her throat. "I'm sure you know we don't believe teenagers should be sexually active. We've taught Jenna that sex is something that should be saved for marriage. But if you and Noah have, um, well . . . I hope this," —she nods toward the condom—"means you've been careful and practiced safe—"

"Mo-*omm!*" Jenna breaks in, slapping her hands over her ears. "*Stahhhp.* You know what Gretchen is like. Faith's not like that. And Noah, geez. He's a total prude about that stuff. If Faith was having sex, I would know about it. And she's not." She drops her hands, and even though her voice remains confident, when her eyes find mine, they hold the tiniest bit of doubt. "Right?"

"Right." I turn back to Mrs. Slade. "Please believe me. I'm still a virgin. And so is Noah." My neck and face are on fire. "The only reason I have that stupid thing is because my sister . . ."

I tell them the whole story. "So, you see? I don't need it, and I don't want it." I pick it up. "I'm going to go throw it away."

"Not here, please. I don't want to take the chance of the boys seeing it."

"Oh. Right." Jenna has twin brothers in middle school, and a middle school boy finding a condom is never a good thing.

"I'll take it with me, then, and I'll toss it the first chance I get. Maybe I'll burn it or something." I bite my lip. This is bad. Very bad. "Please don't tell my mom. She's already watching me like a hawk. And she'd never believe it came from Gretchen."

Mrs. Slade says she believes me, that we'll keep it between us—for now—but something about the distance in her expression argues that Jenna's mom will never look at me in quite the same way again.

Once school is out for the summer, there is no reason for me to study and no more Mom-sanctioned trips to Jenna's. My mother remains almost as cold toward me as she was the day she walked in on the kiss. Thankfully, Gretchen comes home, and Mom's focus shifts to her more pleasing, golden daughter.

Whatever.

After spending the three weeks after she finished classes at the university with Justin's family at their vacation home in—get this—Hawaii, Gretchen's tan makes her look even more like a movie star than usual. Her arrival and the serious nature of her relationship with Justin, the High Prince of Successful Awesomeness, thaw Mom a bit.

Justin is interning at a firm in Iowa City this summer, but he spends a lot of Sunday afternoons at our house, which Mom, of course, loves. It gnaws at my gut, how her affection for Gretchen's boyfriend is based on such superficial things. How can she not notice what a fake he is? Or how easily Justin dismisses Gretchen's brains—her personhood, even—but he obviously appreciates her as his personal arm candy. Ugh. It makes me sick.

I take a summer job working in my grandmother's beauty salon, which gets me out from under Mom's suffocating, watchful eye. It's easy work. From the front desk of the Kanton Korner Salon, I set appointments, field phone calls, stock product, and keep the tanning booths clean. But it's a small town, and Grandma's is not the only salon in town. There's a fair bit of sitting around doing nothing, too.

Unlike some stylists, who can't seem to talk and work at the same time, Grandma Maddie has over forty years of experience doing just that. Her combs slide and her scissors snip through her customers' hair, but she never misses a beat in conversation. My grandma is not the sort of person who can sit still for long. One particularly slow day, she decides I need a trim.

I don't, really, but it makes her happy, so . . . to the shampoo station I go.

"I hear Gretchen has gotten pretty serious with that fancy lawyer boyfriend of hers."

"Justin. Yeah. But he's not a lawyer yet. He still has another year of law school."

"You don't like him." Grandma is very good at hearing the words people don't say.

"Not especially, but my opinion hardly matters. The way my mom fawns over him, you'd think Justin was running for President or something." I breathe in the sweet fruity-floral scent as the woman whose first name I share—on paper, at least—begins lathering shampoo into my hair.

"Gretchen brought him by the house last week. I thought he was nice enough. Why don't you like him?"

"I don't know. He seems kinda fake to me." A bubble floats up from the sink and pops right over my eye. "It's not gonna last. Gretchen doesn't look at Justin the way a girl should look at a guy she's supposed to be in love with."

"Hmm. And how is that?"

"I don't know. It doesn't matter."

But I do know. And it *does* matter. I shake my head to force the thought away.

"Hold still."

"Sorry."

"How about you, Madeleine Faith? Any new boys in your life? Or are you still mooning over that boy your mother dislikes so much."

"How do you know about that?"

"A woman my age doesn't keep doing hair because she likes being on her feet all day, sweetie." She chuckles. "Everybody knows the Kanton Korner Salon has the best gossip in town. "Also," she adds, leaning into my line of sight to give me a wink, "Gretchen may have mentioned it."

Interesting. Then again, Grandma Maddie could pry dirt out of a nun's freshly starched habit, so getting Gretchen to talk about a little family drama is hardly a challenge for her.

"His name is Noah Spencer." I close my eyes to avoid getting water spray and stray suds in them. "And Mom can't honestly claim to actually dislike him as long as she refuses to have a conversation with him."

"Your father said they had words."

"Yeah." I snort. "Basically, she ordered him out of our house. That was about the extent of it."

"That sounds pretty harsh, even for Janet. And nobody does harsh like Janet Prescott, C.P.A."

"You've got that right."

"Oh, bother. Forget I said that. She's your mother, and I shouldn't talk about her like that in front of you. In fact," Grandma Maddie says, chuckling as she massages my scalp, "I shouldn't be talking about her at *all* if I want to keep my blood pressure down. But since she's married to my little boy, the only child of a poor old widow, I can't be expected to be unbiased."

I'm a little disappointed when my scalp massage ends. That's always my favorite part of a haircut.

"Janet is Janet," Grandma Maddie continues as she rinses my hair. "And I'm old and set in my ways. But you, my dear Madeleine Faith, are loved by us both. I must be a better grandma and just shut up about your mother. Is that warm enough? Too hot?"

"It's just right." The spray of warm water tingles through the lather on my head. "I don't know why you even ask. You always pick the right temperature."

I open my eyes just long enough to see my grandmother's smile. "I do my best. So . . . what are we doing today? Just a trim? Or are you feeling adventurous?"

"Just the ends. I like it long."

She drapes a towel over my head and helps me sit up. "Where does your young man get his hair cut?"

"I don't know. Probably nowhere fancy. Noah's pretty frugal. He's saving up to study theatre in England."

"I *see.*"

Grandma Maddie guides me to one of the hydraulic chairs in the middle of the salon. The three other stylists are reading magazines in their otherwise-unoccupied chairs.

"I suppose that begs the question if *you* are now thinking of studying drama in England?"

"Nope." My voice vibrates as Grandma Maddie roughly towel-dries my hair. "I'm still going to apply stateside. Besides, by the time I start college, Noah will only have one more year left."

"Always the practical one, my Madeleine Faith."

"Not according to my mother," I grumble. "She thinks I'm a flake."

"A *flake?*" Grandma Maddie spins the chair around. Planting both hands on the armrests, she leans over to be eye level with me. "Did she say that to you?"

"No." I always feel a little guilty, a little disloyal, when I talk to Grandma about Mom. "But she did compare me to Aunt Becca."

"Hah." Grandma straightens and puts her hands on her hips. "You're no more like Becca than your mother is. I've only met your aunt a few times, but oh *my*. Total opposites, those two. And neither one—never mind."

She spins the chair back around. "Forgive me, sweetie. Your mother means well. Most of the time. And don't worry about what she says. You are nothing, and I mean *nothing,* like your Aunt Becca. Yes, she can sing, but my goodness! That girl is a certifiable dingbat. Becca's put so much junk into her body that if she rubbed two of her brain cells together for an hour I don't think you'd even get a spark."

Wow. Grandma's on a roll today!

I decide to change the subject to one that doesn't make me feel quite so uncomfortable, even though this one is fairly entertaining. "Hey, I heard you say something to one of the clients that somebody new is going to start working here. Did somebody quit?"

"No. I'm expanding. Moving with the times. Do you know Lissa Reynolds?"

"Sure. She was on the dance team with me. She graduated last year."

"And she's just graduated again. Lissa is a certified esthetician."

"A *what?*"

"She does facials, skincare, makeup, that sort of stuff. Sure would have liked to have had her during prom season." Grandma Maddie clicks her tongue. "Oh well, there's always next year. Anywho, Lissa's going to be starting here as soon as I get another sink installed. The guy's supposed to come on Thursday, but we'll see."

She pulls a comb through the back of my hair. "You know, my hair used to be this color when I was young. Back before I went through my 'frosting' phase in the eighties." She sighs. "The eighties fried a lot of follicles in this town, let me tell you. My hair never came back to its former glory."

"I like your hair. The color you have now is really pretty."

"Thank you, sweetie. It's called 186B, officially, but I've christened it Walnut Sunrise."

I laugh. Of course she did. "The name fits."

"It's a new shade we just got in. But you, my sweet Madeleine Faith, don't you color your hair until you have to." She lifts up the back of my hair to put a fresh, dry towel around my neck. "Don't tell my other clients I said this, but you can't get anything this pretty out of a bottle."

"Noah calls my hair 'cinnamon.'"

"Cinnamon. Hmm. I like him already." Grandma nods, smiling. "About a quarter of an inch off, you think?"

"Sure." She's the expert.

"Any boy who compares the color of your hair to an exotic spice sounds like a keeper to me."

"Cinnamon is about as exotic as white flour, Grandma. But you're right. He's a keeper."

"So, is he a trouble maker, this boy?"

"No! Just the opposite!"

"Hold *still*, Madeleine."

I freeze all but my mouth. "He's polite, sweet, caring, and extremely . . . well, *good*. He has strong morals. The problem is," I say, pursing my lips, but careful not to jerk my head, "Mom and Dad think he's too religious and too old for me."

In the mirror, her face scrunches up. "How old is he, forty? Good

grief! I wasn't even out of high school when I married your grandpa."
She laughs. "Of course, there might have been a metaphorical
shotgun in my daddy's hand."

Yes, I know the story. And it certainly doesn't help my case. My
father was born only four months after that hurried wedding.

"Noah's nineteen."

"Nineteen? Pah. My Charlie was seven years older than me, and
we got along just fine. So what's the problem?"

"I don't see a problem. Mom and Dad do. Technically, Noah's
almost twenty. His birthday is in September. I won't be seventeen
until—"

"October sixth. My much-belated twin."

"They don't trust me."

"Ahh. A universal problem for teenage girls, I think. They love
you, honey. They do. I know it probably doesn't feel that way
sometimes, but just hang in there." Grandma Maddie puts a small
mirror in my hand and spins the chair around. "Now, how does that
look."

"Great. Thanks."

Just as Grandma unfastens the cape around my shoulders, the
bell rings, announcing a walk-in. "And just in time, too. Am I good,
or what? Hey, before you leave tonight," she says as she reaches for
the broom, "dig out a coupon for that young fella of yours. I believe
I'd like to meet him. And if he's as frugal as you say he is, he won't
be able to turn down a free haircut now, will he?"

All summer long, conversations at home revolve around romance. Whether it's the catch Gretchen has landed in Justin the Great, Ryan's upcoming wedding, or my parents' thirtieth anniversary, everyone is allowed—and celebrated for—their romantic diversions. Everyone, that is, except me.

Even so, the officially tabooed name of Noah Spencer seems to linger in Mom's mind, showing itself in the restrictions continuously enforced upon me.

My computer and phone are monitored more closely than ever. Thankfully, Mom doesn't think to check for new apps—like the password-required one that gives me a just-for-Noah number. But if I'm even a little late coming home from a voice lesson, my job, or an errand, I'm subjected to the third degree. If invited to Jenna's house, which is happening less and less frequently these days, Mom calls ahead to make sure my plans are legit . . . and that at least one of Jenna's parents will be home to supervise.

But even with all Mom's meddling, Noah and I still find small, safe ways to see each other.

Shortly after I drop the free haircut coupon in the mail, Noah shows up at the Kanton Korner Salon and Spa, as Grandma's new signage now proclaims. Even after his coupon is spent, Noah appears at least once a week—sometimes just for a shampoo. One day, to my amusement, Noah even subjects himself to a facial, just because Lissa Reynolds is the only person with an open spot in the appointment book when he happens by.

I will never let him live that down.

Still, with his departure date drawing ever nearer, it isn't enough. Finally, Noah reschedules his weekly Wednesday night voice lesson for Thursday morning, meeting with Mr. Barron at the high school instead of the church, in a time slot directly before the half-hour allotted for one Faith Prescott.

He tends to linger, after those lessons. Every moment is precious and too short.

And August arrives too swiftly.

Lately, I've been working with Mr. Barron on the songs Ryan and Danielle asked me to sing at their wedding. Today is my final lesson before the big day. Things are going well, even though I will never understand my brother's preference for country music.

In this isolated stretch of moments, as I stand next to Mr. Barron's piano, singing the admittedly touching words of Keith Urban's "Your Everything," everything is right with the world. Of course, I could be perfectly happy singing *Sesame Street* songs with Noah Spencer just a few feet away. His smile is light. Warmth. And entirely for me.

Mr. Barron lifts his hands from the piano keys, chuckling. "It never fails to amaze me how you take this little country love song and make it sound like a Broadway ballad."

"I think it probably helps that I'm accompanied by a solo piano without the fiddle and slide guitar."

"I think it has very little to do with that and everything to do with the person singing the song." He looks over the piano, at Noah. "Am I right, or am I right?"

"You are absolutely correct, Mr. Barron. Faith is an artist."

"Thanks."

"Oh sure," Mr. Barron says, giving me a mock frown, "believe the soon-to-be West End sensation, but not the guy who's been your vocal coach since seventh grade."

He reaches for his coffee cup and tips it up. "Empty. Again." His sigh borders on melodramatic. "Guys. I need to run up to the office and get a refill before my next lesson gets here. I simply *cannot* get through that one without caffeine."

"You are so mean." I laugh. "Poor Alex." The lesson after mine is a seventh grade boy who is experiencing the painful vocal transition of puberty. "His mom still won't let him quit, huh?"

"Nope. She's convinced he's the next Josh Groban."

"Poor kid." Noah chuckles. "I hope he survives the humiliation. He really had that Vienna Boys' Choir thing going last year, but now?" Noah cringes. "Not so much."

"You've got that right." Mr. Barron laughs. "Now, it's more like the Cheese Curd Choir. Squeak! Squoo-eek!"

We all laugh.

"You kids hang here while I get my coffee, and then we'll do one more run through if there's time before Alex gets here." Mr. Barron points a gun-finger at Noah. "I trust you'll keep your hands to yourself, Spencer?"

Noah raises his hands. "Of course. I will maintain a three-foot radius from Miss Prescott at all times."

At the door, Mr. Barron turns back and arches an eyebrow in an attempt at mock sternness. "See that you do." The door shuts on his laughter.

"He's such a dork." I shake my head, smiling toward the door.

"But a lovable dork. So . . . what's new with my favorite vocal artist?"

"Nothing. My life is completely static." It's too true. But I would abandon change forever if I could just keep Noah near. "The wedding is this weekend. But you knew that." I sigh. "Oh, I read *Jane Eyre* yesterday. Bet you're sorry you missed that." I laugh. "I know how much you love that book."

"Yesterday? As in, you read that whole book in a day?"

"It was a slow day at the salon. I also alphabetized the shampoos, painted my toenails, and memorized a new Bible verse."

"Sweet. Which verse? Is it one I know?"

"Probably, since you missionaries' kids are born with the whole Bible memorized."

"Riiiiight."

I grin. "Okay, but I'm pretty sure you know this one. John 11:35."

Noah squints up toward the ceiling as if he might find the verse written on the leak-stained white panels. "Hmm. John eleven thirty-fi—"

His pensive look breaks off in a laugh. "Well, I hope you didn't suffer any brain drain or anything, memorizing the shortest verse in the Bible."

I clear my throat over-loudly and posture myself as if I'm about to read *The Declaration of Independence* to the actual forefathers. "'Jesus wept.'"

"Brava!" He grins, adding a little snooty, half-handed, operatic applause. "Now that you have it hidden in your head, you can work at hiding it in your heart."

"What's the difference?"

"The difference is somewhere between memorization and application. I mean, you had to memorize the Pledge of Allegiance as a kid, right?"

"Sure."

Noah leans back in the metal chair and crosses his feet at the ankles. "We memorize stuff like that because our teachers—or in my case, my parents—make us, and it gets stuck in our brain. But I'd bet my great-grandfather, who volunteered to fight in World War II, had that pledge hidden in his heart. Its meaning sank through to the core of who he was and what he was willing to die for. He was willing to go down in a plane in the south Pacific to help provide liberty and justice for all."

Nodding, I move to the chair beside him. "Okay, but—"

"Ah-ah-ah." Noah waggles a finger at me. "Three feet, if you please, Miss Prescott."

"Right." I scoot over, leaving two chairs between us. "But how do you say, 'Jesus wept' in the same way? It's too . . . simplistic, isn't it? When I think of 'liberty and justice for all' it's so majestic sounding. Saying '*Jesus wept*' is like saying '*Noah sang.*' It's a proper noun and a verb. Not anything really descriptive."

"But did you read it in context? Or did you just look up the verse?"

"I looked up the verse then went back and read the whole chapter. It's about Lazarus dying and being raised from the dead."

"Yeah." Noah uncrosses his ankles and leans forward with his elbows on his knees. "But did you know Lazarus was Jesus's very good friend? When Jesus saw that Lazarus was dead, he didn't say, 'Abracadabra, come back to life, Laz, ol' buddy ol' pal!' did he?"

I laugh. "He most certainly did not."

"No, Jesus *wept*."

Excitement sparks in Noah's eyes. "Jesus didn't just shed a few tears, blow his nose, and get on with his day. He *grieved*. Jesus knew he was separated, albeit temporarily, from his good friend, and it broke his heart."

This is hitting a little too close to home, all things considered. But if Noah notices my sudden difficulty breathing, he doesn't let it show.

"That little verse shows us that Jesus, and through his experience, the whole Trinity, understands grief and pain on our measly human level. For two little words, it's pretty profound. And . . ." Noah pauses to clear his throat, "it's kind of . . . comforting to know that when we're grieving and—and lonely, we're not abandoned."

I nod through the tears gathering in my eyes and the fist clamped around my heart. "Got it." My voice is barely above a whisper. "Jesus *wept.*"

"Yeah." Noah looks down at the floor and clears his throat. Again. When he looks up, his smile warms me to the core. "Jesus wept. But it was only *after* he acknowledged his grief that he reached beyond his humanness and into that giant God-ness of his to whip out a miracle and bring his buddy back."

"Cool." I stare at the carpet for a minute, tossing the two words around in my mind, grappling with the idea of the Creator of the Universe being saddened—no, *grieved*—enough by one person's loss to weep.

"I really like that." I meet Noah's eyes. "It makes him more, you know, *real.*"

"Yeah. It does." We're quiet for several moments before he speaks again. "You have no idea how badly I want to come over there and hug you right now."

"I might."

The hinges on the choir room door squeak, announcing Mr. Barron's return.

"You ready to go through it one more time before Alex gets here?" He raps his knuckles on the top of the piano. "Hello? Uh, guys? Yoo-hoo! Music, remember? Wedding this weekend? This is our last chance before it's go-time."

Noah flinches. I cringe at Mr. Barron's choice of words. *Our last chance.*

A chill moves across my shoulders. *Go-time.* In a few days, Noah will board a plane for London.

"Music." I swallow hard. "Music. Right."

I take my place beside the piano. As Mr. Barron plays the introduction, I silently lay out my heart before a God who knows what it's like to grieve a loss, to weep. *I don't know if I can do this, God. I'm not ready to say goodbye.*

And then it's time to sing.

Even though it hurts, I let the lyrics rip me open. I sing as if every word of this song is a statement of devotion, aimed at Noah's heart.

I love you. I love you. I love you.

I inject that truth—our truth—into the melody, carving the fullness of my heart into every note, the desperation of my hope into each verse.

Skills I've gained through years of training allow me to measure and support each breath through my tears. Raw emotion pours over words and melody, but it's not dreams of the someday-stage of Broadway that sustains these notes, this control. It's a deep knowledge of what the stage of this moment represents: my last chance to sing to Noah.

It could be years before I have this opportunity again.

As I sing, a still, small voice whispers in my ear. It's a familiar refrain, unattached to this song.

Hold on.

I will. I pledge with my eyes, my heart, and through the unsung undertones of this song. *I will hold on.*

My assurance is reflected in Noah's eyes, connecting my heart to his, his to mine, by a thin—so thin—but golden thread of hope.

Too soon, the song is over.

Mr. Barron finishes the last bit of the accompaniment and sits silently staring at the piano keys.

Finally, he lifts his head, pulling a hand across his face. "Faith, that was . . . exquisite. If you sing it like that on Saturday, there won't be a dry eye in the place. Clearly, my work here is done. In fact, I'm gonna need a sec." He spins around on the piano bench until he's facing the wall.

My cheeks are streaked with tears, as are Noah's, but neither of us makes a move to cover the evidence of our emotion . . . until the door of the choir room opens, admitting a gangly seventh grade boy whose feet are much too big for his shoulders.

Wiping his eyes, Mr. Barron spins back around. "Alex. Come on in. We're just finishing up." He waves the boy forward and then steps around the piano. He offers Noah his hand. "Mr. Spencer, it's been an honor."

Noah stands. Their handshake turns into a hug.

Mr. Barron pats Noah's back and steps away, sniffing. "Knock 'em dead over there, kid."

"I'll do my best, Mr. B."

"I know you will." He glances at me, eyebrows raised. "See you next week then, Faith? Same time, new music?"

I nod. My throat is too tight to let a word escape. I'm on the ragged edge of an utter meltdown, and seeing how close Mr. Barron is to losing it again doesn't help.

Noah's eyes are on me. "I'll walk you out."

Words tumble over one another in my mind, but none come until we reach the exit doors.

"Noah." His name is a whisper. It's all I can manage.

"Madeleine Faith." His smile is both strangely full and utterly broken. "Everything you sang? I heard it. And I sang it right back to you, in here." He taps his chest and then cups my cheek.

I close my eyes. *Stay*, I want to beg him, but I don't. I can't. I won't be the thing that keeps him from his dreams.

"Faith, I . . ." His hand slips from my face. "Sorry. I shouldn't have—"

"It's okay."

He sticks his hands in the pockets of his jeans and rocks back on his heels. "I guess you'll be expected home soon."

"Yeah."

He looks up at the ceiling tiles of the entryway. "I don't know if I'll get another chance to tell you good—"

"No." I put my hand on his lips, and then drop it. "Don't say it."

His Adam's apple moves up and down. "Okay." His smile is shaky. "In my head, I'm hugging you. Just F.Y.I."

"Thanks." I let the tiniest smile through, but it's weak and only serves to bring more tears to my eyes. "In my head, I'm hugging you back."

Our eyes lock, and I fight the urge to throw myself into his arms. When the temptation becomes too much to bear, I turn and flee. Pushing the door open, I exit the school on a blind and stumbling run.

Noah doesn't follow.

I don't expect him to.

By the time I reach my car, sobs shake my body so fiercely that I can barely open the door. I sit in my car while Noah fires up old Eliza. I close my eyes as she makes her crass departure, escorting Noah away from Kanton High. Away from me.

Panic strikes. Stealing my air. Curling forward, I hug my arms around myself, arms that ache with the need to hold on to Noah almost as much as my heart aches to realize just how long it could be before I see him again.

I should have wished him well. I should have said goodbye.

This is it. This is really . . . it.

Tonight, my family will head to Des Moines for Ryan's wedding. We won't get back until Sunday night. Monday will be spent moving Gretchen back into her sorority house. Mom has already given me a Cinderella-worthy list of post-wedding chores for Tuesday.

And Wednesday?

On Wednesday, Noah Spencer will board a plane bound for London.

Time has run out.

And I didn't let him say goodbye.

I didn't say goodbye.

Ryan's wedding is beautiful, but even after he and Danielle depart for their honeymoon, the reception goes on. And on. And . . . on. It is well into the wee hours of Sunday morning before we return to our hotel suite, but sleep eludes me. Finally, when dawn peeks through the curtains, I head down to the lobby for the hotel's continental breakfast.

Surprisingly, Gretchen is already dressed and sitting at a table.

Seeing me, my sister lifts one perfectly sculpted eyebrow. "You look terrible."

"Thanks." I plop in a chair and dump cereal and milk into a bowl. "How do you look so good? You had the same weekend I did."

"It's called makeup, honey. You should try it. You look like the living dead."

"Yeah. Feel that way, too."

I pick up the spoon and dig it into the cereal and then pull it out and do it again without taking a bite.

Three days. He's leaving in three days. I can't get it out of my head.

"Who's leaving in three days?"

I blink. Look up. "Did I say that out loud?"

"Uh, duh. So . . . ?"

"Noah."

"Oh, that's right. I talked to him at Smoked Salt a couple of weeks ago. He waited on me and Justin one night."

"How nice for you." I scowl at my bowl. "Mom forbade me from eating there."

Thankfully, Gretchen doesn't respond to my surliness. "You know, you have pretty good taste, kid. I mean, sure, Noah's always been a nice guy. Most guys that cute are just, well . . ." She pauses and then crosses her arms and glares out the window. "They're just so stinking full of themselves."

Gretchen shakes off her scowl and looks at me. "What I mean to say is that Noah's not like that. Not at all. I tell you, Faith, if you didn't still have a thing for him, I might . . ." She laughs.

Classic Gretchen.

"Oh, don't look so murderous. I'm kidding. Even if I chased, I don't think I'd catch one like him."

I stir my cereal some more. "What's wrong with Mr. Perfect?"

"Yeah, Noah's pretty close to perfect. Maybe *too* perfect, if you know what I mean." Gretchen drums her French manicure on the table top. "You know, Mom might be on to something there. I mean, when a guy seems that good, there's usually something seriously wrong with him."

"There's nothing wrong with Noah. Please." I roll my eyes. "But I wasn't talking about him. I meant Justin the Great. Your *perfect* boyfriend. The one our parents adore."

"Oh. *Him.*" Gretchen purses her lips and looks out the window. "Yeah, they do love him. He's purr-fect." She says the word with distaste. "But . . . case in point."

"Gretchen?" I bite my lip. Sure, Justin gives me the creeps a little, but is he worse than I thought? "Justin's not, like, abusive or anything, is he?"

"Abusive?" Gretchen snorts. "Hardly. But thanks for asking." She smiles, and I'm touched by the warmth, the tenderness of it. "That's sweet. My little sister is worried about me."

"I just don't want you to get hurt by some stupid preppy jerk." I wince when I realize how pointed that comment was toward Justin. "Uh, sorry."

"Don't be." Gretchen laughs. "It's actually refreshing to hear someone in this family call Justin a stupid jerk. Everyone else seems to think he's God's gift."

"Where is he, anyway?"

"Still asleep, I guess. I don't really care."

"Oh. Are you guys . . . having problems?"

"Are we having problems? No. Everything is super. Just, super." Gretchen taps her nails again. "Justin gets to show me off to all his buddies and impress his family that my dad's a cardiologist. Woo-hoo." She makes air circles with her index fingers. "And I get to bring him home and have Mom be happy about something I scored that doesn't involve a volleyball. Yay for me."

The way she says it doesn't sound nearly as big-headed as it could have.

"Justin had the *best* time last night," she says, her face a bright beacon of sarcasm. "I mean, who wouldn't love having Janet Prescott take him around and introduce him to all the relatives, gushing about how *wonderful* he is and how *good* we look together, and what a bright *future* he has ahead of him and—"

When I giggle at her impression of Mom, Gretchen stops and grins.

"Mom was laying some pretty serious hints about engagement rings in Justin's ear at the reception," I say.

"Mom had *way* too much champagne. I could have strangled her."

"You and me both. She made me dance with that one old guy. Great Uncle Fester or something."

"Foster." Laughter bubbles through Gretchen's voice. "Great Uncle Foster. Yeah, he's a winner."

"He was trying to look down the front of my dress the whole time I was dancing with him!"

"That sounds about right." Gretchen tilts back in her chair and laughs. "He's a total perv. Mom used to make me dance with him, too, at the family weddings. But now I have Jus-tin." She says his name in a singsong voice and draws an imaginary heart in front of her face.

"Lucky you. When I told Mom that Uncle Fes—Uncle *Foster* was a dirty old man, she compared him to Noah."

"Ha!"

I give her my most poisonous glare, which I'm guessing is pretty scary for real this morning, once you factor in my sleepless night.

"Aw, Faithy." She pats my arm. "Mom had too much champagne. She didn't mean it. Probably." She frowns. "Eat. Your cereal's getting soggy."

"I'm not really hungry." I slump back in my chair. "Noah's leaving for London in three days, and I didn't even get to say good-bye."

"You really like him that much?"

"Yes, I like him 'that much.' He's my best friend." I inhale a shaky breath. "But it's more than that, Gretch." My eyes burn. "I love him. I really do love him."

Gretchen studies me for a long moment. "I'm sorry you're hurting. Really. The way Mom treated Noah was *not* cool."

"Thanks."

"I'm sorry you had to deal with that. And I'm sorry I didn't stick up for you. Not that it would have done any good. I mean, it's *Mom*.

I know how she gets." Gretchen's sigh holds the most compassion I've ever heard from her. "But you're a smart girl. If you really want to see him before he leaves, you'll think of something. You still have three days, right?"

Over breakfast Monday, Mom announces that I am on laundry duty—my assignment toward getting Gretchen and all of her stuff ready to move back in to her sorority house, where we deliver her that night. Once she's moved in, we do a quick check on Ryan and Danielle's apartment before driving home.

I climb into bed, exhausted. Just as I'm closing my eyes, Mom knocks on my door, delivering the happy news that there is a fresh list of chores waiting for me on the breakfast table. Lovely. I set my alarm for seven-thirty.

Tuesday morning, I expect Mom to head to work and give me some breathing room in which I can attend her list in peace, and maybe have a chance to call Noah, even if only long enough to say the words I neglected after my voice lesson. But when Mom wakes me up at six, she announces a change of plan. She's taking me to school registration this morning. After that, I can use the rest of the day to complete my chores.

Oh, joy.

At school, we file through lines, fill out forms, and Mom pays the various activity and book fees. I really don't see why my presence is necessary. Honestly, her presence isn't necessary either, since all of this can be done on the school's website—a fact of which I reminded her on the drive, after I was awake enough to access to my brain.

"It's tradition," she said.

I remember her doing it this way with Gretchen even before I started school, so . . . okay. Whatever.

Finished at last, school supply list in hand, we're about to leave when the volleyball coach beckons Mom from the door of the gym.

As we head that direction, the coach turns, blows her whistle, and yells, "Take a fiver, ladies!"

"Good to see you!" Coach Morehouse says to Mom and then turns to me. "Excited for the new school year, Faith?"

I shrug. "I guess."

"Good, good. Janet, I got your message late last week but just remembered it now, when I saw you. Sorry about that."

"No problem. We were out of town at Ryan's wedding this past weekend."

"Oh, right! I think I saw his engagement announcement in the paper a while back. What can I do for you? Please tell me you've finally talked Faith into joining the team." She smiles at me. "I could sure use some of that Prescott power this year."

"I'm afraid Gretchen was the last volleyball star in this generation of the family. I was calling you about something else. Is it okay if Faith visits with Jenna while the team is on break?"

"Go ahead."

Thusly dismissed, I enter the gym and locate Jenna, who is chugging water. "Hey."

"Look, Prescott. If you're playing on the team this year, you're gonna need to dress out," Jenna teases.

"Right. As if you'd want me."

"Well, there is that."

"Don't tell me. Tell your *coach*. Morehouse thinks I've got 'Prescott Power' or something."

"Ha! The only power you have on the volleyball court is the power to make us lose." Jenna grins and takes a long drink from her water bottle. "How was the wedding?"

"Pretty. Nice." I sigh. "Honestly? It was torture."

"Because . . . ?"

"All I could think about was Noah. He's leaving tomorrow, Jen."

"That sucks. But hey, maybe your mom will finally get off your back."

"Yeah. Maybe."

"Two minutes, Slade," a voice calls from behind me. "Quit gabbing and start hydrating. You won't have another break for—oh. *You.*"

Gretchen's former teammate, Fellowship Community choir member, and all-around sweet Christian girl—*barf*—Kaitlyn Roscoe moves into my line of sight. She crosses her arms over the whistle hanging around her neck. "What are *you* doing here?"

"Registration." I have to work hard to keep from adding the *duh* that's on the tip of my tongue. "What are *you* doing here, Kaitlyn? Shouldn't you be off at college or something?"

"I took this semester off. I'm volunteering as one of the team's assistant coaches this fall. And by the way . . ." Kaitlyn visibly smacks her bright green gum, which is almost as gross as her condescending tone. "The girls are supposed to call me Coach Roscoe."

"Well, I'm not on the team, *Kaitlyn*. So I guess that rule doesn't apply to me."

"From what I hear, you think a lot of rules don't apply to you."

I hold her stare until she looks away.

"Noah says you're not like your sister," she says, after an

uncomfortable pause, "so I guess that includes volleyball, huh?"

"For real." Jenna laughs, but it sounds forced. "If Faith wasn't such a brainiac, I'd be surprised if she could even spell the word volleyball."

"Too bad. The team could use someone with your sister's talent this year. Her talent on the court, I mean." Kaitlyn blows up at her bangs. "We missed you at Noah's going away party Sunday night."

"Did you? Since I wasn't *invited* to the party you threw for Noah, I thought it would be kind of tacky to show up."

"Hmm. I must have overlooked you. Sorry." Her wide eyes and pouty lips reek of falseness. "But you'll be happy to know we prayed for you. At Noah's request, of course."

The joint of my jaw twitches.

Kaitlyn Roscoe, ladies and gentlemen. The perfect example of a 'nice Christian girl.'

Not wanting to stoop to her level, I seal my lips against the Tony-award-worthy soliloquy gaining script in my head.

"Um, Faith?" Jenna fidgets uncomfortably. "I think your mom's trying to get your attention."

"Right. See ya later, Jenna." I don't spare a parting word for Kaitlyn Roscoe.

I climb into the front seat of Mom's car, which is already stifling from the August heat even though we were in the school for less than half an hour.

Mom cranks the air. "I thought we'd go shopping this weekend. Get your school supplies and stuff. Maybe start scoping out some homecoming dresses?"

"Sure."

"Try to contain your excitement, Faith."

"Sorry." I try to inject a little more enthusiasm into my voice. "Shopping. Sounds like fun." But how can the mundane prospect of new pencils and notebooks excite a brain concentrating on the objective Gretchen planted in my brain? I have to find a way to see Noah one last time.

But how?

Numbness steals across my chest as I fasten my seatbelt. How is Noah spending his last full day in Iowa? Is he packing? Visiting friends? Working a final shift at the restaurant?

Mom pulls out of the parking lot and onto the street. "Don't forget about your chore list. It's on the table. And there's a casserole in the refrigerator. Throw it in the oven around five or so. That way you and your dad can eat at six, as usual."

"Sure."

"I've got a late meeting with a client at the Sommerton office tonight, so I'll grab a quick dinner in town. It'll be at least nine, maybe ten, before I get home tonight. And you know your father and his schedule."

"No problem. Can I turn on the radio?"

"Fine. But no rap. Not even that historical Broadway rap stuff."

"I've never heard *Hamilton* on the radio"—but that would be ah-maze-ing!—"so I think you're safe." I push the knob. "AM? Really?" I change to FM. "*And in sports*—" I hit the seek button. Classical music . . . doesn't really fit my mood. The next stop is the shout of a Southern-accented preacher, so I hit the button again.

"*. . . I've got faith in us, and I believe in you and me. So hold on . . . to me tight. Hold on, I promise it'll be alright . . .*"

My heart stutters as Michael Bublé's velvety-smooth voice croons through my mom's car radio. Noah sent me a link to this song within an online playlist he made for me. For us. He sang it to me once, in a spot-on impression of Mr. Bublé, too. But I don't think I've ever heard it on the radio before. Or maybe I have, back when it was new. But not since Noah . . . since we . . .

I suck in a breath, lean back in my seat, and close my eyes against the burn.

The song ends, but the refrain is a familiar sentiment, replanted in my mind.

I know *exactly* where Noah Spencer would want to spend his last day in Iowa. He probably isn't there yet, but—

I steal a look at Mom. Her attention is riveted on the road, but I know her mind is probably calculating the columns of numbers she'll pour over today in preparation for her meeting tonight.

Her *late* meeting. Tonight.

Mom won't be home until nine. Maybe ten. And if I'm right about Noah . . .

A twinge of guilt pokes my conscience. *Just this one last time. I just have to see him long enough to say goodbye.*

Mom drops me off at home and heads in to work. I speed through my list of chores. At six on the dot, Dad and I eat dinner in the living room, watching the local news. I barely taste the tuna casserole, even though it's my favorite—a rare, fat-filled taste extravaganza of only a little bit of tuna, but tons of gooey is-it-really-cheese-if-it-comes-in-a-box? deliciousness with crushed crackers and melted butter on top. After dinner, I wash and stack the TV trays and load the dishwasher. It's only 6:30. Every chore is checked off my list, and there's plenty of daylight yet.

Plenty of time to take a walk to the waterfall.

I chuck a detergent pellet into the dishwasher and start the machine. After washing off the counters, I head back to the living room.

Dad is already half asleep in his recliner as the local news gives way to an episode of *Entertainment Tonight*. With a derisive snort, he adjusts his position in the chair, reaches for the remote, and begins the evening's ritual channel surfing.

"Hey, Dad?"

"Mmm?"

"Is it okay if I take Janey for a walk?"

"Mmm." He scowls, but I assume it's at the television, because his eyes never leave the screen. "Sure. Where are you headed?"

"Um, I thought we'd visit the waterfall. I haven't been there for a while."

"Be careful. Take your phone, just in case something happens."

"Okay." I've never gotten more than a bar of reception at the waterfall, but if it makes him feel better . . .

Dad turns and actually looks at me, taking a moment to focus, as if all his other responses were automated, and he's just now tuning in to the conversation. He probably is.

"You're going for a walk, you say?"

"Yes. To the waterfall. I'm taking Janey. And my phone."

I hold my breath, waiting for him to respond with something like, "*That's what you said the last time, and you ended up making out with Noah Spencer in the foyer.*" But he doesn't.

He gives a couple of little half-nods. "The fresh air will be good for you. You've spent too much time up in your room this summer."

"Um, yeah." I didn't think he noticed.

"Take plenty of water." He turns his attention back to the television. "It's hot."

"Will do."

In no time at all, I've put on my trail shoes and filled a bottle of water for each hand. A quick whistle for Janey, and we're off.

Dad's right. It's hot. Perspiration beads above my upper lip before I reach the Parre Hills trails.

It's too hot to move this fast. Still, I race Janey up the first big hill before trying to pace myself.

Even this early in the evening, it's much darker under the full-leafed trees. The dim light, combined with my anticipation, seems to make the trail a good fifty miles longer than it is. Finally, I reach my favored slope for descending into the creek bed.

The creek is nearly dry now, as it often is in August. Dust spirals up from the weeds as Janey and I find footholds on the crumbling bank. Janey runs ahead, out of sight, but when her happy bark sounds, hope dances through my core.

I pick up my pace.

I'm not quite around the bend when Janey reappears, prancing around a Noah-in-motion.

When our eyes meet, he halts, and his face tilts skyward. I think the words, "*Thank you*" cross his lips in that brief moment before he looks at me again, grinning.

"Well, if it isn't Madeleine Faith Prescott. We've really got to stop meeting like this."

"How right you are," I quip. "How about you move to London or something, then, and stay off *my* waterfall?"

"Your waterfall, is it? And here I thought it was part of the nature preserve." He laughs, but his smile grows pensive as he takes a deep breath in through his nose. "I guess we're ending back at the beginning, aren't we? It's a little . . . weird."

"Yeah." I nod. "At least this time you know Janey's not going to rip out your throat."

"True." He kneels and scratches under Janey's chin. "That is one pleasant difference." His smile widens as he stands and holds out his hand.

The five remaining steps between us disappear. Slipping my hand into its only proper home, I let him lead me across the heat-evaporated creek to our favorite perch.

We stand, hand in hand, looking over the ledge. "Do you remember how I ended up on your waterfall the night we met?"

"You were lost." I smile. "And singing 'Inútil.' But changing the words, of course." It seems decades ago.

"Yes. To fit how useless I felt."

I nod. "I think you said something about being frustrated. That you needed direction or something." I give him the larger half of a smirk. "Pretty ironic, huh? Since you were lost."

"Ironic. Yes. Wasn't it though?" He laughs softly. "But I found new direction when I found you."

"I found you, actually."

"So you did. Serendipity is a beautiful thing. But it was more than that." He rocks back on his heels. "That night could have gone so differently. I came out here to hike off some steam. To sing, yes, since Mr. B told me how great the acoustics were. But I also needed to vent, to yell—or sing or whatever—at God and the world. That was my intention for coming out here, to let it all out, where no one would hear me make a fool of myself. But once I got here and got *lost* here, I was too frustrated with how things were going—or not going, as it were—to even know where to begin. Finally, right before you got here, I prayed. I prayed for faith. And there you were."

"Har, har."

"As corny as it sounds, it's the truth." Noah shakes his head, frowning now at the stagnant water below us. "God has an interesting sense of humor, doesn't he? Now tonight, when all my frustrated hopes and dreams of that night are about to come true, I decided to come back. To try and connect with God, to try and find some peace about leaving you behind."

My breath hitches, and when I speak, it's a whisper. "And what did God say?"

"Well, you're here, so I guess—"

I don't wait another moment to wrap my arms around him. A breath later, his settle around me. I tuck my head beneath his chin.

My heart sings, *Thank you, thank you, thank you.*

All this time, we've held on to the belief that there's more to our pairing than the simple, fleeting nature of romance, and tonight, against all odds and with no communication other than two hearts seeking one last moment together, a way has been made. How can I explain how circumstances aligned today, when everything seemed to be falling apart, but to let that serendipity, as Noah called it, rest in the lap of God?

This embrace is honest. It's *pure.* Even so, it breaks every rule my mom has so strictly enforced this summer.

But if it *was* God who brought us together in the first place, doesn't that make this okay?

At this moment, with Noah's arms tightening around me, I don't have the answer. Is it wrong to think being with Noah is right when it goes against my parents' orders?

Maybe. But regardless of how my parents might interpret our embrace, this is not a romantic moment. This is something far beyond whatever petty "crush" symptoms my mother fears.

No, this is not romance. It's bigger, deeper, and much, much *fiercer* than that.

Tonight, for just a little bit longer, I have Noah, and he has me. Even knowing the peace of these stolen moments won't last, even knowing I might face severe consequences when I get home, I'm overcome with a desperate, *desperate,* gratitude for this moment.

Thank you, God. Thank you, God. Thank you.

Noah loosens his grip just enough to lift my chin. "You're crying."

"I am?" I release my hold on him to brush a hand across my wet cheeks. "Sorry. I'm just so happy you're . . . that I . . ."

My voice breaks, and my face crumples. I bury it in that perfect place where his neck and shoulder meet.

"I know. Me, too," he whispers into my hair. "Me, too."

We stand like that for a long time. "I know it seems like forever right now," he says at last, "but it'll go fast." His voice lacks confidence, and I'm sure he knows it, too, when he sighs, gives me a squeeze, and releases me. "Let's sit."

He waits for me to pick my spot on the ledge and then takes the place beside me.

"You'll be eighteen in just a little over a year. For a while, I thought maybe we could try to start fresh then, but . . . that won't work. You might be legally an adult, but you'll still live with your parents until you graduate, and you'll still be under their authority. Until you're out on your own, you have to respect them and follow their rules."

"Yeah. But they're stupid rules."

"Agreed." He smiles, but the sadness in his eyes cuts my heart open. "But as their daughter, you're called to honor them. And if I'm ever going to be accepted by them as part of your life, so am I." His deep breath shakes on its way back out. "Faith, I think . . . I think we need to stay out of contact until you go to college."

My heart jolts in my chest, as if a hawk's talons have closed around it and yanked. "But—"

Noah stills my argument with a shake of his head. "They've told you to stay away from me, right?"

"But we could still chat, see each other, online."

"How would your mom react if she knew we were?"

His question has a painfully easy answer. "She would confiscate my computer."

"Exactly. I'm off limits, right?"

"So they say, and yet . . . ?" I shrug. And yet here we are.

"If they're ever going to accept you and me being together . . . I hate it, but I think it's the only way."

I groan.

"It'll go by faster than you think. Before you know it, you'll be at college."

"And you'll *still* be in London."

"Yeah. Maybe." He sighs and pulls up his legs, resting his elbows on his knees. "I've been thinking about this from every possible angle, but every angle comes up with more questions, more 'what ifs' than answers. What we have is something special, but . . . we have to admit that we're young. What if . . . what if we're not each other's *only* something special?"

I swallow. It hurts. "You want to see other people."

"No, I do *not* want to see other people. I love *you*. That hasn't changed. I can't even imagine that changing."

His voice is firm, and his words ring true, which pinches my heart even more than the thought of him wanting to date someone else.

He takes a deep breath. "But I think, especially if we're out of contact for the next two years, we have to consider that either one of us *could* meet someone else—could even *love* someone else. You have two years of high school left. Homecomings, proms . . . It would be cruel of me to ask you to commit to a relationship and then jet off to London, knowing we can't even talk to each other without you getting in trouble with your parents."

"I'm already committed, Noah. But you're right. A year ago, if you would have asked who would hold my heart now, it wouldn't have occurred to me to say your name. Last August, Noah Spencer was just some guy who was really awesome in *Guys and Dolls*. And now . . ."

He's everything.

Everything.

"Flatterer. But I get what you're saying. It's so . . . weird. I feel like I've known you forever. That you know me, maybe better than my own family does. And we haven't even known each other a full year."

"And we're talking about a little more than another two years before we even talk to each other again?" I squeeze my eyes shut against the idea and shake my head. "That's crazy."

"I think I heard a 'but' at the end of that sentence."

"But," I say, nodding. "As long as I'm at home, living in her house, eating her food, letting her pay my bills . . . I'm at her mercy." I choke out a bitter laugh. "Mercy. Right. As if she even understands the concept."

His sigh is an unspoken agreement. He leans forward, resting his forearms on his thighs. "So . . . we stay out of contact until you're at college."

I nod, but the thought of two years—two *years*—without a word to or from Noah does not allow me to speak.

"What if . . . ?" He pauses, and the hint of a smile relaxes his brow. "What if, once I get to London, I talk to my advisor and see if I could maybe change from the three-year program to the two-year? Then I would already be finished at the Academy when you start college. I could come to New York sooner. Start looking for work . . ."

"But you wanted to stay in London, use the connections you'll make at school to see if you can get cast in some West End productions."

"Wanted," he says. "That's what I wanted. That was my plan. Before you."

"But it's been your dream for so long."

"Sometimes," Noah says, putting his arm around my shoulder, "a guy's dreams go through a metamorphosis. Sometimes plans have to be adjusted to make room for bigger, fuller dreams."

I scoot closer and lean into him. He tightens his hold.

"I was planning to come back to the States, to New York, eventually. Why not right away?"

"But if we haven't been in contact for two years, how will we manage to find each other? New York is a huge city. And who knows where I'll actually end up for college?"

"True." Noah purses his lips. "Social Media? No, I have a better idea. We won't find each other in New York. We'll find each other here."

"Here?"

"Here. At our waterfall. It's August ninth. Still early August. You probably won't have left for school yet, but soon. Soon enough, anyway."

He's right. A lot of fall terms don't commence until later in August. The only reason Gretchen went back to school so early is because she has to help her sorority sisters prepare for Rush Week stuff. "Two years from today?"

"Sure. It makes sense. Doesn't it?"

I want to say no. But with everything going against every other option . . . "Yes. It makes perfectly horrible sense."

"We'll meet here on August ninth at . . ." Noah pulls out his phone. "8:17 p.m."

My breath catches. "It's after eight? Already?"

"Mm-hmm. What time do you need to be home?"

"There was no set time, but—never mind." If Mom beats me home, I'll deal with it. Right now, I'm with Noah, and I will not let thoughts of her intrude on our time together. Not tonight.

"So . . . two years from now . . ." He stands, paces across the dry creek bed and back. "We'll meet here on August ninth at 8:17."

With a piercing ache of a nod, I reframe it. "Eight, nine. Eight-seventeen."

"Eight, nine. Eight-seventeen." He sighs and holds out his hand. "Deal?"

I slide my hand into his. "De—"

Instead of shaking my hand in the business-like manner I expect, Noah pulls me close and kisses me.

The initial crush of Noah's lips against mine softens but does not end. Gradually, the kiss deepens, but with such tenderness that there's no doubt in my mind—not that there ever was—that I'm cherished. Desired, yet safe. Loved.

"I didn't plan to kiss you," he whispers against my hair a few breathless moments later. "But I'm awfully glad I did."

His lips find mine again, briefly, and then press against my forehead, where I feel his smile fall.

"What is it?"

"I love you, Madeleine Faith. This is . . . it's going to be excruciating."

I nod. "I know."

"Two *years*." He groans. "We won't text. We won't call. We won't . . . anything."

"On the bright side, I guess I'm usually grounded from that stuff anyway. Do you want to take it back? Stay in touch? Even though my parents won't let us?"

"Of course I *want* to."

"But?"

"But I'm afraid it will just make things harder for you here. In two years, when you're on your own, we can just . . . be. Without prejudice. They still might not like it—maybe I'll never win them over, even then. But . . . it's the right thing to do." Noah clears his throat. "In two years, you'll be out from under their control and free to be with me. If you still *want* to be with me."

"Of *course* I'll still want to be with you. When 8:17 comes on August ninth, I'll be here. Even if . . ." I have to say it. "Even if you're not."

Noah opens his mouth to argue, but I put a finger to his lips.

"I love you, Noah. But the right thing to do is to set you free." The last few words come out strained. "If the opportunity comes, if someone works her way into your heart, I want you to consider yourself free to fall in love. To stay in London, if that's what makes you happy. I won't hold it against you. If August ninth rolls around two years from now, and I hike up here, but you don't come, I'll know. And I'll be . . ." I take a trembling breath. "I'll be happy for you."

Noah inhales. Exhales. The quiver in his breath matches my own. When he finally speaks, his voice is thick. "I don't know what the future will bring, Faith. Not for either one of us. I can't imagine loving anyone else. And although it's hard to picture you with anyone but me, I suppose we can't rule it out."

"No, we can't." But my heart doesn't want to listen to reason right now.

"Okay, so . . . we're agreed on the future, but—just for tonight—let's let it go. Tomorrow will come soon enough. Tonight, I want to be right here, right now, in this moment with my Madeleine Faith."

"Right here, right now." *Always*, my heart vows, almost as if daring my brain to disagree. But the only other discernible word swimming around in my mind is *forever*.

We walk the dry creek bed for a while, hand in hand. Eventually, we return to our perch on the waterfall's ledge and go on with our evening as if tomorrow is not the end, as if we haven't just made the most painful promise of our lives.

We talk about the theatre, about what Noah will see in London, and his hopes of being able to afford a trip to see his family in the Czech Republic over the holidays. We discuss the pros and cons of the various shows Mr. Barron is deciding between for the KHS fall musical this year, and whether or not I'll go out for the Leopold Community Theatre again. But even with all the topics we cover, time passes too quickly.

"We should probably go." Noah says. "It's after ten."

Pain grips my throat. I croak, "What time do you leave?"

"My flight departs at 8:10. Mac is driving me to the airport in Moline. We're leaving at five."

"I wish I could go with to see you off."

"If you were there, I might not be able to get on the plane."

Tears well, hot and weighted with love. "I would *make* you get on the plane."

Noah stands and pulls me to my feet. Without verbal agreement, we head back up the creek.

I whistle for Janey, and even though the weak breath barely makes a sound, she comes. Just shy of the place where we need to ascend opposite sides of the creek bank, we pause.

"No matter what happens two years from now or in between," Noah says, pressing my hand to his lips, "I will never regret meeting you, Madeleine Faith Prescott. I will never regret a single moment I spent with you, or even thinking about you. I will never regret loving you."

I just nod. I can't speak, but I trust he knows the meaning of—

and cherishes—the singular tear that spills down my cheek as my silent agreement with every word.

Noah wipes the tear from my cheek with his thumb. Lifting my chin, he kisses me slowly, reverently.

"We broke some rules tonight," he whispers.

"I know. I don't care. Maybe I should, but I couldn't let you go without saying—"

Noah pulls me into his arms so suddenly that it steals the rest of my words—the one word I was unable to say, that I would not let *him* say, before.

"Goodbye, Madeleine Faith," he whispers, pressing me tightly to his chest.

And then . . . he releases me.

It's more than just the physical release of his arms letting me go. It's a splicing. A severing. We both know it. And it hurts.

It hurts so much.

Without another word, without looking back, Noah turns and strides farther up the dry creek bed.

My hand flutters to my throat. As his shadow retreats against the night, my response is a stage whisper.

"Goodbye, Noah."

A slight hitch in his step is the only indication he's heard me, but it's enough.

It has to be.

31

My hike toward home is slow. Each hill is steeper, more difficult than the last. Each step away from the Nature Preserve is another thousand miles between me and Noah.

When our house finally comes into view, it's dark. No doubt Dad fell asleep watching TV. And since, as he so truly stated, I've spent so much time in my room this summer, by the time he woke up to shuffle off to bed, he probably forgot I went for a walk. If Mom's home by now, she, too, has likely assumed I'm up in my room. It's a relief, but a dull one, considering the two years stretching before me without Noah.

The front door is locked. I punch in the code to the garage door and enter that way instead, waiting for it to shut all the way before opening the door to the house. When the latch on the inside door catches, I wince, knowing how easily sound carries through a dark house at night.

Janey's claws click against the slate floor, but that's not an unusual sound, since her food and water dishes are in the mudroom—and that's where she goes.

On cautious feet, I tiptoe down the short hall, passing Dad's study on my way to the stairs, but with only patches of moonlight guiding me through the house, it doesn't register that someone is standing just inside the study until a cold chill sweeps down my neck.

"Where in God's name have you been?"

"Mom!" I jump inside my skin. "Geez! You scared me!"

"I scared *you*?" She steps through the door. "Answer the question."

"The waterfall. I went to the waterfall."

"Right. You sneak into the house like that after eleven o'clock at night and expect me to believe you've been at the *waterfall*, in the *dark*, this whole time?"

"I *was* at the waterfall!"

"Were you alone?"

My heart rate speeds as if trying to propel itself out of my body. I hesitate a moment too long.

"Were you with Noah Spencer?"

"Yes." I will not lie about it. "I was with Noah."

"I knew it!"

Mom grabs my forearm, like she's going to drag me to the time-out chair. Or the execution chamber, maybe, if her stony, wrathful expression is an accurate indication of her plans for me.

"You've been sneaking off to fool around with that boy behind my back all summer, haven't you?"

"No! I didn't even know for sure that he'd be there tonight. I—"

"Don't you *dare* lie to me!"

The pressure of Mom's grip eases from my arm, but the look in her eyes is Medusa-deadly.

"You've been sneaking around with that boy for months. I know you have." Her whisper is a hiss. "You've been carrying condoms around in your school bag, for God's sake. Your *school bag*!"

A gasp rakes my throat. *How does she . . . ?* "That wasn't even mine!"

"After everything we've done to break his hold on you, to keep you away from him, I can't believe you're still so intent upon throwing away your future—not to mention the reputation of this family—by behaving like a cheap, reckless little *slut!*"

The insult shocks all ability to argue from my mind, but she doesn't stop there.

Her voice is barely above a whisper—so Dad doesn't hear?—but her insinuations and accusations reverberate against my ears. She spews venom, describing what she assumes about the nature of my relationship with Noah. But those vile phrases can't come close to the shock of feeling—*hearing*—the smack of her palm, striking the side of my face.

I stagger backward, blindly grabbing for something to help me catch my balance, but my hands find only air. I fall hard onto the slate floor, my cheek scraping against the corner of a side table on the way down.

Tears of pain and disbelief spring to eyes I had thought were spent from the grief of saying goodbye.

She hit me. Not only that, but the things she said . . . *She called me a—*

God! My heart cries through the sob exiting my lips.

Spare patches of moonlight spill through the sidelight windows of the entry door. Towering over me in the half-light, my mother looks almost inhuman. Malevolence drips from her shadow. Her eyes are enraged, but also focused, intense, like those of a predator. From my position on the floor, she appears twice as tall as she should.

I've feared displeasing my mother many times. But never before have I been afraid of *her*.

I lift a hand to my throbbing face. Along my right cheekbone, warm moisture—sweat, tears . . . or blood?—meets my fingers. Did I hit the corner of the side table hard enough to break the skin? I don't think so.

Mom hit me. The stark realization plays over and over in my mind. Physical violence is something I never imagined. Not from one of my parents.

She hit me. My mother hit me. My mind cannot wrap around what has just happened.

When Mom steps forward, I flinch. I can't help it.

"I've confiscated your car keys," she says. "You're grounded until further notice. You will not leave this house unless another member of the family is with you. If *that boy* comes within two miles of you—or even within two miles of our property—I will call the sheriff and press charges of statutory rape."

What did she say? Rape? *Oh, God! No!*

"This is—how can you—how can you be so . . . evil!" My heart stutters back into motion, freeing my tongue.

"Keep your voice down!" She grips my upper arm. "Your father has an early surgery tomorrow."

And she doesn't want him to know what a horrible, evil ogress he married? "Noah would never hurt me!" I whisper. "Never."

"You're a minor. He's an adult. It doesn't matter if you wanted it or not!"

"I didn't *want* anything!" I cry out, but when her fingernails dig in to my triceps, I lower my voice. "We haven't *done* anything! How can you even think I would—?"

"Save it, Faith. Save the innocent act. I know the truth."

"No, you don't! You don't know anything! And you certainly don't know *me* if you think I—"

"I'll tell you what I *do* know. Your father was already in bed when

I got home, and since I couldn't find you in the house, I decided to give you the benefit of the doubt. I called Jenna's mother to see if you were with her, which, of course, you were *not*."

"I told you. I was at the waterfall."

"Jenna's mother told me about the condom you had in your schoolbag. Your *schoolbag*? Really?" Her tone is coated in disgust. "And that was months ago, which means you've been fooling around with that boy for at least that long. But that doesn't mean you used it. My God, Faith!" Mom's voice breaks. "Please tell me you at *least* used protection with him. And whoever else."

Whoever else?

I can't . . . She can't think I . . .

Shoulders shaking, teeth chattering, I drop my gaze to the floor. "We didn't need to use pro-protection." I hiccup on a sob. "It wasn't necessary."

"Not necessary? Why? Because he said you were the first? Ha! If you believe that, you're a bigger fool than I thought. I'm sure you're not the first girl Noah Spencer has sweet-talked into the back seat of his beat-up old car. You've taken Sex Ed, Faith. You should know better! You *always* need protection. When you're sleeping with someone, you're sleeping with every other person they've ever—"

"But we're *not* sleeping together! We never did!"

"Save it."

Recognizing the stony expression on her face, I clamp my lips. No argument in the world will alter what Mom believes about me now.

My face throbs where I bumped it against the side table. A strange prickly heat resides on the other side, where my mother slapped me.

Mom drones on about my supposed stupidity, what a disappointment I am. I keep my eyes locked on the floor until one phrase catches my attention.

"You'll what?" My head shoots up. "What clinic? Why?"

"I'm taking the day off tomorrow. After your dad goes to work, I'll take you to the women's clinic in Iowa City. That's far enough away that we won't risk running into anyone we know." Mom looks as if she's just caught the scent of rotten garbage. "You'll have to be tested, of course."

"Tested? For what?"

"Did you even pay attention in health class?" Mom mumbles and looks at the ceiling. "You'll need to be tested for herpes, gonorrhea, chlamydia, HIV, and all the other various STDs girls like you might come in contact with. And pregnancy, of course."

"Girls like . . . like *me*?" My hands fist at my sides.

"Yes, Faith. Girls who are so promiscuous that they feel the need to carry condoms, even in their schoolbags. Girls who sneak out of the house to fool around with boys in the woods. Girls who . . ."

Blood pounds in my ears as Mom lets loose with a vivid stream of words and descriptions, all variations of the same contemptible accusation. By the time she's finished, I am numb.

She flips on the light. I blink against the sudden brightness.

"I've been down this road before." Mom leans against the door frame. "I should have expected this. I wanted so much more for you. But with all your music and drama, and your head always in the clouds . . ."

"I'm not Becca."

"Save it." Mom repeats, holding one hand up, like a crossing guard. "You may be a pretty good actress, *Madeleine*, but I'm not a fool. Or maybe I am, for believing you were old enough to be rational." She lets out a long breath. "In any case, I'm sure you need a shower after the evening you've had, so get cleaned up and go to bed. I'll expect you in the car and ready to leave at eight a.m. sharp."

I push myself up off the floor and take two steps toward the stairs.

"Stop. One more thing. Come here." She pivots and enters the study, flipping on the light. I follow.

"Close the door." She goes to Dad's desk and grabs the handset of the landline phone. "Call him. Now."

"Who? Noah?"

She nods. "Now." Mom's voice is iron, encased in ice. "Tell him what I told you. Tell him you're through. Tell him if he comes within a hundred feet of you, I'll have him arrested."

She shoves the phone toward me.

My hands shake, but I dial Noah's number.

He answers on the second ring.

"Noah?" His name is a breath, barely a whisper.

"Faith? Is that you?"

A jagged inhalation betrays me. "Yeah. It's me."

"What's wrong? Are you hurt?"

"No. Yes. Noah—" My voice breaks on a sob.

"I'll be right there. Hold on, Faith. I just got back to my car, so I'm still close. I'm heading back into the preserve now." I hear Eliza's door creak and slam. "Did you fall? Is anything broken?"

Yes! I want to scream. *Everything is broken. Everything!*

"I'll be there as fast as I can. Reception will be bad once I go down into the gully. Can you give me a rough idea of where you are from the waterfall, in case I lose you?"

"Don't. You don't need to go—I'm at home."

"At home?" he pauses. "Okay. I'll go back to my car, and I'll be there in ten minutes. Hold on."

"Okay," I say, but then his words register. "No! You can't come here."

Each breath is a little harder to grasp than the one before, thinner. The room tips, eerily. The light dims, keeps dimming, but when I glance at Mom—*tipping*—her arm is at her side, she isn't anywhere near the dimmer switch.

My field of vision narrows. I pull at gasps of air, but there's not enough. The room spins.

"Faith, tell me what's wrong!" The same panic that's closing my airway is in Noah's voice, but I can't catch a big enough breath to exhale a word.

"Oh, for the love of—You're going to hyperventilate. Give me the phone, Faith. Now." Mom wrenches it from my ear. She clears her throat. "This is Janet Prescott. Faith's mother." She pauses. "Don't you dare 'ma'am' me, young man. No, you may *not* talk to Faith. *Ever.* You will not be seeing her again. My daughter will be remaining at home until school starts. She will not be allowed to have any contact with you. Ever. Again." Mom takes a breath. "Do not interrupt me!"

Never have I seen my mother's face so red. It borders on purple. A vein pulses at her temple.

"Mr. Spencer, let me make myself very clear. I will be filing a restraining order against you on Faith's behalf. If she turns out pregnant, God forbid, you will be hearing from my lawyer, and whatever measly wages you earn will be garnished until this situation is resolved and your obligation is met. In the meantime, I give you fair warning that if you come within a hundred feet of my daughter, I will have you arrested for statutory rape."

I lean against the built-in bookcase, cupping my hands in front of my mouth to catch my breath. There's a pause in Mom's tirade, but I can't make out what Noah is saying on the other end of the line through my own respirations.

"Two years? Do not patronize me, Mr. Spencer. I'm not an idiot. I've heard your lies before." Another pause. "Oh really? Well, I happen to remember interrupting a certain make-out session in my foyer when the two of you were supposedly 'just friends.' Enough! This conversation is over."

As Mom pulls the phone from her ear, I hear Noah's protestations.

Sudden indignation—*righteous* indignation—surges through my oxygen-deprived blood, propelling me forward.

Stealing the phone from Mom's grasp, I press my left hand against her sternum and extend the reach of my right, holding the phone as far away from my mother as I can.

"Noah—I'm sorry!" I shout toward the mouthpiece. "Please, don't try to come here before you leave. She's serious. She'll have you arrested!"

Adrenaline courses through my body, boiling my anger into strength and evasive agility as Mom tries to grab the phone away from me.

Time stalls and stretches as the agreement I made with Noah comes into clearer focus, and a faint, desperate hope sparks within the hollow coldness in my chest.

Hold on.

There it is again. But with Noah gone, *truly gone* from my life for the next two years, it will be like holding a pause button down with a lead weight . . . or like waiting backstage for an absent orchestra to cue the end of an intermission.

I draw a quick, deep breath. Soon, she'll find a way to break my hold, but with the right few words, Noah will understand.

"We can do this, Noah." My throat is raw from hyperventilating, so I push the air harder, from my diaphragm, make my plea louder. "Eight, nine. Eight-seventeen. Hold on, Noah. Hold. On."

There's a pause of pure silence. Mom stares at me as if I've just crossed the border into crazy town. If I have, she's the one driving the car.

"Eight, nine. Eight-seventeen," Noah says. "I'm holding on, Madeleine Faith." His voice is anguish . . . and hope. "For you, I'll keep holding on."

The heft of mom's threats joins the weight of time. Both descend, threatening to destroy the little strength I have left. Still holding Mom at arm's length, I close my eyes and bring the phone to my ear.

"Noah." I can't say goodbye again. I don't have the strength. But I can say something else. Something Noah will understand, but she—this monster, my mother—will not.

"Noah," I whisper his name again. "Break a leg."

"You, too." His voice is resigned, but I know he heard the *I love you* in that benediction. "You, too, my Madeleine Faith. Break a leg. Always."

"Break a leg." Mom scoffs. "I'll break more than that if he dares to show his face around here."

With a grunt, Mom pushes my restraining hand away, but I hang up and toss the phone at her. It drops to the floor and comes apart.

"Are you satisfied?" I ask, putting my hands on my hips. "It's over. He's leaving for London tomorrow. *Tomorrow!*"

"I suppose that's what tonight was about, then. He wanted something to remember you by."

"You're wrong. But you've made up your mind to believe the worst. Fine. So be it. We're done."

I turn my back on my mother and head for the door.

"Don't you dare turn your back on me, Faith Prescott!"

A red flush of anger accompanies the sudden onset of a deep ache that pulls from the base of my skull and traces skid marks across my scalp. Clenching the door handle with one hand, I meet her seething gaze with my own.

"My name," I say, clenching my teeth, "is *Madeleine*."

I take the stairs two at a time and slam—and lock—my bedroom door. I turn around, letting the door take my weight as my legs give out. I slide down to the floor, where I curl into a ball around my drowning heart.

While Noah Spencer travels to the Moline International Airport, I read the instructions on the home pregnancy test my mother purchased at a 24-hour pharmacy in Sommerton sometime after I went to my room last night.

I examine my reflection in the mirror, hoping there's evidence that my mother hit me, but there's none. There is a little scrape on my cheek from where I fell against the side table, but even that little abrasion is gone after I wash my face, exfoliated off by the washcloth.

While Noah checks his bags at the airport, Mom lectures that even though this test was negative, and even if the one I will be taking at the clinic is negative, I'll need to take another in three or four weeks, just to be sure.

When Noah's first flight of the day takes off for Chicago, I'm sitting in my mother's car, headed toward a women's clinic over two hours away.

I stare out the window, barely seeing the small towns or noticing the miles of corn and soybean fields. Every once in a while, I blink, but that's the only change to the view.

Occasionally, Mom interrupts the news radio drone to name a

new restriction she's been inspired to add to her list of ways to cripple my social life.

No phone. No computer. No car keys. Mom vows to do whatever it takes to make sure I have no means of contacting, or of being contacted by, Noah Spencer.

Not that it matters, of course. Noah and I agreed. No contact for two years.

Eight, nine. Eight-seventeen.

"When we get home, I'm going to call the school," Mom says, "to see if I can put specific restrictions in place for your computer usage there."

I don't care.

"I know you don't understand this now, but I'm doing this for your good. For your protection. Your future," she says. Adding, "God willing, you're not pregnant, of course," under her breath.

"The test was negative." And I'm a virgin, which makes the whole pregnancy thing a non-issue, not that she cares.

"Yes, but you were together last night. It takes what? Two, three weeks for a positive test? Besides, you can't always trust those things you buy at the pharmacy."

Then why did she bother?

I tune out. I'm well beyond the need to argue. My heart is thirty thousand feet up and several hundred miles away. Each moment takes it—and Noah, who's holding it—further from my reach. Why should I care about computer restrictions at school or having to pee on another stick or whatever?

At the clinic, my mother waits in the lobby, as instructed by the staff. I sit in the doctor's private office, fully clothed, for a "chat." It's supposed to be a "safe place" for me to divulge the truth about my sexual history.

I answer the doctor's embarrassing questions with shakes of my head. Negative. Negative. Negative. When required, I use words, but as few as possible, and most of them consisting of the letters 'N' and 'O.'

After the Q&A session with the doctor, I'm directed to an examination room. A nurse explains how to fasten the gown and steps out while I disrobe.

Five minutes later, the doctor returns. She asks the same questions, only phrased differently, as if my answers might have changed now that I'm without the armor of my clothing to protect me.

The doctor calls for the nurse and explains the state-mandated protocol for the examination. *They're just doing their job*, I remind myself as I place my feet, as directed, in the stirrups. *They're just doing what my mother told them to do. Just like everyone else.*

I stare at the ceiling tiles, trying to find faces in the texture—a vain attempt to separate myself from what's happening beneath the sheet draped over my knees. I wish I'd worn shoes that require socks, instead of flip flops. If I had, at least a small part of me would still be hidden.

Tears leak from the corners of my eyes, but I make no move to acknowledge them or wipe them away. I try to distance myself from the violation of this unnecessary examination.

I dress. Endure the discussion of birth control options by concentrating my thoughts on the illusory map in my head, plotting where Noah might be, moment by moment, and picturing the ocean he'll soon fly over, the landmarks he might view from the air, flying into London.

Big Ben. Buckingham Palace. That huge Ferris wheel thing . . . What's it called, the London Eye? Yes, that's it. I wonder if he'll be able to see the West End theatre district from the air.

The doctor is nice enough, I guess.

She does agree, at my request, to share her findings with my mother. Sort of.

"Your daughter has expressed that she is not sexually active. After my interview with her, and from the condition of tissues I observed during the exam, I am inclined to accept that assertion."

That's as much as she can say, she tells me, as it is virtually impossible to prove a girl's virginity, considering today's active lifestyles.

My mom only nods. She thanks the doctor for her time but says nothing to me that would indicate she's accepted my innocence as truth.

Because that would prove she's a monster?

I don't care. I am numb. An empty shell of flesh. My heart is safer outside my body, on its way to London, where no one can touch it.

After the appointment, Mom makes a quick call and arranges to meet Gretchen for lunch. After lunch, the three of us go to the mall to do some back-to-school shopping.

Shopping.

Mom goes to the counter to pay for a deep pile of stuff she's buying us at Forever 21. Gretchen grabs my arm. "Are you going to tell me what's going on?"

"It's nothing."

"It's not nothing. You're walking around like a soulless zombie, and Mom's acting like she's on a triple dose of happy pills."

"I don't want to talk about it."

She stares at me, pursing her lips. Her mouth drops open. "Oh! Geez, I'm sorry. Noah left, didn't he?"

"Yeah. This morning."

"You're sad, and she's thrilled. Makes sense."

"I guess."

"Well, there's no better cure for a broken heart than making Mom's credit card melt." Gretchen links her elbow through mine. "For whatever reason, she's feeling generous today. We might as well fill our closets while the card is hot!"

We hit all of my favorite stores and Gretchen's. When my level of enthusiasm doesn't lead to a dressing room, Gretchen leads me there, sometimes even yanks me there.

"Faith." Gretchen pulls me into a dressing room. Again. This time, she comes in with me. "Seriously, kid. Are you okay? What aren't you telling me?"

I swallow. I want to spill my guts, but I can't. She won't believe me.

I don't blame her. If I hadn't lived it, I might not believe me either.

Sure, we both know Mom can be moody. Temperamental. Kind of vindictive sometimes. But she *hit* me. She said horrible, vile things. She made me go that clinic and . . .

I meet my sister's eyes. Concern lines her brow. There's compassion there, too.

What if Gretchen *did* believe me? Could she . . . help?

"Why are you shaking your head?"

I stop. "Sorry." If I tell Gretchen what Mom did to me, and if she believes it, she will absolutely say something to Mom. Maybe even make a scene, right here in this store.

And I'll be the one to pay for it later, at home.

"I don't want to talk about it."

Her frown deepens. "I want to respect that, Faith. But the way you've been acting today? It's not like you."

"I'll be fine. Really." Every detail is on the tip of my tongue, begging me to let it out, but . . . what's the point? It's not worth the effort.

I'm on my own.

"Okay." She sighs. "But if you change your mind . . . I'm here."

I have to swallow again. "Thanks."

We go to a few more stores. I try on the things she and Mom tell me to. I nod or shrug my acceptance of the purchases. But viewing the excursion through a fog of humiliation, a haze of shock, and an overwhelming sense of loss, I don't truly notice the excess of our shopping trip until we're home, unloading the bags from the trunk.

Hollister, Abercrombie, Old Navy, Dillards, Scheels, Forever 21, Sephora . . .

Bag after bag after bag . . . It's ridiculous.

Wait. Scheels? The sporting goods store? I don't even remember darkening the door, but I must have, because I have the Under Armour and Adidas to prove it. In fact, this one shopping trip has added enough clothes, shoes, and accessories to my closet that I could probably outfit myself and five of my friends and *still* have clothes left over.

I stare into my closet, remembering what my sister said earlier in the day. Is this evidence that Mom feels some sort of guilt?

Maybe.

I don't need this much stuff. I don't want this stuff. Yes, I will enter the eleventh grade in style, but for reasons that make me sick.

School starts two weeks later.

I'm nominated for Student Council again, and without putting an ounce of effort into my campaign, I score enough votes to be named Junior Class Vice President. I know it'll look good on my college applications, but I can't make myself care. All I think about is Noah.

What is his flat like? Has he made friends? Of course he's made friends. He's *Noah*. Does he like his classes? Has he been to see a show on the West End yet?

In October, I take a calculus test without bothering to study for it. When I receive the test back, a harsh red C- mars the white page, startling me back into my life.

I'll be filling out college applications soon, and every single grade counts toward my dream.

My escape.

If I'm going to get into a good college, if I'm going to get away from this place, I have to wake up and work for it.

Broadway. First, a good college with a great Musical Theatre program and then Broadway.

And in the meantime . . . Eight, nine. Eight-seventeen.

Noah.

Someday, Noah.

I dive into my studies and do piles of extra credit to ensure the 4.0 G.P.A. my parents expect—and my dreams require.

I'm cast as Lili in KHS's fall production of *Carnival!* and get great reviews—if you count local comments and a review in a 3000 paper circulation hometown newspaper.

When the Leopold Community Theatre announces try-outs for *Guys and Dolls* in November, I have every intention of auditioning. But when the appointed day comes, I sit outside the Opera House in my car, sobbing. I can't do it. The memory of seeing Noah Spencer cast as Nathan Detroit on the KHS stage is too vivid, and the memory of sharing that particular Leopold stage with him is still too fresh. I drive back home without ever having left my car.

Jenna tries to be there for me, but she's varsity everything now, and the few weekends we do hang out are becoming increasingly awkward. We're drifting apart, but neither of us wants to admit it out loud.

Winter rolls in, and Jenna's basketball schedule collides with my speech and dance team rehearsal schedules in the usual way, but it's different somehow.

I feel more alone than ever.

I ask permission to go to the Wednesday night youth group at Fellowship Community. I figure with Noah gone, what's the problem? My request is denied. Mom does, however, buy me a personal Bible study guide on the subject of obedience.

Go figure.

I expect to hate it. I don't. In fact, I learn a lot, and it helps me better understand some of the things Noah was conflicted about when we were "not-really-dating" dating. Clearly, Mom didn't read it before purchasing. She was trying to make a point and likely assumed I'd never crack it open. But I did. And I'm glad, because God used her arrogance to slip past her, to reach me.

Still, I'm lonely.

But I'm holding on.

It's a dreary December afternoon in French III. This is the only class Jenna and I have together this semester, but she hasn't even made eye-contact with me since we came in. It's weird, but it seems to confirm the strange vibe I've been getting from her all week.

It's a small class, since most people only take two years of foreign language, and we're spread out enough that I don't worry that anyone will overhear our conversation, as long as I keep my voice low.

"Jenna," I whisper, leaning across the aisle. "Is everything okay?"

She looks over for just a second before her eyes return to the top of her desk. "Sure. Why?"

"Have you been avoiding me?"

"No. I've just . . . I'm busy. You know."

Jenna bites her lip. She won't look at me.

"Jenna, did I do something? If I did, I'm sorry. Just . . . will you please tell me what I did?"

When she finally looks up, I'm shocked at the betrayal in her eyes.

"I don't know what you did, Faith." Her brow furrows. "But my mom does. Or she thinks she does. I don't know."

What? "That doesn't make sense. What are you talking about?"

Jenna licks her lips. Her gaze meets her desktop again. "Look, my mom doesn't want me to hang out with you, okay? Not that we hang out that much anymore, anyway."

"But . . . why?"

"She thinks you're a bad influence on me."

Oh . . . oh, no.

"I let Cole come over when they weren't home," she whispers, leaning close so no one else will hear. "My dad came home early, and . . . bad timing, you know?"

"You mean you . . ."

She scoots her desk closer to mine. "Not . . . totally. But far enough that I didn't exactly want my dad to walk in!"

"Oh." Wow. "Are you okay?"

"Grounded."

"Okay . . ." Not what I was asking, but . . .

"I guess your mom called my mom a while back. She was worried you were pregnant."

"But you know we never did anything."

She shrugs.

"Ever."

"There was that condom in your bag last year."

"That was Gretchen's!" I hiss. Is she serious? "Come on, Jen! You know me better than that."

"I thought I did." Jenna's eyes are filled with accusations. "But my mom made some good points actually, that made me wonder if maybe you didn't tell me everything."

I can't believe this. I can't . . . believe this. "Like what?"

"Like how when you were with Noah, you acted like I didn't exist until you needed an excuse to meet up with him."

I can't deny it. I didn't know I was doing it at the time, though. "I'm sorry."

"Yeah, whatever. And I know what you *told* me about the condom, and about why your mom made you go to the women's clinic, but . . ." She shrugs and looks away. "I mean, how many times did you ask me to lie so you could be with *him*? You lied to your mom. You used *me* to lie to your mom. Why would it bother you to lie to me, too?"

My eyes slide shut. "Because you've been my best friend since elementary school."

"Have I?" Jenna's jaw twitches. "Because the way you were with Noah, I think maybe he took my spot."

"Is that what this is about?" My jaw drops. "You're jealous of Noah?"

"No, Faith. Noah is gone. This is about me not knowing if I can trust you. I don't even know if I know you anymore. We've changed. We've grown apart. I mean, really . . . what do we have in common? Nothing."

When she meets my eyes, her expression is one I've seen many times through the years, but never before has *that look* been directed at me. Not seriously.

"My mom made a really good point when we were talking about this last night."

I don't think I want to know, but I have to ask. "What's that?"

"She said you seem awfully attached to Noah Spencer for someone who claims to have never gone past first base."

What is she saying?

"There's a private women's clinic in Sommerton. Geez. I mean, your dad's a doctor at the hospital, too. And as far as privacy goes, there's that hypocritic oath or whatever. They have to keep things private."

Hippocratic, she means, and it's not really about privacy, but I don't correct her.

"So why would you go that far unless something happened and you wanted to make it . . . you know, go away?"

I . . . I can't . . . How could she think . . . ?

She's supposed to be my best friend. We have history. She knows me. She knows I would never . . .

"Jen." Cold spirals through me. "I told you everything. I wasn't . . . I never . . ." When I inhale, everything shakes. "I'm sorry I asked you to lie for me about Noah. That was wrong."

And I *did* apologize. Months ago. Before Noah ever left.

"But I never lied *to you*, Jenna. Noah and I never—you know. Mom made me go out of town because she didn't want anyone to recognize me at a local clinic."

"Maybe." She shrugs. "Or maybe you've just convinced yourself that's what happened. Blocked it out or something. Maybe you feel guilty, and you're in denial."

"You think I could just *forget it* if I had sex? If I got pregnant and—"

"I don't know. Maybe." She crosses her arms and blows a puff of air up toward her bangs. "Or maybe you're more like your sister than I thought you were."

Jenna could have punched me in the gut and shocked me less. In the throat, and I could more easily breathe. But this?

Anger, disbelief, and betrayal dot my vision. "You know, my sister might be a lot of things, but at least she's loyal."

"Oh, you're one to talk about loyalty."

"Fine. But explain to me exactly how you getting caught with Cole became about me and Noah? How can you just sit there, acting all offended, making accusations against me, when you're the only one of us actually doing the deed?"

"Mademoiselle Prescott. Mademoiselle Slade."

We look to the front of the classroom.

"Do you two have something you'd like to share with the rest of the class?"

"No." Jenna's response sounds like it's coming through two rows of teeth.

"No, Madame Danforth," I answer, but by the shocked, slightly predatory looks on my classmates' faces, it seems I already have.

A cold rush of dread paints a line across my neck.

"Jenna," I whisper later, when we're told to partner off for dialogue. "Jenna, I'm—"

"I'm partnering with Paige. Right, Paige?"

"Uhhh . . ." Paige looks back and forth between us. "I guess?"

"Jenna, I just—"

"Don't talk to me."

For the rest of the class period, my eyes keep straying toward the clock.

When the buzzer rings, I try to catch Jenna so we can talk, so I can apologize, but she shoves by me and won't let me get a word out.

After I get my phone back, she doesn't answer my calls.

She won't respond to my texts.

She's blocked me on all the socials.

We've more than drifted apart. After what she said and what I said and how it was overheard . . . I'm not sure our friendship can be saved.

I'm not sure I want it to be.

Gossip has always moved through our school halls like wildfire. What I said too loudly was both match and gasoline. Still, I don't expect the extent of the fall-out from my overheard words—which is but a spark, eclipsed by Jenna's quite successful attempt to smokescreen my unintended announcement with lies—and carefully tainted truths—about me.

Like a virus dancing across a world without soap, the rumors involving me and a women's clinic mutate as they spread, killing what little of my friendship with Jenna might have been salvageable, as well as my reputation as one of "the good girls" in the small town of Kanton, Iowa.

My life constricts.

And yet . . . two words flutter like whispers in my soul, sustaining me through the spring.

Hold.

On.

$g$oing into the second semester of my junior year, I load my schedule with AP college classes offered through an agreement between KHS and Sommerton Community College. I've been on the AP track all through high school, earning college and high school credits this way. But now, when I'm so desperate to escape this place, knowing that each class completed is one more class I won't have to pay for myself—if Mom and Dad stick to their guns and refuse to help me with my Musical Theatre degree—gets me through the nightmare of homework that swamps me every night.

But it's worth it. If Mom and Dad agree to let me take three more classes online over the summer, I'll be on track to receive my associate degree from Sommerton Community College a semester *before* my KHS class receives their high school diplomas, and my college general education requirements will be complete—and paid for—before I ever leave home.

Under that heavy workload, the cold loneliness of winter melts into spring, the season of college visits and guidance appointments. Within the guise of encouragement, my parents try to interest me in studying marketing or public relations—any course of study they believe could make good use of my more creative gifts. But the more Mom and Dad try and cajole me away from thoughts of pursuing a stage career, the more determined I become—not that I ever wavered. By the time the end of my junior year is in sight, my head pounds from carrying the weight of my dreams alone, but I've made a plan . . .

It's a plan I'm not about to let my parents in on. I can't risk them trying to squash it.

It's a good plan, though.

Solid, I think. I hope.

The kind of plan that might finally prove I'm not some flighty, artistic dreamer, but a mature and capable almost-adult.

At seventeen, however, I'm not an adult. Not legally, anyway. To pull this off, I need help.

And I know just where to get it.

It's a Saturday afternoon, three days into summer vacation. I stand on the porch of Grandma Maddie's Queen Anne-style two story and breathe in the scent of blooming peony bushes for a minute before I knock. Grandma hates doorbells. She says they jar her nerves—which is more than a little odd, considering she isn't at all bothered by visitors just walking on in. But that's Grandma Maddie for you.

A popped-out disco tune floats through the open window. I know the song, of course. Not only because it's been one of Grandma's favorites for as long as I can remember, but also because it was retrofitted in the late 1990s as the title song for the Broadway musical *Mamma Mia!*

More than likely, Grandma Maddie is knee deep in some sort of project. She finally took herself down to part-time status at the salon over the winter, but her days off don't slow her stride. If she isn't doing hair, she's volunteering somewhere or crafting or playing

Texas Hold 'Em with the group of friends she refers to as her "Bridge Club," although she openly admits to never having played Bridge. At seventy-five, Madeleine Prescott the First isn't a woman who can sit idle.

I heard, through the ugly-but-effective Kanton grapevine, that she shut down someone who was gossiping about me and Noah in her salon a couple of months back. We've never spoken of it, but I don't doubt she full-on roasted them right out of their chair.

I open the door. "Grandma!" I shout over the music. "Grandma!"

"Why, Madeleine Faith!" She appears, wearing an apron that says *I kiss better than I cook.* "What a sweet surprise. Come on in, honey. I was just throwing together some lemon bars to take down to the Hospice House."

No surprise there. Grandma Maddie has been taking treats to the Hospice House in Sommerton ever since Grandpa Charlie spent his final days in that facility over ten years ago.

I let the screen slam shut behind me, knowing Grandma doesn't care. "Is anyone you know in there this week?"

"Mm-hmm. Rachel Donovan. Cancer. So sad. And her daughter just got married last year. I did the hair for the bridal party."

"Oh. Sorry to hear that."

"You want to throw those crusts in the oven, hon? I'm going to whip the filling together while it's baking. Ouch!" Grandma Maddie swats her leg. "Darn flies have been biting me all afternoon. You know what that means. There's a storm on its way."

I glance out the window as I pick up two pans of pressed graham cracker crumbs. It *is* getting a little cloudy. Mom says it's just an old wives' tale, but Grandma is almost always right about biting flies and rain.

I slide the pans into the preheated oven. "How long?"

"Oh, ten minutes. Fifteen maybe. I usually just watch them."

I set the timer for ten. Grandma has been known to forget about things in the oven once she starts chatting.

"How are the college plans coming along? Is your dad still pushing for the U of I?"

"Go Hawks," I say, with very little enthusiasm. "Since both Ryan and Gretchen went there, I think he just assumes I will. Mom's pushing pretty hard for it, too."

"Well, that's their alma mater or whatever you call it, so of course they favor it." She shrugs. "It's a good school. And it keeps you close to family, what with Ryan and Danielle and Gretchen up there."

"I know."

"There's a 'but' in there, isn't there?" Grandma pulls a small juicer from a bottom cupboard and plugs it in. "Go grab me a couple of lemons out of the fridge, would ya, hon?"

"Sure."

"So you're still pushing to go to one of those fancy New York colleges, huh?"

"Not . . . necessarily."

"No?" A can of Sweetened Condensed Milk slips through her fingers. She jumps back, keeping her metallic purple pedicure out of its path.

I have to admit, Grandma Maddie makes seventy-five look pretty swag.

"Whyever not?" She picks up the can, inspecting it for dents. "I thought New York was your big dream."

"It is. Well, part of it." I take the lemons to the cutting board to slice. "My dream is to sing on Broadway someday. That hasn't changed. It would be great to be in New York, but living there is crazy expensive." I gather the sliced lemons and deliver them to the juicer. "Since I'll be paying for it on my own, I'm widening my options."

"Paying for it yourself? Your parents won't help at all?"

"Not if I major in Musical Theatre."

"But with all those classes you've already taken, you'll only have two years left on your bachelor's degree!"

"Something like that. Maybe a little longer, depending on how I can schedule all my major classes and the required recitals and all that while holding down a job. But I *will* get to New York"—and Noah, the other half of my dream—"eventually."

"After all your hard work, they won't help you pay for two measly little years of college." Grandma Maddie grinds her teeth as she juices a lemon. Then another.

When she turns back to me, her anger has relaxed into concern. "Honey, I know it's what you want to do, but I don't see how you can go to school full-time *and* make enough money to pay for it without their help. There aren't enough hours in the day. I don't suppose Musical Theatre's one of those things you could do online, is it? If it was, I'd say you could just move in here with me, get out from under your mother's . . . Well, you know."

If only it were that easy. "Thanks. Really. That means . . . a lot." I clear my throat. "But I need to be on campus. It's a performance studies program, so I have to be where I can perform. I'm applying to several schools with good Musical Theatre programs, and I'm going to apply for every scholarship I can find, at all the schools I'm applying to." I take a breath. "I've decided to graduate a semester early. I'll be eighteen, so Mom and Dad can't really stop me."

Grandma sighs and puts a lemon-scented hand on my cheek. "In any case, my door is always open to you, honey. Always."

"I know. And I appreciate that. I do. But at least for now, they're paying the bills, so . . . I'm going to try to tough it out at home. If they let me stay after I've told them my plans."

Her eyebrows lift, but she doesn't say anything.

"I'll go to college for Musical Theatre—somewhere—next fall. But in the meantime, I'm thinking . . . I'd like to go to La Bella and earn my esthetician's license."

She blinks. "La Bella College of Cosmetology?"

I nod. "That's where Lissa Reynolds went."

"Yes, I know." Grandma Maddie nods several times, slowly. "An esthetician's license, you say. I see. So *that's* why you've been spending all that time talking to Lissa at my shop."

"For not being there most of the time, you sure know what's going on."

"It's what I do best. But what does a career in esthetics have to do with Musical Theatre?"

"Stage makeup!" I flourish my hands around my face. "But that's not all. Estheticians make pretty good money in bigger cities. I can have a good job through college and gain experience to hopefully get a job in theatre makeup once I get to New York and start auditioning."

"Hmm . . ." She nods with a thoughtful expression that seems to approve of my plan. At least, I hope that's what it means.

"I've talked several times with the college rep from La Bella. Did you know it only takes twenty-seven to thirty weeks to be eligible for an esthetician license?"

"I think Lissa might have mentioned that."

"Right. Well, a new term starts right after my birthday. I'll be eighteen, so Mom and Dad can't say no. And if I start then, I can be finished and fully employable by May. I'll have decided on a college by then, so as soon as I find a job in a day spa, I can move to . . . wherever and start earning money. The La Bella rep said they would help me with licensure in another state, if I need it. Which I will."

The timer goes off. I check the crusts and put them back in for a few more minutes.

"There's only one hitch," I say, grimacing. "La Bella needs a fifty percent deposit by June fifteenth, and I don't have it."

I'm sweating. And not because it's hot in the kitchen. This is so weird. I've never had to ask for anything like this before. My heart is pounding.

I take a big breath. "I was hoping you might consider giving me a loan. A short term loan."

"How much are we talking about?"

"Umm . . ." I gulp. "The deposit is four thousand dollars. I've applied at a few restaurants in Sommerton to make some extra money this summer. If I get hired, I should be able to pay you back in full by the end of the summer. But," I add, "I totally understand if you can't or you don't want to. It's cool. I'll figure out another way."

The timer beeps. As I pull the graham cracker crusts from the oven, my back tingles where Grandma Maddie's eyes are surely drilling into it. What does she think of the idea? Will she help? I know I said I would figure out another way, but I haven't yet, so . . .

I send up a quick prayer, one of many I've breathed in and out while forming this plan.

"The cream cheese is on the counter. It's all softened up," Grandma says. "You start whipping it with the powdered sugar, and then we'll sit down and talk about the specifics. I think we can probably work something out."

My last summer at home passes in a flurry of online classes, voice lessons, working as a receptionist at Grandma Maddie's salon, and waiting tables at a restaurant in Sommerton—not The Smoked Salt Grille—in the evenings. Things have relaxed at home, probably because I stay in my room a lot and give my mother no reason to suspect me of . . . whatever. Outside of work, my social life is nonexistent and my expenses, few. Grandma is adamant that I'm not allowed to pay her back until I'm all finished with college and settled with a job in New York, so by the time school starts, I've saved enough to pay the remaining balance that will be due to La Bella when I start night classes in October.

Back in school, I keep working weekends at the restaurant in Sommerton. The first two months of my senior year fly by. Three days after my eighteenth birthday, I get up extra early to pray, something I've been doing more and more often these last few months. Today, I'm going to finally unveil my plan to my parents, and I need God's help with that—if only to stop the shaking of my hands.

At breakfast, I pick at my egg white omelet for a good five

minutes before I work up the nerve to blurt out, "I've decided to graduate early. At the end of this semester."

I wait for the explosion, but it doesn't come. Instead, my parents exchange a glance. Dad sets down his newspaper.

"We know," he says. "The school counselor sent a letter at the beginning of the year."

My pulse thrums. I can't believe they've known for two months but didn't say anything.

I swallow and rearrange the silverware around my plate. *Stay calm. Stay . . . calm. You're an adult now, so be an adult.*

I nod, trying to act like I'm not as surprised as I am. "I'll have all my credits completed this semester, as well as my associate degree from Sommerton Community College. There's no reason to stay in high school."

I inhale a tight breath. I've practiced my speech for weeks, but it's hard to force out the words.

"Since I'm eighteen now, I don't really need your permission, but I would like your blessing."

"Our blessing? Hmm," Dad says, and the fact that he's doing all the talking while Mom remains silent is freaking me out a little. "Honestly, Faith, we were hoping you would change your mind."

"What about all your college applications?" Mom chimes in, and I let out a breath. "You've applied for admission next fall, right? Not in January."

"Right." I nod. "I'll start college next fall, as planned. I'm not sure where yet, but I'm planning to major in Musical Theatre." I hold up my hand to silence Mom's inevitable interruption. "Since you've made yourselves clear about what you will and will not pay for in regards to my education, I've made some additional plans to help pay for my own schooling."

I hate that I can't look my parents in the eye, but if I do, I might lose my nerve, so I continue to stare at the omelet on my plate.

"Starting next Monday, I'll be taking night classes at La Bella College, studying esthetics. I've already put down a deposit, and I have the remainder due in my savings account."

"Beauty school?" Mom's jaw drops. "Tell me you're kidding, Faith. You got a twenty-one hundred on the S.A.T.!"

As if intelligent people with good test scores shouldn't consider a skilled trade? *Careful, Mom. Your snobbery is showing.*

"Yes. And I hope those scores will put me in the running for some good scholarships toward my Musical Theatre degree."

"I'm lost." She splays her hands and leans away from the table. "What does beauty school have to do with Musical Theatre?"

"*Cosmetology* School," I correct as gently as I can, considering my teeth are clenched.

I make an effort to relax my jaw, my voice, and my body language. "As a licensed esthetician, I can work in a spa or a salon. I can even work as a makeup artist for theatrical productions after I finish college and start auditioning in New York. It's a respectable skilled trade that a lot of people make really good money doing."

"But . . . why?"

"Haven't you always preached about—" I cringe. Bad word choice, probably. "Er, told me that I won't be able to make a living in the theatre? That I need something to fall back on? Well, I don't believe that. But I do know I need marketable skills to support myself *until* I'm able to make a living in the theatre. Not only that, but this is a skill I can actually use in a theatrical setting, doing stage makeup."

Their expressions aren't exactly open, but they're listening, so I continue.

I explain how esthetics is a growing field, even pulling a spreadsheet from my pocket, listing the average incomes of estheticians in all the cities where I've applied to colleges. I explain the length of the program and why it makes sense.

"So you see?" I say at last. "It's a solid plan. I can still have a viable career option in the theatre, if—" I cough and take a drink from my water glass. "*While* I'm establishing myself as a performer."

"Faith." Dad takes off his glasses. "You don't have to support yourself through school. We helped pay for Ryan and Gretchen's undergraduate degrees, and we'll help you, too."

"If," Mom butts in, "you pick a course of study that isn't a complete waste of our money and your time."

"I know you want what *you* think is best for me." I silently pray for patience. For fortitude. "I've been drawn to the stage all my life. It's who I am. I can accept that you won't pay for my schooling. I'm willing to pay my dues in order to follow my dreams."

"You're very talented, Faith. No one will argue that." Mom's tone is her version of tender, I guess, but the prevalent Faith-directed chill I've grown accustomed to is not entirely absent. "But you're so young. You have too much potential to waste it on a long-shot like show business." She sighs. "I know you feel grown up and wise now. Everyone does when they're eighteen. But you don't realize how sheltered we are here in small-town Iowa, honey. We all know you are, inarguably, the most talented singer and actress in your high school of five hundred students. Here, you're a big fish in a tiny pond. But it's an ocean out there in the real world, full of other, possibly *more* talented, fish and a good many sharks. The odds are stacked against success before you even start."

"I know it won't be easy, but I'm not a coward. I won't quit just because it's scary or competitive."

"Naiveté often masquerades as bravery when you're young," Mom says, her voice taking on the tiniest bit of condescension—at least to my ears. "You're a small-town girl from Iowa, not some worldly-wise urbanite." She nods. Agreeing with herself? "Your dad and I don't want to punish you for being talented. We want to protect you. To make sure you're safe and that you're preparing yourself to have a good life and a career that can support you."

"If I try to live the life you want, it will kill the part of me that makes me . . . well . . . *me.*" I take a breath and remind myself to keep my cool. "I believe God has given me the talents he has for a reason and that I need to develop those talents with proper training and education—not smother them with practicality."

Mom opens her mouth to interrupt. I hold up my hand.

"No, please. Just listen. Yes, I'm young," I say. "And yes, I'm probably pretty naïve. But I only get one shot at being young, and I don't want to waste it being afraid. Don't you understand? If I don't pursue the dreams God has put in my heart, I'll not only be letting myself down, but God, too."

"You believe God wants you in show business?" Mom scoffs. "I imagine most of the stuff that happens backstage on Broadway would make Jesus Christ roll over in his tomb."

"Well, I guess it's a good thing he's not in there anymore, isn't it?" My tension spills, staining my words with angry sarcasm. I close my eyes. *Breathe, Faith. Breathe.* "Sorry. That came out a little strongly. What I mean is . . . maybe he wants me there for that reason."

"So you want to be a Broadway missionary?" She snorts. "Or an evangelical makeup artist?"

I sigh. "I want to live the life I've been called to live, in the way I've been called to live it. I want to use the gifts God has given me, recognizing that the most important of those gifts is himself. No, I don't know what that's going to look like yet, but I know I need more training—professional training and experience—to be ready when I figure it out. If I'm accepted into a musical theatre program at a university, I can get that training. And by working as an esthetician while I'm doing it, I can also have a job to support me through the hard times after I go to New York."

"You've obviously given this a lot of thought, Faith." Dad puts his glasses back on, only to pull them off again. "I'm proud of you."

He's . . . what? I blink. "Really?"

"Yes, I am. But I still have to agree with your mother. Spending thousands upon thousands of dollars, not to mention several years of your life studying something in which the odds of finding success are slim seems like a waste. Not just of our money and your time, but of your potential."

Mom nods. "I know your head was filled with a lot of religious stuff over the past couple of years, Faith. And that worries me. You're young. You're vulnerable. You'll be surrounded by all these volatile, artistic people who are going to find out your dad's a doctor and you come from a family with money. What if you go off to college and get dragged into some cult?"

Like Aunt Becca did at my age. Minus the college part. "You're kidding, right?"

"No, Faith, I'm not. You don't know what kind of crazy stuff is out there in the world. I do. My sister ran off to California to be a rock star, and she ended up making jewelry for Jesus while she bounced in and out of rehab clinics. Now, she's a Denver pothead, barely making enough money to stay alive."

"I'm not an idiot, Mom. And I haven't bought into a cult. I'm a Christian."

"But you're basing your future plan on"—Mom makes air quotes—"'God's will.' Do you know how many times I heard that from my sister? I will not—" Her fist slams into the table, and I jump. "—let the same thing happen to my daughter."

"Janet." Dad puts his hand over Mom's clenched fist. Mom

closes her eyes, inhales through her nose, and lets the breath out slowly through her mouth before opening her eyes again.

"We want you to get a good education," she says, her voice calmer. "To use the brain God gave you—yes, God—to live up to your potential. I know you think you're a better Christian than I am, Faith. And maybe you are. But my parents dragged me to church enough when I was a kid that I at least know the Ten Commandments. And one of those commandments says 'honor thy mother and thy father.'"

"Following my dreams does not dishonor you." I close my eyes for a moment to tamp down the defensive arguments that tease the back of my tongue. "I cannot pretend to be something—or someone—contrary to what God created me to be. That doesn't honor *him*. And it doesn't honor you, either. It only appeases you. And that's not the same thing."

There's no immediate rebuttal, so I continue.

"This isn't some wild dream. It's what I believe I'm *meant* to do with my life. I'm applying for scholarships. I'm going to work really hard to be ready for my auditions. And . . . I'll be happy with whichever school wants me enough to offer a financial aid package I can live with."

"But why beauty—er, cosmetology school?" Dad asks. "You're already burning the candle at both ends with your community college classes in addition to the high school requirements. And you've never talked about wanting to be an esthet—" Dad clears his throat again, "a *makeup artist* before."

"I've always helped with makeup for the shows at school. And I've gotten to watch Lissa a lot—she's the esthetician Grandma hired last year. I think I'd be good at it."

Mom inhales sharply. "I should have known." She crosses her arms. "This was *Madeleine*'s idea, wasn't it?"

"No. This was my idea. All of it." I was worried this would happen. "I *did* talk with Grandma about it. Since she owns a salon, it seemed like a good idea." I look back down at my plate and the omelet that's turned to mush from all the fiddling I've done during this conversation. "She did loan me the money for the deposit to La Bella, but I'm going to pay her back as soon as possible."

Mom shoots a seething glance at Dad. As if he has any more control over Grandma Maddie's decisions than over his wife's? Please.

"It was *my* idea," I reiterate. "I know it seems a little sudden, because it's the first you've heard about it. But it's not sudden. I've been planning this for months. I was just waiting to tell you until I was eighteen so you couldn't tell me no."

Mom sniffs. She won't make eye contact with me.

"I'm not going into this blindly. I know it'll be rough this fall, adding night classes at La Bella to all I've got going on already, but it's only for a couple of months, and then I'll switch to days in January."

Mom presses her lips together, and a fast breath exits her nose "Aren't you going out for the musical this fall?"

"Yes. Most of my practices are right after school. My classes at La Bella don't start until six. Mr. Barron said he would work around my schedule."

"Well, isn't *he* helpful."

I ignore Mom's sarcasm. "I'll finish up at La Bella in early May. That gives me plenty of time to find a job and a place to live wherever I end up going to school."

"Why are you *really* doing this, Faith?" Dad asks. "Graduating early, I mean. Racing into adulthood before you've finished the time allotted for being a kid?"

An ache presses around my throat. "I left 'kid' behind a while ago. Last year was really hard."

"But you did fine! You were at the top of your class!"

"I know, Mom. It wasn't school that was difficult. Well, not exactly. There were a lot of rumors, and—"

"It's a small town. You were the flavor of the month for a while, but it's over. You need to move past all that."

Heaven forbid she should take an ounce of responsibility.

"I know the last year or so has been . . . ah, difficult for you," Dad adds. "Socially speaking. But you've kept your grades up under a heavier course load than either Ryan or Gretchen could have handled. I suppose there's no reason why you shouldn't graduate early if that's what you really want."

"It *is* what I want. The sooner I can get out of KHS, the better." I set my fork down. I really need to stop messing with this omelet. It's gross. "There's nothing for me here. After Noah left, I—"

Noah.

The shock of saying—hearing—his name aloud after so long is intense.

I pull in my breath, wishing I could remove that last phrase from the air before it registers in my mom's ears with as much resonance as it did mine, but it's too late.

I cannot believe I said his name. Out loud. To *them*.

Why, *why* did I have to go and bring Noah into this?

"Oh, for the love of . . . This is about *him*? Unbelievable." Mom huffs. "Now we get to the truth, Joseph. This isn't about wanting to go to beauty school or wanting to put herself through college. This is about that Noah Spencer again."

She says his name like it's a disease. The hairs on the back of my neck prickle upward.

"There is still a restraining order in place. Have you been in touch with him? If you have, I—"

"I haven't spoken to Noah Spencer in over a year." But now that I'm eighteen, I can—and will—have that restraining order rescinded.

"I bet you got online with him as soon as you got your computer privileges back."

"No, I didn't." I blink at her accusing stare. "You don't believe me?"

"I've heard about those privacy apps and things kids can get now so their parents don't know what they're doing on their phones.

Faith, I told you that if I he contacted you I would—"

"You would have him arrested. I know." I grind my teeth. "Why would I risk that?"

"Joseph, get our lawyer on the phone. This whole ridiculous plan is that no good Noah Spencer's doing. I bet he's the one who's talked her into graduating early as well as this beauty school nonsense." A mocking laugh exits her nose. "He's probably hoping that *she'll* be able to support *him*!"

"Enough." I push back from the table. "What is *wrong* with you? Do you think I'm incapable of having an original thought? These are *my* plans, not Noah's! As far as he knows, I'll graduate in May, with the rest of my class!"

"I don't believe you." She stands, heading toward the stairs. "And I'm going to your room to find the evidence. You've only been eighteen for three days. If he so much as—"

"Evidence?" I rise and follow her upstairs. "Evidence of what?"

In my room, I watch in disbelief as my mother rifles through my desk drawers, looks under my bed . . . even between my mattress and box spring.

"Your relationship with him was unhealthy from the very beginning," she says. "He was a charmer. You fell for him just like Becca fell for every sweet-talking drug-pusher who played a guitar. Noah Spencer is using you now, Faith, just like he did when he was here. You can't trust people like him. They'll crush your heart and spit on everything you do for them as if none of it matters until they need the next thing."

Mom moves to my dresser, pulls out the top drawer, and dumps it out on my bed.

"He's using your infatuation with him to manipulate you. Don't you see? It's like I said, he probably wants *you* to support *him* while he chases after his own stupid acting career."

"Stupid acting career?" Blood pulses against my temples. "Tell me how you really feel, Mom. My dreams of a stage career *define* me. They've made me who I am. If Noah is stupid for wanting to be an actor, then so am I."

"You're certainly acting it!" She shoves my underwear back into the drawer and grabs the next drawer down, repeating the process.

"Why are you doing this? This is *crazy*! Why won't you believe me?"

"You lied about him before. Why wouldn't you lie now?"

My chest heaves with every breath, and my vision begins to tunnel, just like the first time Mom threatened to have Noah arrested. I take a deep breath in, close my eyes, and let it out slowly.

"That's it, then."

I walk down the hall to Ryan's old room, open the closet, which is now used for storage, and pull out the luggage set Ryan and Danielle gave me for Christmas last year.

"What are you doing with those?"

"I'm eighteen, Mom, and I'm done."

"Done? Done with what?"

"Done with this argument. Done with trying to measure up to Ryan and Gretchen and whatever picture you've drawn in your head about what I should be. I'm done with being compared to your loser sister, no matter what I do. And more than anything, I'm done with trying to tell you the truth about me and Noah."

"This *is* about him. I knew it."

"It is now. But it didn't have to be." I am out of emotion and nearly out of time. "Look," I say in a calmer tone. "You're going to be late for work, and I'm going to be late for school if we keep going over this now. I'll come by and get the rest of my stuff—and Janey—after school. That way I'll be out of the house before you get home, and we can avoid being awful to each other."

Mom blinks several times. "Where will you go?"

"I guess . . . Grandma Maddie's, for now. Then . . . we'll see."

"Of course that's where you'd go. But you'll be back."

"Maybe." I plop the biggest suitcase on my bed and unzip it. "Do you believe what I said about Noah? That he isn't involved in my school decisions? That I haven't spoken to him for over a year?"

"No." Mom leans against the door frame, crossing her arms. When I start filling my suitcase, she says, "Give me one good reason I *should* believe you, Faith."

My hand stills on the suitcase zipper. Regret is bitter, replaying every white lie and omission, every vague or outright dishonest action.

"I can't." I zip the suitcase shut. "I wish I could present evidence that would make you believe me, but I can't."

"That's what I thought."

"I'm sure it is." I heave the overnight bag off the bed and onto the floor beside its empty mate. "But things aren't always what they appear. I have spent the last year trying to earn back your trust—or at least your respect—but you have none to give. Not to me." I pick up the empty suitcase and open it on the bed.

"Faith Prescott, you put your things back where they go this instant and desist with this childish running away game you're playing. It's infantile. And it won't work on me."

"I'm sorry it's come to this."

"Grow up, Faith. You've had your sport. Now put that luggage away."

"I'm eighteen, Mom. I *am* grown up." I grab the overnight bag. "And by now, you, of all people, should know that I don't play *sports*."

Leaving the two bigger suitcases behind—I'll come back and

finish packing after school—I slip by my mother and head down the stairs . . . and out from under her expectations and accusations for good.

INTERMISSION

ENTRÉ ACT

ONE YEAR LATER

August 9th
Present Day
Somewhere between Michigan and Iowa

*T*ick-tick-tick-tick. *Tick-tick-tick-tick. Tick-tick-tick-tick. Tick-tick-tick-tick.*

I tear my gaze from the highway's hypnosis-inducing rhythm that took me to such a dangerous, mind-numbing place. I've spent these last hours driving through even more miles of my subconscious than I have trekking through Michigan, Indiana, and Illinois. I've practically driven drunk, intoxicated on memories. It's a little scary actually, just how absent I've been, how little I recall of the drive.

"Get it together," I tell myself through gritted teeth. How ironic it would be if Noah showed up, but I absentmindedly drove my car off a cliff and ended up at a hospital instead of at the waterfall.

Not that there are that many cliffs along the interstate in this fairly flat part of the country, but still.

I take a deep breath. Just another few miles, and I'll cross the border into Iowa. Eventually, I'll trade the interstate for a crisscross quilt of rural highways that will take me to familiar gravel roads.

I can do this. And I'm close enough to home now that I might be able to find a non-country station on the radio.

I hit one of the presets I never took the time to reprogram in Michigan and . . . *voila!* I'm two measures away from the beat drop on Beyoncé's latest single.

Music. Distraction. I can do this.

Within thirty minutes of crossing into Iowa, I reset my cruise to sixty-two—the fastest speed I'll risk on these bored-country-cop highways.

At the end of a commercial-free hour of music—thank you, God—I'm in the home stretch.

Literally. I keep my focus steady, forward, as I pass the blacktop turn-off for Parre Hills.

As I slow for the first of two gravel roads, my stomach tightens. My chest, too.

Dizzy. I try to blink it away, but when Janey nudges my shoulder with her nose, I realize my breathing is keeping up with my blinks.

She whines.

I'm scaring her. "Sorry, girl." I take a deep breath. In. Out.

Inhale. Exhale. "*Noah.*"

Noah.

Gravel dust chases my taillights, layering off-white waves on the rear window. Out my side window, the sun is descending, teasing the blue of the sky with shades of melon and lavender.

Lavender. Like those roses Noah sent me, for being a dumb hotel.

I shake my head. "We're almost there, Janey."

Caught up in memories as I've been, these hours have seemed to take little more time than a hike to the waterfall.

A hike I will soon make, but from a different direction than I used when I still lived with my parents.

A stretch of fresh rock bullies the tires. The tread loosens its grip, sending the back end into a fishtail.

I lift my foot from the pedal and yank the steering wheel to the right. Memory tempers sudden panic, and I gently pump the brakes, regaining a hold on the road just in time to make the final tight curve. The road straightens, and my mind wanders back to where my memories left off.

Maybe living with Grandma Maddie was not the ideal solution to my problems with my mother. Or maybe it was. And maybe they aren't my problems so much as hers, but I bore their brunt. When God says, "Honor your father and your mother," I don't think he means for his children to submit themselves to abuse. Until I enforced distance from Mom, I didn't truly recognize that abuse was what I had experienced. Emotional, verbal, and—

My hand moves from the steering wheel to my cheek, remembering her slap. My resulting fall. That forced, unnecessary, invasive clinic visit.

Direct and indirect physical abuse.

Accepting Grandma's open door was a mode of survival I probably should have sought sooner, instead of continuing to live in an arena of fear and under a microscope of distrust.

I don't know if my leaving affected my mom to the point that she regretted her own behavior, but by Christmas, a tentative sort of peace settled between us. Still, it was a bit awkward when I left Christmas dinner with Grandma Maddie.

Yes, I had questioned my decision to move out. More than once. But every time I thought of going back home, only to pack up and leave again in May, that soul-deep whisper of "Hold on" found me, and I decided against it. My plans hadn't changed, and neither had my parents' objections to them.

It hadn't been easy taking buses and trains to audition for the various musical theatre programs to which I applied. It hadn't been easy finishing high school while taking classes at La Bella. And it most certainly had not been easy—although it had been satisfying—to tell my parents I won a full-tuition scholarship to the University of Michigan.

I smile now at that memory. With the scholarship, my parents assumed I would quit La Bella, but I kept to my plan. I finished the program the first week of May and immediately began the application process for my Michigan esthetician's license. Before my old KHS classmates even flipped the tassels on their graduation caps, Janey and I had moved into an apartment with three other musical theatre majors, and I'd started working at a day spa near the U of M campus.

It's been a busy summer, but I've made some like-minded friends, and I've gained a steady stream of regular clients at the spa. Even after classes start up in a couple of weeks, forcing me to scale back my hours at the spa to part-time, I should have a little extra left over every month to build my savings.

The savings that will be necessary when, two years from now—hopefully—I'll be moving to New York.

The two days I've taken off work this week will pinch a little bit, but that pinch won't matter once Noah . . .

Eight, nine. Eight-seventeen.

Anticipation swells in my chest like the feeling that rises each time the first notes of an overture sneak under the curtain to tickle the ears of the actors waiting backstage.

God, please let him come.

The angle of the sun glints off the brown sign for the County Nature Preserve like the wide lens of a spotlight. My eyes follow the late afternoon's glow as it extends down the road and up the lonesome tree-line. I look at the clock.

5:38 p.m.

I'm almost three hours early. In August.

"Idiot." Good thing I picked up a few more bottles of water when I stopped for gas. The heat index is probably in the triple digits.

I glance in the rearview mirror, where Janey's ears have perked up. "Not you, sweetie. Me. I'm the idiot."

I pull off into the sad excuse for a parking area. Unlike the dusty path behind us, the forward view isn't marred by the passage of a recent vehicle. In fact, there's not another car in sight.

"He's not here yet." Taking a deep breath, I check the dashboard clock again. "Of *course* he's not here yet, idiot." This time, I'm sure Janey knows I'm not talking to her.

I angle the rearview mirror toward my face. Purplish blue smudges from several sleepless nights—anxious, anyone?—join with the long drive to stain the thin skin beneath my eyes. A patina of fatigue dims the gold flecks in my brown eyes, to the point of shadow.

I wrinkle my nose at my reflection. I have the skills and the products to camouflage my fatigue, but in this heat, I would probably just sweat them off, anyway. Why waste good makeup? Especially while I'm in the midst of learning several quite pointed lessons on how frugality helps pave the path to dreams.

A wet tongue glides up the side of my face. My scowls relaxes into a smile.

Janey thumps the silver tip of her long white tail against the back seat. Looks at the gate. Whines.

"You're ready to go, aren't you, girl?"

One more moment of artificial coolness . . . and I open the door.

As soon as the car's protective seal is breached, a thick wave of heat sucks the breath from my lungs. Not patient enough to wait for me to open the rear door, Janey ambles over the console, jumps out the driver's door, and immediately heads for the grass, curved tail in motion.

I chug the rest of my half-full bottle of water and then retrieve my backpack from the floor of the passenger side, stuffing the extra water bottles and Janey's portable water dish in the backpack. After securing my keys in the outside zippered pocket, I shoulder the pack and slide my phone in the back pocket of my shorts. I don't bother turning up the ringer volume. Mom had my number changed the same week Noah left for London. He's not going to call, and I don't want to know if anyone else does.

I shoot a glance back up the road.

"Do you think he's close?" I retrieve my just-put-away phone and check the time.

Wow. I've made it to a quarter to six now. A full eight minutes since I last checked the time. "It's still early. He's probably miles and miles away."

My abdominal muscles tighten. A sour twinge seeps into the joints of my jaw. I recognize the sensation, but I can't reconcile it with the current geography.

Stage fright? Here?

It makes sense, I guess. But this isn't just another performance, on just another stage. This is my *life*. Tonight, my past, my hope, and my future will collide.

Eight, nine. Eight-seventeen.

The refrain reverberates in my head with determined, desperate hope.

Inhaling through my nose, I pull the breath deep into my diaphragm. The well-exercised muscle expands. As Mr. Barron taught me, I picture the tissues stretching thinner and thinner, giving me permission to exert both volume and control. Choosing "ah" as my sound, the G above middle C as my note, I crescendo the breath over fifteen seconds and then repeat, taking the note up a step, to an A.

Even though I have no need to warm up my vocal chords, the exercise usually calms my coiled nerves.

And it does help, some. Still, I have to rub my arms as phantom gooseflesh prickles against the heat.

After all this time, this long intermission is almost over. The Entré Act music is swelling. At 8:17 p.m., the curtain will rise for Act II and reveal its players.

Earlier, if Noah stays true to pattern.

If Noah stays true.

I close my eyes, aiming a heavily weighted whisper toward the sky, and then head for the gate.

"Ready, girl? Let's go."

Janey races ahead, moving with pup-like excitement through the stacked logs that serve as the entrance gate. I follow, smiling at my dog's exuberance to be leash-free in an old, familiar place.

Nose to the ground and curved tail in constant, happy motion, Janey ventures ahead, doubling back now and then to make sure I haven't strayed off the path. The trail cuts through heavily timbered hills, down into washed out gullies, and back up again. It's kind of a mess. As I negotiate overgrown weeds, ruts, and natural debris along the trail, I start to wonder if my memory has failed me.

I don't remember the path to the creek as being this long, even from the entrance gate. Did I take a wrong turn somewhere?

Just when I'm about to whistle for Janey and turn around to make my way back to the entrance and start over, the trail curves around an old oak tree.

I know this tree.

My gaze roves slowly up the trunk and back down. At its base, deep orange fungi with ruffled edges ring the tree, each wider than a dinner plate. They're beautiful, like some sort of other-planetary, science-fiction flowers, and they make the tree seem as if it's been professionally landscaped by God.

I suppose it was.

I inhale, closing my eyes and opening my mouth. Yes, there it is. The loamy mushroom aroma I remember.

Janey nudges my palm with her nose. She knows this isn't our destination.

At the bottom of the next hill, I veer off the trail and toward the creek, hidden beyond the brambles. We walk along the bank, searching for the best place to go down, into the creek bed.

I'm not as familiar with this side of the creek.

Finally, we find a less-severe incline with some decent rocks peeking out of the dry clay bank for footholds.

But for a few stagnant pockets, the creek is dry and much easier to travel along than the trail had been. In a wetter season, I would hear the waterfall long before reaching it. Now, I come upon it in silence only broken only by the buzz of insects.

It isn't really a waterfall, of course. Not in August. Tonight, it's only a waterfall in *theory*. It's probably been weeks since even a drop of water has trickled over this ledge. Tonight, it's just a precipice. A dark, dry cliff.

An empty stage, awaiting its players.

I sit on the ledge awhile, letting disappointment tighten my throat. Despite the absence of a car at the entry gate, not to mention the earliness of the hour, a small part of me expected Noah to be here, sitting on the ledge, waiting for me. Just as he so often was when we lived on the same continent.

I pull out my phone and check the time. It's just past six-thirty.

It's darker in the woods than the hour allows elsewhere. My gaze roves the twilit bank. I stand. Pace.

Yes, to the naked eye, the waterfall looks empty. But for me, this place is filled with *him*.

"Noah."

His name rides the current of my breath, and the sound of it is a punch in the gut. Emotions surge with such force that I'm almost forced to take a step back. In November, it will have been three years since we met here, atop this waterfall. Not a day has gone by in which I've not thought of Noah Spencer.

Dreams of him, of us, dangle from this ledge, where they've waited two years this side of our goodbyes.

I press my palms to my eyes. I'm not crying, but . . . I'm wrecked.

To be here, now, back in the place where it all began, where it could end, if he doesn't come . . . the memories are sharper. Clearer.

Does he think of me as often as I think of him? Does he think of me . . . at all? What changes have these years brought to Noah's life? To Noah's *heart*?

My hands tremble. So much can change in two years.

I've changed.

I'm sure he has, too.

Will I even recognize him when he comes? And what will he think of me after all this time? I swallow and relieve my pacing legs, setting them dangling again.

When I was sixteen, Noah said I was beautiful. But I'm sure he's met many more sophisticated beauties in London than the simple Iowa girl he once loved. And we agreed. If one of us fell for someone else, we were under no obligation to return tonight.

What if he . . . ?

"Please, God," I whisper. "Please, let him come."

I fight my fear, my disloyal-feeling doubt, but it comes anyway, eking its dulled coldness into my blood. This date, this place— they're sacred.

Eight, nine. Eight-seventeen.

But will those numbers mean anything to Noah Spencer across the chasm of two discarded calendars and an exciting life abroad?

"Hold on," I whisper over the ledge.

He said he would come.

A flash of brightness catches my eye and turns my head. What is that? A flashlight?

I suppose it *is* dark enough on the trail by now to need one.

Hope rises, and so do I. "Noah?"

The sun still gives the evening light, but it's set well below the tree line. I look up and west, expecting the oranges, purples, and pinks of sunset . . . but there is only streaked gloom and dark gray. Farther up, the high clouds are puffy and full. And they're moving, fast.

Another flash. I groan. The light was not from a human invention, but a more celestial source.

"Ouch!" I slap at a tiny pinch on my arm that leaves a mushy fly in its wake. As a distant rumble resonates through the sky, I flick off the nasty remains and wipe my arm with the corner of my shirt. What was it Grandma Maddie used to say? *"Flies only bite when it's going to rain."*

The air is thick with humidity. Too thick. I know how fast a hot August day can turn on you around here. I've known the temperature to drop twenty degrees in a quarter of an hour, just before the sky rips apart. If that's the sort of change moving through the darkening sky, if a cold front meets this heat, it'll result in one wallop of a storm.

"God, please. Not tonight. I know it's dry. I know people around here are probably praying for rain. But if you could please, please hold off that storm. Just until eight-seventeen. No, nine. Nine would be better. That way we'll have a little time to get out of here."

We, I pray, believing.

I pace.

I sit. I stand.

I pace some more.

I check the time on my phone.

7:47.

Half an hour to go.

Noah is always early.

Drawing my legs to my chest, I hug them, resting my head on my knees. After a moment, I need to lift my head to catch my breath, but my inhalation lacks the control of normal respiration.

The air is too thick, too wet, for a place this dry.

A twig snaps from the direction of the trail. Janey perks up, and a low growl rumbles from her throat.

"Easy, girl."

It's a simple command to give, a more difficult one to obey myself. As I stand, I tighten my ponytail and smooth my hair. Butterflies fiesta through my midsection.

Backing away from the ledge and toward a better vantage point, I dab the hem of my t-shirt across my damp forehead and then rub my sweaty palms against the fabric of my shorts. I wait for Noah to appear.

A hesitant step or three later, only a young doe stands at the turn in the creek. My shoulders drop. I click my tongue, and the doe scampers up the bank.

Thick quiet descends once again.

I pull the phone from my pocket. In the upper right corner of the screen, a small shape blinks.

Low Battery. Wonderful.

"It's almost eight, Janey. But I guess he could be running late." I snort a laugh. "Or on time."

Janey tilts her head, her unspoken question reinforcing what I already know.

Turning away from where the doe fooled me into hope, I resume my post at the ledge of the waterfall, cracking open a bottle of water for me and one for Janey as well.

The breeze is stronger now. Cooler. The flashes and rumbles are steady, though. Not too close yet. Maybe the storm will go around us. *That would be awesome, God.*

Far above the absent cascade, the breeze's attentions are fickle. Like a homecoming queen candidate the week before the vote, it moodily flirts with the treetops. High, sun-scorched leaves whisper like oracles of hope and doom.

My heart vacillates between the two.

He'll be here.

He's forgotten me.

He'll be here.

He's forgotten me.

I check my phone.

8:09.

I cap my empty bottle and stand.

Pace.

People change. Just because someone was unfailingly prompt two years ago, doesn't mean they've kept the habit.

8:16.

My phone emits three loud beeps, startling an unnaturally high-pitched bark from Janey. In turn, her bark causes me to almost drop my phone.

The battery icon blinks at me, empty. The display blackens, but I don't need to see the numbers to know what they would have said within seconds, anyway.

"Well, Janey," I whisper, "I guess he's not coming."

I need to sit down, and do—right where I stand.

Cross-legged on the rocky creek bed, the phone rests between my hand and head as if it can support the weight of my loss.

Blackout.

And, *scene.*

ACT II

an intermission is supposed to give the actors a chance to recoup, to change costumes, to get ready for the second act and its climactic resolution. But the curtain is up. Act II is in motion, and I am . . .

I am alone.

This is not the script I wanted.

Noah.

I thought his heart was seared to my heart. His dreams to my dreams.

I was wrong.

Oh, God. This hurts. It *hurts.* Why?

Why?

I did not audition for a one-woman show.

"Noah." His name is a moan, an ache, a death. "You said you would come."

I unzip a pocket on my backpack and drop the useless phone inside.

Useless.

Inútil, in Spanish.

I draw my knees up, tight to my chest.

Cold washes through me like an arctic wave, contained inside my body. My muscles tremble at its force. Janey scoots closer.

My chest seizes to the point of pain, and I fist my hands in my shirt, near its source, but the sob refuses to be contained. It erupts, splitting my heart. Blood pounds through my veins, awakening my brain to the truth, but it's a cold rush . . . and vicious.

He didn't come.

He didn't come.

I roll to my side, tucking my elbows in, clasping my hands below my chin. I'm cold. So cold.

Janey curls around me. Whines.

I cannot comfort her.

I cannot comfort me.

I curl further, deeper into my pain, until I can taste its brokenness. Defeat. Despair.

. . . and love.

Still, love.

It is rich and real.

It is wide and terrible and deep.

It is mine.

As he was.

Until eight, nine. Eight-seventeen.

It may not have been sleep that took me away from the knowledge of my surroundings and the passage of time, but when I awaken, it is to a shout of thunder. My body is curled around Janey, who has positioned herself precariously between me and the ledge's drop.

I'm sore, spent, exhausted, and as depleted as if the very marrow has been sucked from my bones.

A strong, chill wind shakes the treetops.

When did it start raining?

My hair and arms are damp but not soaked. The heat is as gone as if it were nothing more than a figment of my imagination.

A burst of light illumines the sky. An echoing *crack* follows close behind. I flinch at the nearness of the sound.

"Janey." I stand. "It's time to go."

My dog rises with a pitched yawn. I reach for my backpack, pull out the flashlight, and flip it on, roving the bank with the beam. The phone is dead, so I can't check the time. How long have I been here? What sort of creatures watched me mourn? Watched me exhaust myself, sobbing toward sleep?

The light reveals nothing I didn't expect, only the sheen of fresh wetness on rock and clay and parched brambles, until . . .

On an outcropping of rock, tiny white shapes shiver in the wind.
No.

I blink.

No. It's too late in the season. And much too dry for the delicate
spring wildflowers to survive.

But there they are, those defiant little Dutchman's breeches,
sadly hanging over the rocks on long, droopy stems. And hidden
behind them is . . .

"The Dutchman's pocket."

I inhale a sharp hope through the thick, storm-chased August air.
I thought of our secret mailbox on the drive down from Michigan,
but once I arrived, other memories crowded in. "I never came back
here after Noah left. What if . . . ?"

I stand in indecision until a series of horizontal spider veins cross
the sky, accompanied by near-immediate crackles of sound, sparking
my feet into motion.

It's been two years. I push the flowers this way and that.

"Where is it? Where *is* it?"

Hot, angry tears form and spill. I rip at the flowers now,
desperate to unveil the little cave.

A stubborn handful of sagging white blooms gives way, revealing
our secret mailbox, but I lose my balance and land, quite hard, on
my derriere.

"Stupid flowers! Stupid Dutchman's pocket! Stupid—!" I gasp,
running out of wrath.

Bigger drops of rain fall now, spaced apart. Each hits the dry
creek bed like a slap.

The sky lights and booms. Janey whines, her tail between her
legs.

"I know, Janey. We need to get going. But if I don't look, I'll wonder forever. Don't worry. I'll be quick."

I brush off my backside, glad I stowed my phone in my bag. It's the one monthly bill my parents still pay for me, and I'm not due for an upgrade if it gets crushed by my bum in a fit of temper.

In my anger and grief, I've made a mess of these tenacious little wildflowers, and I feel guilty for the destruction. Carefully, I push the remaining flowers aside and shine the light into the wide crevice.

A spider's web sparkles in the corner of the opening, and its oversized occupant scuttles out and up the rock. I squeak back a scream and grimace, but the jar is still there, safe within the Dutchman's pocket. *Our secret mailbox.*

I grasp the jar and pull it free from the miniature cave. It's filthy, to be sure. But I have to know. Did he leave me a parting gift?

This jar has seen so many little things, proofs that Noah went out of his way to let me know I was on his mind and in his heart. Notes, funny doodles, song lyrics, a tin of cinnamon-flavored candies . . .

I have to smile, even though it hurts. Two years of muddy rain splatter have rendered the outside of the jar nearly opaque. I tilt it. A tiny *clink* . . .

"There's something in there!"

I try to turn the lid, but it won't budge. I wrap the hem of my t-shirt around it for a better hold, bend at the waist, and groan with the effort until every nerve in my neck is about to pinch. It won't give.

I switch hands and twist hard. Nothing. And it's getting slippery now, with the rain.

A loud boom shakes the ground. Janey's bark ends on a whine. Enough.

I shove the jar in my backpack. Flashlight in hand, I lift my face to the sky. "God, I know better than to go under a tree in a lightning storm, but I don't have much choice. If you could just hold off any direct hits until we get to the car, I'd appreciate it."

Janey stays close at my heels as we trudge back up the creek's path. The rain is falling harder now, faster. Wind drives the big drops, stinging the earth and my face on their descent. The flashlight's glare illumines the rain almost as much as the path. By the time we reach the spot where we entered the creek bed, hours ago, the rocky clay of the bank has taken on a sheen.

"It's going to be slippery, Janey." My voice is drowned out by a rumble. "C'mon, girl."

Passing the flashlight into my left hand, I grab onto a low-hanging branch for leverage, but just as I place my left foot higher on the bank, the slick surface of my old sneakers gives way. My body *thunk*s against the bank, and I slide, stomach-to-the-wall, back to my starting position.

I angle the flashlight over my shirt front.

Ruined.

I reach for the branch again, but my wet hands slip down its length, stripping off several leaves.

"Arrgh!" I growl. "I can't even get a grip on the stupid thing."

Hold on.

The familiar words caress my mind, but over the last few hours, they've grown thorns.

"Hold on?" I tilt my face toward the source of the rain. "Hold *on*?" Anger laces every syllable. "Are you *kidding* me?"

The rain stings my upturned eyes, but I ignore it. Every muscle tightens with anger, disappointment, and . . .

Betrayal.

"He didn't come." My hands clench into fists. "He didn't come! It's *over*." My teeth clench around a guttural shout, a sob that scalds my throat. "There is *nothing left* to hold on to!"

Huge, stinging drops of rain plunge from the sky.

God-sized drops. As if his tears are joined to my sorrow, but . . . bigger.

My anger deflates upon a double-edged sword, hidden in my heart. I drop to my knees, letting it penetrate my soul and spirit, each joint of my body, to the core of every bone.

Jesus wept.

A corner of my soul senses warmth. I cling to it.

"He didn't come," I whisper, and even though the storm is loud, I know I'm heard. "But you stayed. You've always stayed."

I think back to the moments I clung to words I'd hidden in my head and, later, my heart. Of how I learned a truer, more loving meaning of obedience through the spiteful gift of one who meant to use that concept as a punishment and a means of control.

"I held on . . . and you've held me. You know this feeling, don't you? Your heart's been broken, too."

Peace. There is still pain—so much pain—but within it, peace.

I push to my feet and reach for a sapling, higher than the limb I tried the first time. It's thin, but green youth gives the living wood strength and flexibility, and its roots stretch deep enough to support my weight. It bows as I lean back, but it doesn't break, and that bend allows me to hang on and walk my feet up the steep slope.

With the baby tree supporting most of my weight, my sneakers have an easier time finding traction in the clay. I throw one leg over the top of the bank and then the other. With four sets of claws to help her ascent, Janey scampers up more easily.

"Double time, Janey. Let's get back to the car before the storm gets any worse."

Each blast of thunder pulses in my chest. Keeping the flashlight trained to the ground in front of me, I break into a reluctant jog to keep up with Janey's stride along the trail. By the time we break through the clearing by the entrance, my sides ache, and my legs are rubber.

With shaking hands, I unlock the car. Janey jumps in the backseat. I've barely closed the door when the *ping-ping* of white pebbles begins to dance on the hood of my car.

"Hail?" I'm thankful we made it to the car in time, but . . . "This can't be good."

I fumble to put my key in the ignition and then spin the heat knob to the opposite setting I needed upon arrival.

Janey shakes, splattering the car's interior with cold water and mud. This is going to be murder to clean, but I don't care. We have heat.

Tiny spheres of ice bounce on the hood of the car, like Mexican Jumping Beans. I execute a five-point turn. We need to find shelter, someplace safe to wait out the storm.

I'm exhausted, filthy, wet, cold, and more than five miles from Grandma Maddie's which, judging by the angle of the hail, will be driving into the storm.

I just want to go home.

The thought crunches against my better judgment. I release the accelerator. The car slows. Stops.

It's so close. I could go in, take a hot shower, sleep in my old bed . . .

But how would I explain my appearance at this late hour? Uninvited, unannounced, filthy . . .

I don't want to lie.

But Mom will have a field day if she knows the truth.

A sudden return of anger warms my blood. *No. Freaking. Way.* I would rather get swept up in a tornado than be forced to tell this story to my *mother*. One taste of heartache per day is enough, thank you very much. My foot presses the gas pedal, and I hum "Ease on

Down the Road" from *The Wiz*. It's way more upbeat than how I'm feeling, but it seems appropriate on so many other levels.

The slight reflection of the green road sign is all I can see through the mix of rain and hail. I slow to make the turn toward the highway.

Yes. I'll drive through the night. Eventually, I'll get ahead of the storm.

I stop just short of the turnoff.

What if the hail gets worse and damages my car? Will I get in an accident? Or have to file a claim on my insurance?

Does my insurance cover hail damage?

I don't know, but I cringe at the thought of dipping into my meager savings to pay the deductible.

The one-thousand dollar deductible.

Dollar signs multiply with each teensy grain of ice that hits my car. The hail is small now. Not large enough to cause damage. But it could get bigger. Not to mention the visibility issues of rain and wind, and both increase the possibility of an accident. I have to make rent and pay for my share of utilities, groceries . . .

When I turn on the radio, I'm greeted by the automated voice of the National Weather Service Alert System. "*. . . with damaging winds up to seventy miles per hour and—*"

I turn it off, hit the brakes, rest my forehead on the steering wheel, and groan.

There's no other choice. I swallow hard, forcing my pride into my stomach.

I'm going home.

40

My code still works at the gate to Parre Hills, but my hand stings from getting pelted by hail as I punch it in. It's like the storm is moving at the same pace and direction I am, driving me toward doom.

I drive as fast as I safely can through the gated community to my parents' house and pull under the carport back by the garden shed.

"Stay here, Janey. I'll be right back."

One swipe of the wind's breath steals the car's warmth. I run up to the garage, lift the protective cover of the keypad, and pray my parents haven't changed the code.

The keypad blinks twice, and the door lifts. "Yes!" I run back to the car, grab my backpack, and then open the back door for Janey. "Come on, girl! Come on!"

Frozen spheres bounce across the cement driveway as if God has dumped out a barrel of gum-machine bouncy balls. In the brief time it takes me to get back to the garage with Janey, the hail's size has increased, but at least my car is protected from the worst of it.

It isn't until I press the interior button to close the garage door that I realize both of my parents' cars are missing.

My parents aren't home.

My parents. Are not. At home.

Mercy.

Janey shakes. A fresh coat of rain and mud—and maybe a little fur and drool—fly my direction.

"There's no getting around it, pup. You have to get a bath before you go much further. It's straight to the shower, okay?"

Janey whines and tucks her tail between her legs but follows me into the house. Her claws click on the slate floor of the mudroom that connects the garage to the rest of the house. She stops by the washing machine and sits, as if obeying that particular command.

"Shower, Janey." My voice is firm as I flip on the light. At the far end of the large mudroom, a pocket door leads to the smallest bathroom in our house.

"Go on, now."

I pull open the glass shower door and turn on the water, testing it with my hand to make sure it's not too hot or cold. When Janey doesn't move, I straddle her, put my hands on her hips, and push. "Shower. Now."

She obeys. I follow her in, shut the glass door behind us, and spray as much mud off Janey as I can before applying the shampoo, which takes quite a while to rinse out of Janey's thick fluff. Finally, after she's shaken a few more times, I let her out and towel her off as best I can.

Lukewarm water may have been fine for Janey, but it isn't nearly warm enough to shake the chill from my bones. I turn the faucet handle closer to the "H" mark.

The mirror is completely fogged over by the time I exit my wonderfully steamy shower. I dry off, tuck a fresh towel around my body, slide the door into its pocket, and . . . scream.

"Mom! I didn't know you were home."

My mother stands in the doorway of the mudroom holding a cast iron skillet above her head.

"*Faith?*"

Janey growls, leaning back on her haunches, her attention riveted on the person she perceives as a threat to her master.

"Janey, sit. Mom, put the pan down. You're scaring her."

Mom blinks and lowers the skillet. "I'm scaring *her?*" She takes a shaky breath and sets the skillet on top of the dryer. "You scared me half to death!" Her hand flutters over her heart. "I thought some crazy homeless person had broken into our house to take a shower! And then you opened the door and *that dog*—"

"Didn't you see my car outside?"

"Your car . . . ? I didn't think to look for a car."

"Please tell me you didn't call the police."

"I didn't." Mom blinks again. The corner of her mouth twitches. "That was pretty stupid of me, though, wasn't it?" She laughs and looks at the skillet. "I mean, what was I going to do, invite some vagrant into the kitchen for a grilled cheese sandwich?"

I can't help myself. I laugh. "Sorry. I should have called or something, but my phone died a couple of hours ago. When I opened the garage door and saw your cars were gone, I just assumed . . ." I shrug and reach for another towel. "I didn't think anyone was home."

When I move to the side, Mom peers past me.

"What in the *world* happened to you two?"

"I'll clean it up. I promise. We got caught out in the storm. In the woods."

"You were in the woods? *Tonight?* For heaven's sake, Faith, we've been under a tornado watch since three o'clock this afternoon! They've been sighting funnel clouds along the path of this storm since it started to move up from Kansas. And the lightning!" She leans against the dryer. "You could have been killed."

"I didn't know the weather was going to be this bad. I didn't think to check the forecast before I came down. Sorry."

"Well," Mom says, crossing her arms, "maybe if you had *called* and told me you were coming, I could have warned you about the weather."

"Well, maybe not everybody freaks out over a little storm like you do." I bite my lip, wishing it would have been my tongue, about two seconds ago. "That came out a little harsher than I intended. I'm sorry, I'm just . . . tired. I hadn't planned to—"

I don't finish the sentence. But from the hurt look on her face, I realize I don't have to.

We stare at each other in silence for a long moment.

"You planned a trip to Kanton, but you weren't going to come *here*."

There's knowledge in my mother's tone, but strangely, no recrimination.

"No. I was going to go right back home." I bite my lip. "To Ann Arbor, I mean. I have to work tomorrow night."

"At the spa?"

"No, my other job."

Mom nods. "That's right. Ryan said you met some kids from that program you're going into and got a job singing with them somewhere."

"Mm-hmm. One of my roommates got me the audition. They schedule us together usually, so we can drive over together. To Detroit. The club is in Detroit."

"And it's a jazz club, right?" Her voice is soft. "That sounds . . . interesting."

She's trying. She's actually . . . trying. "It's a cabaret club. We do a little jazz, a little blues, some standards, a few show tunes . . ." I shrug. "It's fun. Good experience, too. A few other students from the program work there. It'll be nice starting school in a couple of weeks, already knowing some people."

"Yes, I suppose it will." Mom takes a deep breath. "I guess I should let you get dressed."

"Do you think I could borrow a robe or something? Everything in my backpack is soaked."

"Sure. Actually, I just washed one of mine." She opens the dryer and sorts through, pulling out a white terrycloth robe and hands it to me

"You can bunk down in the family room with me. This storm front probably has a couple more hours of energy in it, and there's no sense taking any more chances with your safety tonight than you already have."

"Okay." I nod. "Can Janey come, too?"

She sighs. "I suppose. She'll just lie at the top of the stairs and whine, otherwise."

It's true. Janey hates storms almost as much as my mom does. "We'll be down as soon as I get this cleaned up."

"Leave it. It'll be there in the morning."

"But—"

"It's after eleven, Faith. It just hailed half an hour ago, and we're under a tornado watch. We should be in the basement."

"Okay." Back when I lived here, the house could have been on fire, and Mom would have expected me to stay on task until every last germ was sanitized. Now, it seems almost as if Mom cares more about . . . me.

Maybe the distance was good for both of us.

My eyes burn. I blink them. "I'll just throw the towels and my clothes in the washer. I'll be down in a minute."

Mom nods and leaves me to it.

I set the robe on top of the washing machine. With the towel still wrapped around me, I grab more towels and try to dry my wet mop of a dog before wiping down the areas where noticeable mud has clung. When I'm satisfied, I slip into the robe and throw my clothes and the dirty towels into the washing machine.

Taking a deep breath, I gaze around the bathroom and mudroom. There's nothing here that can't wait until morning, no other tasks to put off my trip downstairs.

It's time to face my mother.

"You painted."

Mom looks up from the photo album in her lap. "Mm-hmm. New carpet, too. Do you like it?"

"Yeah." I tuck a leg and sit on the leather sofa. "It's kind of soothing."

"The color is 'Vermont Olive,' whatever that means. But I think it's more of a sage."

"It's nice."

"Gretchen hates it." Mom glances back down at the album. "She said this color went out of fashion a decade ago."

"Do *you* like it?"

She tilts her head and looks at the walls, as if seeing them for the first time. "Yes. I do."

"That's what matters. It's your house, not Gretchen's, right?"

"You're right."

I snort softly. "Never thought I'd hear *that* statement come out of your mouth." I clap a hand over my lips. "Sorry. It's been a long day. I guess my verbal filter took a break."

Mom waves a hand in dismissal and closes the album. "Old

habits are hard to break."

A boom of thunder makes us both jump.

"I hate storms. Especially when your father's not home."

"I know."

"I didn't think to ask earlier, but are you hungry? Thirsty?"

"Water sounds good. But I can get it." I get up and walk around to the small beverage refrigerator behind the built-in bar. "Do you want anything?"

"I'm fine, thanks."

The glasses are still where they've always been, and the pitcher of water looks fresh. There are even a few cucumber slices floating on top.

I pull out a Styrofoam bowl from one of the cupboards. "Can I use this to give Janey some water?"

"Sure. Faith, did your grandmother know you were coming to Iowa?"

"No." I fill the bowl with tap water and set it on the floor.

"Ryan? Danielle? Gretchen?"

"No, no, and no."

"You mean to tell me that you just drove six hundred miles and didn't tell *anyone?*"

"Yeah, I guess. I mean, I told my roommates, but—"

"What if something would have happened to you?"

"Nothing happened." My throat tightens at the truth of that statement. "Nothing."

Mom is silent for several extended moments. "I know we haven't always had a great relationship, but I'm still your mother. I still worry about you."

I exhale. "I know you do. But this was . . . personal."

I drain my glass and pour another. "I should have told someone, but I guess after waiting two years, I didn't want to have to explain myself if this trip turned out to be totally pointless."

"And did it turn out . . . the way you wanted?"

"No."

"I'm sorry."

Sorry?

Gee, thanks Mom, but your 'sorry' is about two years too late. I take a sip of my water, mainly to keep my mouth occupied with something other than the words that want to come out. It's not powerful enough to wash away the bitterness welling on the back of my tongue.

"You said you've been planning this, uh, trip, for two years?"

I nod. I don't trust myself to speak.

"But you've only been in Michigan for three months."

"Yeah. Never mind. It doesn't matter."

A sudden awareness lights my mother's eyes. "Two years," she whispers, lifting her hand to her throat. "This was about that Noah Spencer, wasn't it?"

That Noah Spencer. I press my lips more tightly together. What should I say? What *can* I say that won't result in being either scolded or mocked?

When my fingernails have dug a series of crescents into my palms, I say, "Yes. But it's over. For good this time, I guess."

"You saw him?"

"No." The word claws through my throat . . . and my fragile hold on composure. "No, I didn't *see* him, Mom. I haven't seen or heard from Noah Spencer since the night you slapped my face and called me every imaginable variation of the word 'whore.'"

Mom's eyes round. Her face blanches.

"Never mind." I grind my teeth. "I shouldn't have brought it up."

"I've never known how to . . . I thought—hoped—that . . .

maybe you would forget about it."

Forget about it? That night—and its many repercussions—gutted me. *Gutted* me.

My mind races through hundreds, no *thousands* of moments I've tried to forgive my mother, each like rehearsing a scene over and over without being able to discover the character's true motivation. Flat. A performance without heart. The forgiveness I've recited to myself, with the hope that it would come true, is nothing but insincere dialogue—or a prop that's misplaced every time I think about how she treated me. About how she treated Noah, when he was a part of my life.

"I tried to forgive you. I thought I did, so many times." I shake my head. "But every time I think about how the last few years *should* have been, I . . . I unforgive you." I grimace. "I don't even think that's a word. But it's how I feel."

"I see. That's a long time to hold a grudge."

Says the grudge-holding champion of Kanton, Iowa.

"Yeah, well, I guess we have something in common after all."

Mom opens her mouth but closes it just as quickly. Her gaze moves to the carpet.

When I finally look—*really look*—at my mom's face, what I see there surprises me.

Delights me, on some level.

It's pain.

Her pain.

Finally.

A strange, ugly sort of satisfaction stirs in my belly.

Without warning, she stands. "You're going to need a pillow and blanket." She doesn't meet my eyes. "I'll go get them. Upstairs. Be right back."

I know very well that she keeps blankets in the storage ottoman, not two feet away from the couch, but I don't argue. Instead, I silently watch her retreat up the stairs.

Every muscle tenses around my bones. Accusations boil within my brain. Tonight's crushing disappointment rushes through my blood, gathering under my skin.

Where would I be right now if she'd had the courtesy to meet Noah? To trust us? Would we still be together, in a committed long-distance relationship? Or would we have gradually, naturally discovered—on our own—that ours was not a romance that was meant to succeed long-term?

As Noah discovered for himself, I guess, at some point during the past two years.

But what if . . . ?

What if we had been allowed to be together? What if that amazing connection had survived? Deepened?

The grief of that possible future, lost, sucks away the air I want to use to scream. At her. *This is your fault! Your! Fault!*

Poisonous words form in my mind, thickening my tongue with their venom, begging for release. *I hate you! I HATE you!*

The ugly passion of my own emotion jolts me back from the precipice of rage.

Is it true? Do I hate my own mother?

Hate is such a short, pointed little word, but its tip drips puddles—no, *oceans*—of death.

I have hidden your word in my heart that I might not sin against you.

It's one of the verses I memorized right after Noah left.

Another verse scrolls through my head. And another. Passages I'd hidden first in my head, as Noah had explained, and later in my heart as well.

Hate and murder are equated in some of those verses.

Do I wish my mother dead?

Of course not.

I have hidden your word in my heart that I might not sin against you.

The verse from Psalm 119 plays over and over in my mind, the final few words seeming to hold extra emphasis. *That I might not sin against you. That I might not sin against you.*

Silently, I argue with the voice in my heart. *I tried, Lord. I tried to forgive her. It didn't take.*

"I'm not like you, Jesus," I whisper, closing my eyes. "You can forgive and forget, but I can't. I just don't have it in me." A groan tears through my lips. "I can't do it. It's just too big. I can't forgive her. I don't even *want* to forgive her!"

And there it is, at last.

The truth.

"I'm so *tired* of this." I don't wipe away the tears that spill down my cheeks and into the terrycloth robe covering my knees. "It's so . . . heavy. It's drowning me. Please, help me. I want to be done with this. Please, make me *want* to forgive her."

My yoke is easy. My burden is light.

Another verse, recalled from its hidden place within my heart. And it's as sonorous in my spirit as the thunder that rattles the high-set basement windows.

"I don't want to hate her anymore. Teach me how to love her like you love her," I pray. The thickness in my throat painfully pulls at each whisper, but I have to get the words out. "Help me forgive her like you forgave—forgive—me."

My grace is sufficient for you, for my power is made perfect in weakness.

A tingling rush crosses my shoulders. I don't open my eyes, but in my own request, I finally see the thing I've been willfully blind to.

Asking for help implies I'm doing most of the work and only require assistance. And here, now . . . with her . . .

I just don't have it in me to forgive her. At all.

Warmth alights, feather-light on my skin.

"I have hidden your word in my heart," I whisper. "And you live there, alive inside it. I can't do this on my own. If it's ever going to be real, it has to be all you, Jesus. Not me. All you. Plant *your* mercy in my heart toward my mother. Let it flow in and through me."

I'm out of words, but full of truth.

I cannot forgive my mother. Not alone. But . . .

I am not alone.

I am held.

I rest my head on my knees and let peace surpass understanding.

"Faith?"

I lift my head when Mom sits on the floor beside me.

"Oh, honey." She reaches for the box of tissues on the coffee table and hands it to me. "Faith, for what it's worth, I'm sorry he didn't— I'm sorry things didn't go as you'd hoped."

For what it's worth.

Does her vague apology count for anything now? Or is it too little, too late?

And yet . . . the peace is still there, embracing and defying my pain, surpassing understanding as it nudges my breath into words.

"Thank you. It's worth more than you can possibly know."

Mom's rapid blinks can't dry her eyes fast enough to keep a tear or two from spilling. She looks away—and I do, too, knowing her aversion to letting anyone see her cry.

"Mom," I begin softly. "I know I did things I shouldn't have when Noah was still here, but I didn't do a lot of the things you thought I did."

"You were young. It was unpleasant, but it was natural. All

teenagers rebel in some way. It's over now."

I rest a hand on Janey's still-wet fur and take a deep breath, exhaling a silent prayer to let go of the words I want to hear—her words, seeking forgiveness for having set the stage for my pain tonight and so much more. But those words are not offered. They may never be offered. And my disappointment has no home but where I must leave it now, at the feet of a grace-offering God, who desires me to reflect his heart.

"I know you think Noah and I were . . . intimate, but we weren't. I've never, well, *you* know." I lift a hand to my heating cheek. A dry laugh escapes my lips. "Good grief! I'm almost nineteen years old, and I can barely even say the word 'sex,' let alone *do* it."

"But he was so much *older* than you. Surely you can understand why I would think he might—"

"You didn't know him. We never even came close."

For several breaths, I wait. Mom does not swerve her gaze.

"I believe you," she says.

Invisible light pours into my chest.

"But someday, when you have a daughter of your own, maybe you'll understand how I came to that conclusion."

Deep breath. "You were trying to protect me. I know." I sigh. "Noah was one of the good ones, Mom. He really was." A cold chill travels down my spine. I cross my arms at my waist and dig my fingers into the robe, trying to suppress a shiver—but fail. "I hate how that sounded. It sounds like he's—" I swallow. "Like he died."

I close my eyes. *Oh, God!* A fresh tear rips across my heart. *Please, not that. Let him be safe. Let him be . . . happy.*

I truly want that. I want Noah to be happy, even if it means I have to redefine the word for myself.

Yes, Lord. I nod my amen, feeling the smile of the Holy Spirit. *Wherever he is, and whoever he loves, please pour out joy on Noah*

Spencer. Pour out love on him like crazy, Jesus.

Peace flutters across my ribcage, up my shoulders, and down my arms like tingles of light beneath my skin. It doesn't disintegrate my pain, but it warms it. Manages it.

"I'm sorry Noah let you down tonight."

"Me, too." I open my eyes and relax my arms. "Me, too." When I blink, each eye releases a tear. "Maybe God had a different plan for tonight than reuniting me with my first love."

Mom stiffens. I'm not surprised, but her discomfort doesn't let me off the hook. There are things that need to be said. Closure that can't be claimed until I've done the hard thing, said the true words. Owned them.

God. I drop my chin and close my eyes, releasing streams of saltwater down my cheeks and silent whispers from my spirit. *I am so broken, but I feel like you've opened a door. Please, give me the courage to walk through it. Give me the words I need to say. Help me speak the truth . . . in love.*

I wipe a hand across my face. "Mom?"

"Hmm?"

"For the past few years, I've blamed you for every hard thing in my life. I've—"

My voice breaks. I've been honest with God, but it's much harder to voice ugly truths to the one who's given them their sting.

"It was not okay, the way you treated Noah. And it was worse, how you treated me. The vicious accusations, the name-calling . . . You hit me, Mom. And you made me go to that clinic, and—" My throat is dry. I have to swallow. "You did those things—*abusive* things—and that is not okay."

"I didn't mean to—I was angry, Faith. And maybe I overreacted. I shouldn't have slapped you. But everything else? It was for your safety. I was doing my job, as your mother."

She truly believes that. It's a little hard to swallow, that truth. But I will not be held captive by it. I allowed myself to wallow in bitterness and hate for way too long. Now that I'm finally free of that ugliness, I refuse to allow it to have a hold on me again.

"I forgive you, Mom. For all of it."

Mom blinks several times, opens her mouth, and closes it. "It's over. In the past. And I can't . . . I can't do much, I guess. You don't live here anymore, so we just need to . . ." She shrugs. "We move on."

It's not the response I hoped for, but . . .

I nod. "We'll figure it out as we go."

Mom yawns and tilts her head. "I think the storm's over."

A great crash of thunder pulls a yelp from her, and I almost drop my glass of water.

"Or maybe not."

Our laughter is soft but heavy-laden and cut off by my own wide yawn. "I don't know about you, but it's been a long day. And a long night," I add as I stand and offer Mom a hand up. "Do you want the sofa, or would you rather take the recliner?"

Mom groans. "I'll take the recliner. If I sleep on that sofa, I'll be stiff for a week. You're young. You'll bounce back more quickly."

"Time for bed, Janey."

"Please tell me that wet lump of fur is not going to sleep on the sofa with you."

"It's a sectional. We'll each get a section." I clasp my hands and bat my eyes.

"Oh, fine." Mom rolls her eyes, but the expression holds a semblance of a smile.

I arrange the blankets and pillows Mom brought downstairs and settle into the sofa. "Goodnight, Mom."

"Goodnight." Mom settles into the recliner and pulls the chain on the lamp. "Sleep tight."

"Geesh, Mom. I'm not six years old."

"I know, Faith." She sighs. "I know."

The next morning dawns clear and sunny. Except for a few downed tree limbs and puddles, there's little evidence of the storm. My internal alarm clock has me up before seven. Mom is still asleep in the recliner when I set to work cleaning the mess upstairs.

When I'm finished, I cast a critical eye around the bathroom. The brushed-nickel fixtures sparkle. The glass and mirrored surfaces are finally streak-free. Even the toilet's been scrubbed, just to be thorough.

"You really didn't need to do that, Faith," Mom says as she puts a load of whites in the washing machine.

She must have switched my clothes to the dryer sometime during the night because I found them there when I went to do it myself.

"You did an admirable job wiping everything down last night. Besides, the cleaning service is coming later. They could have gotten what you missed."

"You have a *cleaning service?*"

"I won a month of service in a raffle last winter and . . ." She ducks her head. "I guess I got spoiled. I signed a contract and everything. They come once a week. Keep the place neat and tidy."

"Sweet." I laugh. "I wondered how you managed without me around to do the dirty jobs."

"That's one of the privileges of being a parent, Faith. Free slave labor." She smiles. "But then they grow up, and you're stuck cleaning your own toilets. It's so unfair to—"

The doorbell rings.

Mom looks at her watch. "That's probably them now. Oh, dear." She frowns, wide-eyed. "Janey's still outside, isn't she?"

"Yeah, why?"

"Does she still do that thing where she sneaks up behind people and growls?"

"Um . . ."

"I better let them in before Kay has a heart attack. She's petrified of dogs." Mom slams the door of the washing machine. "Do you mind starting this up for me? The soap's in the—"

The doorbell rings again. "I've got this. Go let your cleaning lady in before she files a lawsuit against me."

I start the machine. My ratty old backpack leans against the wall by the pocket door to the bathroom. It didn't make it into the washer last night, but I have a spare in my apartment, the one I've been saving for school. Rather than take the filthy thing home, I decide to chuck it, but when I pick it up to deliver it to the trashcan, it's heavier than it should be.

Our mailbox.

How had I forgotten it was in my bag?

I try turning the lid, but it's still stuck. I take it to the sink, tossing the now-emptied backpack into the nearby trashcan as I go by.

The dirt washes off quickly. Inside the jar, I see a tiny piece of paper and . . . a small, silver charm—the comedy/tragedy masks, atop a treble clef—on a matching chain. The paper is a . . . receipt? Yes. From The Smoked Salt Grille. And there's writing—

familiar penmanship—on the other side.

Still holding on, Noah.

But . . . he didn't come.

Apart from breaking the jar, there's no way to get that charm and note out. But do I really need to?

Does it matter?

Noah may have left a token of his promise for me to find, but whatever it meant when he put it in the jar, it clearly no longer carries the same meaning.

If it did, he would have come.

Closing my eyes, I hug the jar to my chest. I have to accept this. He made his choice, and it isn't me. I have to let him go.

In just three steps, the jar and its contents can join the backpack in the trashcan. But I can't make myself take those steps.

Yes. It's the right thing to do.

Eyes still shut, I take one step.

Please. Lord. Let him be safe and happy.

I loosen my grip on the jar, holding it away from me in one hand, as I take the second step.

"So *that's* where it went."

My eyes snap open. My knees lock. Every bone in my body jolts to attention.

In the doorway of the mudroom, in white socks, with mud caked onto the hem of his jeans and splattered across his gray t-shirt and tentative smile, Noah Spencer stands, twisting the brim of a red baseball cap.

"The jar, I mean." He clears his throat. "I tried to get here on time, Faith. Really, I did. But the—the weather. My flight was diverted to St. Louis, and I—I thought maybe you'd left a note for me in the Dutchman's pocket. But the jar was missing, so I decided that rather than go back out to my car, I'd hike the other way, toward Parre Hills, and hope the restraining order had expired. But I got a little turned around in the woods—not so familiar with your side, I guess—and I . . ."

I gape, blinking rapidly, like the opening and closing of my eyes will make this illusion disappear. That one of these blinks will eventually prove him a figment of my imagination. But he stays.

He's explaining something about hail and a rental car with a broken windshield, but his words come so quickly, like a flowing velvet river.

He's picked up a bit of an accent.

And he needs a shave.

But he's here.

Here. In my mother's house.

"So, as you can see, I got rather filthy in the process. I'm sorry."

He's not real. He can't be. I'm still asleep and caught in the clutches of a cruel dream.

But if I'm dreaming, why does he look . . . older?

Tired.

Taller. Not much, but maybe an inch . . .

Agony and bliss ripple through my body. Noah. Is. Here.

The jar slides from my grasp.

I take a step forward.

"Faith, stop! The glass! You're barefoot."

"Faith?" Mom sticks her head around the doorway. Her face has lost all color. "Faith? Are you okay? I thought I heard—Oh, dear. Don't move. I'll get the broom."

Every breath reverberates in my ears, each inhalation and exhalation faster than the one before. My head is as light as a helium balloon. Love, joy, desperation—my brain is infused, saturated, with so many emotions, but it refuses to settle on just one.

I look down. *Sparkly.* Someone spilled diamonds on the floor.

Diamonds on the floor? Impossible.

Tears flood my eyes. *Cruel dream.*

My vision pin-holes. Oohh . . . dizzy.

I look down, at my locked knees.

I'm a performer. I know better than to lock my knees. But I can't seem to . . .

So . . . so dizzy.

I try to lift my head, but the sensation of falling steals the strength from my neck.

43

"Don't cry, Madeleine Faith."

Noah's breath is sweet against my face. *Spicy.* His voice is even richer than in my dreams.

"Wake up, Faith. Open your eyes now. Come back to me."

Oh, his arms! They're stronger now. *Thicker.* And warm, as if he's just come in from the sun.

How did I land in his arms?

Noah's hand caresses my cheek. His lips press against my forehead. "I'm sorry, Faith," he whispers. "I'm sorry it took me so long to get here."

The wet skin on my cheeks lifts.

"Ah, there she is. My Madeleine Faith." A soft, cinnamon-scented tune sends wisps of words—something about a corner, my smile, home—into my hair. The tune is familiar, but the words are . . . not quite right.

"Noah." His name is an exhalation, a breath—my breath—held inside far too long.

He's here.

He's . . . real.

"Noah." I open my eyes. "You're here." I press my hand to his cheek. "And you're still a hack. You cheesed up that song from *Thoroughly Modern Millie*."

"Busted. I guess I can't get anything by you."

Noah's smile. Noah's smile is everything. It's *everything*.

"You're here. You came."

"Yeah." The blue of his eyes is brighter than I remembered. Wetter.

Mom clears her throat. "I'm going to run upstairs and get some bandages. I'll . . . be right back."

I don't move except to blink. I think I might never move again.

But what did Mom say? Bandages? For what?

"What is she talking about?"

"Do you remember dropping the jar?"

I bite my lower lip. I do vaguely remember the sound of glass shattering. I nod. "I think . . . I locked my knees."

"Ah. Well, when you fainted, I . . ." Noah's voice is a little strained but so beautiful, "I had to catch you."

I lift my head. There's a bright red stain on Noah's left sock. "You're bleeding!"

"It's not that bad. Are *you* all right?"

"I'm fine. *I'm* not the one bleeding." I move to sit up.

"Careful now." Noah's arms tighten around me. "Broken glass, you know. Give yourself a minute. Get your bearings."

"Does it hurt? Is it deep?"

"My understudy will probably be disappointed, but I think I'll live."

"Good. But still, we should . . . I'm sorry, but did you say *understudy*?"

"Yes." Noah grins. "We're still in rehearsals, but starting next month, and then for the next eight months, I'll be playing the part of Jimmy in an off-Broadway revival of *Thoroughly Modern Millie*. And in case you wondered, I do sing the correct words on stage."

"You're in *Millie?* Wait. You said off-Broadway. You mean . . . you're in New York? But you're supposed to be in London for another year!"

"Remember when I said I would try to switch to the two-year program?"

I nod.

"I finished in April, packed my bags, and headed back to the States. Long story short, I started auditioning and . . . got this part."

"That's . . . wow! Congratulations!"

My cheeks ache with sheer joy. With Noah back in my life, I should probably get used to the feeling.

"I can't believe you're really here. You're in my mom's house, bleeding on the laundry room floor."

"It's quite romantic, isn't it?"

It kind of is. "You sound like a Brit."

I run my fingers over the goldish-brown stubble that lines a more defined jaw than I remember. Noah Spencer is no longer a boy. He is a man. The romantic lead in an off-Broadway musical. It's . . . surreal.

"Are you sure I'm awake?"

"If I am, then you must be as well. So . . . what are you doing for dinner?"

"*What?*"

"Would you have dinner with me?"

"Noah, it's not even nine o'clock in the morning."

"Madeleine Faith Prescott, I am officially asking you out on a date. In case you're unfamiliar with the concept, it's the usual course of action when two adults who are romantically inclined toward one another share a meal in a restaurant. I am asking you out. On a date. A *real* date."

"A real date." My grin spreads wide. "I would like that."

"Good." He winks, and my heart spins and flops over on itself.

"I hear there's a pretty decent place in Sommerton," I say. "It's called The Smoked Salt Grille or something weird like that. Except—" I smack my hand against my forehead. "I have to be at work at nine."

"So we make it an early dinner."

"No, you don't understand. I have to be at work *in Detroit* at nine. It's a ten hour drive, if I go *really* fast, plus I have to drop Janey off at my apartment in Ann Arbor. If I don't leave pretty soon . . ." A strangled noise exits my throat. "I can't believe you're here and I—"

I squeeze my eyes shut. I don't want to cry again. Our time together can't be so short! Not after two years! Not after the night I just spent and the strides I've made . . .

"It's okay. I'm not expected back in New York until the thirteenth. I'll go with you. I can change my flight from Moline to . . . where did you say? *Detroit?*"

I nod.

"Detroit. Huh." When Noah shifts position, he winces. Reaching down toward his foot, he pulls an inch-long sliver of glass from his sock. "So while I've been combing every theatre-student haunt in New York this summer, you've been in . . . *Detroit?*"

"No, I work in Detroit. Well, one of my jobs is there. I live in Ann Arbor. I moved there in May because I'll be attending the University of Michigan this fall. Long story."

And I will tell it all. Someday. But . . .

"Wait, why were you looking for me in New York this summer?"

"Now that's a fun story." He frowns. "In retrospect. It wasn't at the time, I assure you. Anyway, I flew in for your high school graduation, but you weren't there—"

"You came to my high school graduation?"

"I did. But *you* didn't."

"Oh, yeah. I graduated early."

"As I learned. Unfortunately, I only had a few hours in town." He lifts a shoulder. "Money was tight, but I'd found a really cheap round-trip fare I couldn't pass up. Anyway, I showed up at graduation, and Jenna told me you'd left town, but she didn't know where you were. I guess you guys didn't keep in touch?"

"No. We . . . drifted apart. Another long story."

"Ah." Noah nods but doesn't ask for details. "Well, that silly little charm, wherever it landed, was going to be a graduation gift."

"But I wasn't there. Sorry."

"No worries. We'd agreed to stay out of touch. You had no way of knowing I would come to graduation, and since my time was limited, I decided to leave it in the Dutchman's pocket and hope you'd come home over the summer and find it."

I can barely wrap my mind around it. He came back for me. *Twice.*

I'm bursting with a thousand variations on the theme, "*I love you, Noah Spencer,*" but Mom picks that moment to return with the first aid kit and a broom and dustpan, so I say, "Thank you," instead.

As soon as Mom has swept away enough of the broken jar that we can safely stand, I help Noah hobble over to the dryer, and he boosts himself slightly up to sit on it. While I see to Noah's foot, Mom runs the vacuum over the floor to pick up any stray glass fragments, and then she makes a quiet exit.

"Your mom is different than I expected her to be."

"The part where she let you in the house was different. That's for sure." My tone is dry but not bitter.

He nods. "People change."

"Yes. They do. *We* do."

He exhales a long breath. "Two years is a long time."

"It seemed like fifty while I was in it, but now that you're here . . . not so much."

"Can we pick up where we left off?"

"Like you said, we've changed." I taste the trueness of my words.

"We're not the same idealistic young dreamers who met at the waterfall. Picking up where we left off doesn't really seem possible."

Noah's eyes cloud. "Oh."

"But," I add, squeezing his hand and smiling because I don't recall when our fingers entwined. "Someone once told me that dreams can go through a metamorphosis and come out bigger and fuller on the other side. And there's no one in the world I'd rather build a big, full dream with than you."

The spark returns to Noah's eyes. "It'll take time, getting to know each other again. Especially with me in New York and you in Michigan."

"Yes. But we'll have technology at our disposal now. And I'll have school breaks."

"My contract with the production company is going to keep me busy for almost a year." Noah groans. "A *year*."

"What's *almost* a year compared to the past two years?"

"Ask me that a week from now."

I'm not sure if music begins to swell, and I can't name the exact moment Noah wraps his arms around me, but when our lips meet, I know that somewhere, beyond this temporal stage on which we stand, in a realm we *can't quite see*, a sold-out crowd has leapt to its feet and is shouting for an encore.

We comply.

CURTAIN

CURTAIN CALL

THREE YEARS LATER

A not-quite-packed house turns to watch me escort Faith's mother to a front row seat at the Leopold Opera House. Once I've seated her next to my mom, I turn to the stage and ascend the stairs to where Pastor Bryan waits, grinning.

I give a nod to Dr. Jeremiah Hitchings. He lifts his baton, directing the Leopold Community Theatre's small pit orchestra to begin "Ten Minutes Ago" from *Rodgers & Hammerstein's Cinderella*.

Ushers open two sets of doors at the rear of the auditorium, allowing a short stream of silver-gowned bridesmaids and their tuxedo-clad counterparts to waltz—literally—down the aisles, toward the stage. Of the six waltzing couples, only one and a half needed help with the choreography—Ryan, Danielle, and Gretchen Prescott—but a quick lesson from one of the other bridesmaids, an aspiring choreographer, took care of that yesterday. The Prescott members of the wedding party are, perhaps, not dancing as smoothly as the others, who—like Faith and me—are all theatre nerds of one variation or another, but they're doing all right.

It took Faith only about two and a half years to finish her degree, thanks to the college credits she earned in high school. I proposed eight months ago—the same day she moved into her first New York apartment. Next week, while we're on our honeymoon, some of the guys who share this stage with me now will be moving Faith's belongings into her *second* New York apartment. Mine.

Ours.

While I wait for the star of this show to make her entrance, I mentally rehearse the lines I'll recite—perhaps the most important lines of my life—in just a few moments.

The theatre seats are filled with a colorful mix of family, friends, and strangers—an interesting blend of locals, school chums from London and Michigan, and theatre friends from New York, as well as several business associates of the Prescott family and sponsors of my parents' mission work.

A pause in the music and . . .

There she is. My own Cinderella. My bride.

Madeleine Faith Prescott.

"Thank you." The whisper through my lips is the sincere shout of my heart, but those syllables feel somehow insufficient to express my gratitude. This beautiful woman, my Madeleine Faith, is my bride at last.

With one hand nestled in the crook of her father's arm and the other slightly lifting the hem of her wedding gown, Faith ascends the steps toward me, where my heart pounds upstage, center.

She is simply . . . radiant. I know I should take a moment to look at and appreciate the one-of-a-kind gown—provided at cost as a gift from another theatre friend, a costume designer—but I can't take my eyes off her face.

"Friends, family, beloved," Pastor Bryan says, stepping forward. "Today, we gather together to witness the joining of Noah Thomas Spencer and Madeleine Faith Prescott in holy matrimony. Who gives this woman in marriage to this man?"

"Her mother and I."

Faith winks one cinnamon-colored eye at me, just before leaning toward her father's cheek and leaving a kiss behind. My smile quirks to one side. Oh, how we struggled not to laugh when that line came up at rehearsal last night!

Dr. Prescott places Faith's hand in mine—*perfection*—and then turns, descending the steps to take his place beside his wife.

I turn to face my bride. Her beauty, always stunning, shines with a brilliance that makes me weak.

The ceremony is a blur of her love meshed with mine. All we've been through, together and apart, is culminating right here, right now. I'm not ashamed of the tears that fall as I pledge my vows and slip freshly soldered rings on Faith's finger, and I cherish each of her tears as a platinum band slides onto mine.

"By the power vested in me by the State of Iowa, as witnessed by our Triune God and these friends and family members, I now pronounce you husband and wife!" Pastor Bryan takes a step back.

I am hers. She is mine. And we're going to kiss to prove it.

"This has become something of a habit," I say, closing the little bit of space between us. "Kissing you on this stage, with an audience."

"No, that was Liesl kissing Rolf, not me kissing you. But Madeleine Faith *Spencer* has never been kissed by anyone, anywhere." She inches forward. "Not even her husband."

"Hmm. I can change that."

I cup the side of her face with my hand, loving the flutter of her eyelashes as she tilts her smile toward mine.

"I love you," she whispers as a breath against my lips—words I return before claiming her kiss.

I am determined to make this first kiss one Madeleine Faith *Spencer* will remember for all of her days. But one perfect kiss is not enough for my bride. I pull back, but Faith grips the lapels of my tuxedo jacket and presses her lips to mine again.

Our second kiss is a rather rousing encore—at least in my opinion.

The audience agrees, breaking into laughter and wolf-whistles above the cheers and applause that began with our first kiss as husband and wife.

We're both laughing when our lips finally part. My right hand takes her left, and then, as one would expect from two actors on a stage, we raise our joined hands and take a bow.

Last night, we rehearsed the recessional to an instruments-only version of "I Do, I Do, I Do, I Do, I Do" from *Mamma Mia!*, but when one of my groomsmen shouts a series of nonsensical but familiar 1950s-esque syllables and the pit orchestra begins the reprise version of "We Go Together" from *Grease,* we realize our plans have been hijacked . . . perfectly.

Grinning, we glance at each other and shrug. Though we didn't plan it, couldn't have, Faith and I execute a perfectly synched hand jive before rejoining our hands, descending the stairs, and running out of the Opera House toward . . . life.

Dear Reader:

I sincerely hope you enjoyed Faith and Noah's story, that it moved you and left you feeling warm and loved. But the darker themes within this tale cannot be ignored . . . especially when so many early readers have told me how they've wept over this book, some having experienced similar—and worse—pain to what Faith suffered due to her mother's words, actions, and attitudes.

There is a fine line between honoring adults and appeasing them, but a much thicker line between respecting adults and fearing them. Unfortunately, it can be difficult to identify either delineation when you have no opposing frame of reference.

Do you, like Faith, feel trapped beneath the control of an abusive person? Is fear, panic, or anxiety your default response to the approach of a family member, guardian, caretaker, or significant other due to past or ongoing verbal, emotional, physical, or sexual abuse? There are people who will believe you. There is help available. Please talk to a trusted adult. If there are no trustworthy adults in your life right now, look farther, beyond your usual circles. They do exist.

Although I am not affiliated with the organizations listed below, they all offer services which include counselors who are available 24/7:

- The Hope Line: https://www.thehopeline.com.
- Youth Crisis Hotline: 1-800-448-4663.
- Crisis Text Line: To connect with a crisis counselor at Crisis Text Line, text GO to the number 741741.

- National Child Abuse Hotline: If you are a minor, you can also call 1-800-4-A-CHILD (1-800-422-4453) or visit them online at childhelp.org.
- National Domestic Violence Hotline: Adults can also find information and assistance at 1-800-799-SAFE (1-800-799-7233) or online at thehotline.org.

Share your story. Find hope. Live in love.

Hold on.

For you,
Serena

Serena Chase is the author of the critically-acclaimed Eyes of E'veria epic fantasy series. A lifelong performer who often changes the words of songs to fit the moment, Serena, like the lead character in *Intermission,* was cast as "Liesl" in *The Sound of Music* when she was sixteen (going on seventeen.)

During her college years at Belmont University in Nashville, Tennessee, Serena not only earned her B.B.A. with Concentration in Music Business, but appeared in a music video and earned several album credits for background vocals. Since moving back to her home state of Iowa, she has indulged her love of performing by singing at weddings and special events and participating in local community theater productions, including her most recent role playing "Eliza Doolittle"—opposite her husband as "Professor Henry Higgins"—in *My Fair Lady.*

Although she loves the stage, these days Serena is most often found in her writing cave, playing with her imaginary friends, rubbing the head of her 100 lb. goldendoodle and exchanging random quirky texts with her two teen daughters.

Serena loves connecting with readers! Please visit her website, find her on Pinterest, Twitter and Instagram (@Serena_Chase) and "like" her official author page on Facebook to keep up-to-date on new release news.

Did you enjoy Intermission? *Please consider leaving a review at Goodreads and/or at the website of the retailer from whom you purchased the book. Thank you!*

ACKNOWLEDGEMENTS

This book began about eight years ago as a short story assignment within the Apprentice Course in which I was enrolled through The Jerry B. Jenkins Christian Writers Guild. Therefore, I want to thank Jerry B. Jenkins and all the authors, editors, and mentors who designed that program.

Sandra Byrd: A decade after CWG placed me under your mentorship, I still consider you my mentor, but you have become so much more. You've seen this book from short story to finished product and through many incarnations and drafts over these many years, and you've believed in it—in me—and pushed me out of my comfort zone to make it deeper and truer and barer and better. Not only that, you've invited me into your life, your home, and your circle of encouragement. Thank you will never be enough.

Jenny Quinlan of Historical Editorial: You came in around draft three and pushed me to bring each of these characters more fully to life. You talked me through some rough plot spots and gave me priceless insights toward what the final product, several drafts later, has become. Thank you so much!

Jenny Zemanek: That. Cover. Beautiful! Thank you for being so wonderful to work with and for creating such a beautiful image for people to associate with Faith and Noah's story.

My critique partners: You three are my how-did-I-survive-before-you friends. Your honesty, encouragement, talent, and prayers have encouraged me through the last few drafts of *Intermission* . . . and life itself. Jessica Keller/Jess Evander, Charity Tinnin, and Amanda G. Stevens: I love you guys. So much. So. MUCH.

Heather Perdelwitz: As always, you've read more versions of this story than anyone should ever be forced to suffer through. Thanks for your constant encouragement.

Erynn Newman of A Little Red Ink: Thanks for your excitement for *Intermission* from the moment I told you this story would be coming your way and for the attention you gave to the book's copyedit to ensure I wouldn't be sending my baby out into the world with dirt on her nose. I'm so excited that you, Bethany, and I will be traveling and teaching together *IN IRELAND!* in 2018!!!

Charity Tinnin of ibleedbooks: Thank you for giving such attention and care to the final proofread—and also for identifying with Faith and Jenna's love for Louis Tomlinson's pirate/angel voice.

Lori Twichell: Our chats may be few and far between, but you refresh me, sistah. Thanks for being an early reader of the almost-there version and for that chat after.

To the Muddy River Writers group (and the patient staff of Dunn Brothers Coffee in Burlington, Iowa): My "writerly black hole" isn't dark anymore. I'm looking forward to many more mocha frappes in the company of my new story-crafting friends.

To my small-town musical theatre friends in southeast Iowa and beyond, from the 1980s through now: Thanks for the laughter, the music, and the golden memories. Let's make some more, shall we?

To Broadway and West End composers and performers, past, present, and future: You light up stages and sound recordings with artistry and buckets full of amazingness. You provide songs to sing when I run out of words. You grab my emotions and beat them senseless, beautifully. I may sometimes adjust your lyrics to fit a moment. I may not have the range to reach your heights. But I have ears to hear and a heart to feel, absorb, and embrace your intent. You have my undying gratitude. (And to the lovely and talented Susan Egan, who followed me on Twitter a couple of years ago for some unknown reason that caused me much *squee-ing* for several days after, I give you a fangirl's loyalty.)

To Dave, Delaney, & Ellerie: All the love. And show tunes. Lots and lots of show tunes. Even at the dinner table.

Last, but certainly not least: to both my established reading audience and the new readers who were willing to pick up this book and read it to the end, thank you. You are in my heart, my thoughts, and my prayers. Hold on.

Affectionately,
Serena